Monsters, Tricksters, and Sacred Cows: Animal Tales and American Identities

Monsters, Tricksters, and Sacred Cows: Animal Tales and American Identities

Edited by A. James Arnold

With an Afterword by

DEREK WALCOTT

A. James Arnold, Series Editor

New World Studies

University Press of Virginia

Charlottesville and London

THE UNIVERSITY PRESS OF VIRGINIA

First published 1996

Library of Congress Cataloging-in-Publication Data

Monsters, tricksters, and sacred cows : animal tales and American identities / edited by A. James Arnold : with an afterword by Derek Walcott.
p. cm. — (New World studies)
Includes bibliographical references and index.
ISBN 0-8139-1645-3 (cloth : alk. paper). — ISBN 0-8139-1646-1 (pbk. : alk. paper)
1. Indians—Folklore. 2. Animals—America—Folklore. 3. Human-animal relationships—America—Folklore. I. Arnold, A. James (Albert James), 1939- . II. Series.
E59.F6M66 1996
398′.0973—dc20 95-33391
CIP

Printed in the United States of America

Contents

Acknowledgments

The editor wishes to extend heartfelt thanks to the Virginia Foundation for the Humanities and Public Policy, which funded the Columbian Quincentenary symposium on which this volume is based.

Josephine V. Arnold provided invaluable assistance in running down difficult references. She knows how much her work is appreciated.

Monsters, Tricksters, and Sacred Cows: Animal Tales and American Identities

A. James Arnold

INTRODUCTION:

Monsters, Tricksters, and Sacred Cows: Animal Tales and American Identities

Models, Metaphors, and Minefields

Where to begin writing about cultural identity in the Americas after the 1992 quincentenary? The years leading up to and immediately following the events, variously described as a *celebration* or an *encounter* between the New World and the Old, saw a further polarization of hardened positions that express a heavy ideological investment in one or another idea of America. The culture wars continue to rage. Precious little common ground remains; the field has been so thoroughly mined by the opposing camps that editing a volume such as this one approximates an exercise in tactics. Tactically, in order to advance in such a situation, it is necessary to clear the minefield. That can only be done by exploding the mines already laid in one's path.

Pots and Crocks

"The historic theory of America . . . has been . . . the creation of a *new* national culture and a *new* national identity. . . . Europe is the *unique* source of these ideals . . . " (Schlesinger, "Dissent," 630, 633). So affirms, quite peremptorily, a general leading the Eurocentrist forces, Arthur M. Schlesinger, Jr. "The melting pot is a crock," quips Gregory

Jay, in the hope that ridicule may undermine the Eurocentrists' position (Jay, "End," 5). In his 1991 *Partisan Review* polemic against a recent report by the New York State Social Studies Syllabus Review Committee, Schlesinger took up the cudgel against the thesis that "ethnicity is the defining experience for most Americans" ("Dissent," 630), and he did so in the name of assimilation. Eventual assimilation into WASP society has always been the goal of the melting-pot model. Assimilationists subscribe to a mode of identitarian thought that posits one root, or stock, which it locates in northwest Europe. Recent polemics on both sides of the culture wars have focused on whose roots are invoked, not on the problems attendant upon the model of single rootedness for describing or theorizing culture (and differentiating it from race) in the Americas.

Root and Stock

If one looks at the principal competing positions in the culture wars in terms of the societal models they propose and the metaphors they use to express those models for ready consumption by the public, then the Afrocentrist model propounded by Molefi Kete Asante and others can be seen for what it is, the reverse image of assimilation. Like Schlesinger's model, Asante's appeals to a common root (our culture is African because our ethnicity is African), and that root is unique. In this view, people of color in the Americas, other than Native Americans, are "Africans in America [who] have been dislocated—that is, taken off their own terms for the past 345 years" (Asante, "Center," 46). At the risk of pushing a paradox to its limits, I would propose quite seriously that the postulate shared by Asante and Schlesinger has resulted in positions that represent a dead end in both cases. The positions do not correspond to reality, and they are incapable of engaging those who do not already share the ideology expressed by the taproot metaphor that expresses their presumed uniqueness.

Taproots, Rhizomes, and Triptychs

Initial planning for the 1992 Columbian Quincentenary symposium at the University of Virginia took into consideration the fact that competing claims of Eurocentrists and Afrocentrists all derive from the specific history of the United States of America. Taken together, these two mutually hostile views of culture in the United States, both of which ground themselves ultimately in ethnicity, represent recto and verso of the same page of history. Neither position is fully comprehensible without the other; each implies the other. It is finally for this reason that each position demonizes the other.[1]

The idea of America is, of course, larger and more complex than this Manichaean vision of cultural Good and Evil. Therefore it was necessary, first of all, to broaden the field of investigation of cultural identities in the Americas in both time and space. Geographically, we were able to take in the two American continents, as well as Mesoamerica and the Caribbean archipelago. Temporally, we strove to represent the precontact period—including the imaginary geography and monsters that European explorers brought with them to the New World—and some of the myriad ways in which cultural adaptation, accommodation, and resistance have taken place in the five centuries since 1492. As initial plans for our symposium were being laid, Tzvetan Todorov published the Paris edition of his book *On Cultural Diversity,* which has brought these questions into the center of the public debate on culture.

Contributors were selected from several academic disciplines—cultural anthropology, history, comparative literature—without regard for conformity to any specific methodology or world view. Indeed, all contributors were unfamiliar with the work of most of the others before the symposium took place. The organizer of the symposium and editor of the present volume did have a hypothesis in mind, of course. Available evidence suggested that all cultural systems in the Americas were already, and had long been, modified by the presence and pressures of other groups with which they had been in contact over long periods. To the extent that it might be possible to demonstrate that if a process of cultural modification, whether born of violent contact and domination or of mutual exchange, was a constant in the Americas, then it could be shown that the Manichaean vision of the culture wars in the United States corresponded not to reality but to political ideologies designed to control populations while retaining as much power as possible.

A viable alternative to the *Roots* model of culture had been around for about fifteen years, but it began to make its way into discussions of culture in the Americas only after our symposium had been planned.[2] The metaphor of the rhizome had been circulated by the French philosophers Gilles Deleuze and Félix Guattari in the mid-1970s.[3] Between 1990 and 1992, it became the cornerstone of two important books by the Martinican writer Edouard Glissant and the Cuban writer Antonio Benítez-Rojo. Benítez-Rojo gives this description of the metaphor and its implications for our purposes:

> The rhizome state can be understood starting from the rhizome of the vegetable world. It is a botanical anomaly if compared to a tree. It is subterranean, but it is not a root. It sends out multiplications in all directions. It is a labyrinth in process. It can be understood also as a burrow, or as the system of tunnels in an anthill. It is a world of connections and of trips without limits or propositions. In a rhizome one is always in the middle, between the Self and the Other. But, above all, it should be seen as a nonsystematic system of lines of flight and alliance that propagate themselves ad infinitum. (Benítez-Rojo, *Island,* 291, n. 24)

The in-betweenness posited by the rhizome state corresponds nicely to the position taken by Henry Louis Gates, Jr., in the debate over Afrocentrism in the U.S. In the same issue of *Newsweek* cited earlier, Gates stated: "We need to explore the hyphen in African-American, on both sides of the Atlantic" (Gates, "Pharaohs," 47). It would be hard to find a clearer, more incisive example of the pertinence of the rhizome over against the totalitarian root metaphor.

Ethnicity per se plays a relatively small role in Benítez-Rojo's study, whereas Glissant never loses sight of the results of the forcible transport of millions of Africans to the New World and the violent process that created a creolized, or syncretic, culture in plantation America.[4] Indeed, that process is his point of departure and his principal subject as he surveys the contemporary world scene:

> Gilles Deleuze and Félix Guattari have criticized the notion of *root* and . . . of *rootedness.* The root is unique; it is the stock that takes everything to itself and kills all around it. Over against this notion they set the rhizome, which is a multiple root, spreading in fibrous systems through the earth or the air, without any stock developing into an inevitable predator. Thus the notion of *rhizome* would maintain the fact of being rooted but would challenge the idea of a totalitarian root. Rhizomous thought would stand in relation to what I call a poetics of Relation, according to which all identity extends itself in relation to an Other. (Glissant, *Relation,* 23)

At this point, one can see clearly that the choice of metaphor we make to discuss cultural processes can determine every proposition we develop in our reasoning on the subject. Contrariwise, the metaphor used to communicate in simple terms a complex system of relations is rigorously implied by our prior investment in a social, political, and economic system. Such metaphors are neither innocent nor merely literary. People choose to live and, sometimes, to die for such notions. What are the implications of the taproot and fibrous-root (rhizome) metaphor?

Taproot	*Rhizome*
unique origin (stock)	multiple points of rooting
culture identified with ethnicity	culture as history
return to one source (Soul)	connectedness (Relation)
totalitarian logic	dialogue as the norm

One contributor to our symposium developed his own metaphor to account for the evolution and history of African animal characters in folktales that are disseminated throughout former plantation America. Kandioura Dramé preferred the image of the triptych, which retains a sense of the sacred from its use as a three-paneled painting used in religious ritual. In reviewing theories of folktales originating in Africa, he pointed out the inadequacies of the survivals model, which correlates with the taproot theory of culture; he then examined the continuities model, which correlates with a theory of multiple rootedness. Finally, the image of the triptych, which can be folded with the three panels overlaid for transport from place to place, has the advantage of allowing for one or another aspect of the complex ritual object to be displayed, depending on the audience or the occasion. This is perfectly in keeping with the notion that cultural forms sharing a part of their heritage with others have developed singular features that root them in the historical place of development. At the same time, these cultural forms connect or relate to a more or less distant past in various points on the globe. Their rootedness is thus multiple and complex; it relates these cultural forms to many others in both time and space.

Simple Figures, Complex Manifestations

On the day he received the Nobel Prize for Literature, Derek Walcott addressed an overflow crowd at the University of Virginia to set the tone for the symposium. He stressed the universality of animal figures in myth and folklore, drawing illustrations from both the classics of Western cultural tradition and the oral and written culture of the West

Indies. After publishing his epic poem *Omeros* in 1990 and preparing his adaptation of *The Odyssey* for the Royal Shakespeare Company, the new laureate sketched in a theory of multiple rootedness that neither Glissant nor Benítez-Rojo would disavow: "Odysseus's qualities are precisely the qualities one ascribes to certain animals in folklore. . . . I tend to think of Odysseus as the equivalent of someone in Jamaican or Caribbean folklore, as someone elusive and small, as someone who can get out of things. And the confrontation . . . that might happen between a small animal and a very big one: the cunning that is there as opposed to size" (Walcott, "Afterword," 270). Clearly, Walcott has refashioned an archetypal text of the Western tradition in terms that approximate those of the new cultural anthropology championed by James Clifford, Richard Handler, and Renato Rosaldo. The poet, like the anthropologist, finds that he can no longer function as the agent of imperial ideology in a native setting.

Walcott's presentation of Odysseus, the culture hero of a European foundational epic, connects him to the trickster traditions of the Americas. *Traditions* must be written in the plural because the results of our symposium demonstrate that neither in Afro-Caribbean or African-American cultural tradition nor in Native American tradition can we speak of one trickster figure. The essays by Dramé and the editor demonstrate how the development in the New World of a trickster figure like Anancy depends upon the historical circumstances of the cultural region in which the development occurred. Anancy cannot be seen as a uniform, stable figure inherited from a unified African source, which, as it happens, does not exist. Likewise, the essays by Gary H. Gossen and Dell H. Hymes show conclusively that there is no one Coyote, either in Mesoamerica or in the western United States. The richness and variety of these traditions, then, militate against any representation of *the* trickster as *the* representative of a culture of resistance to which an oppressed group ought to lay claim. Relation and connectedness are affirmed by the collective weight and incisiveness of these analyses at the expense of Soul.

The question of Soul arose during the question and answer session that followed Walcott's reading on 8 October 1992. Gossen pointed out that Walcott's comments on the interconnectedness of literature and orality in the Caribbean and in his own writing was reminiscent of the twentieth-century Spanish poet Federico García Lorca. He asked whether Walcott felt any affinity with García Lorca. In reply, Walcott began by affirming the multiple rootedness that, in his view, all poets experience: "The twentieth-century poet has an affinity with every poet who has lived or who is alive in the twentieth century, so it's all an exchange that goes on, of picking things up. Obviously, yes, Lorca is just one of scores of people who are an example and an influence" (Walcott, "Remarks," 18). He then broached the subject of Soul, in the precise sense that term took on in the wake of the Black Aesthetic movement in the U.S. during the 1960s and 1970s.[5] For Walcott, every culture has its version of Soul. He elaborated:

> But Lorca's point is *duende,* which is Soul, really, in the same sense that the black speaks without boasting about having Soul—not, "You can't do it because you're white, you ain't got Soul," I don't mean that—but that Soul is the depth of the black experience. That's peculiar to the black experience in the same way that *duende* is characteristic of gypsy music or the flamenco. If you ain't got *duende,* you ain't got it. So each race has its own pure core. The string of the soul is touched by that reality within the race. It may be a Jewish thing; it may be this or that, whatever the name is; but that's the vibration that comes out of the race. It's not a self-separating thing; it is a reality of the voice. For instance, you can say of [Allen] Ginsberg's poem "Kaddish" that it's a powerful Jewish lament, particularly, and it's particularly Jewish. And that's the strength in it. The lament for his mother is a magnificent elegy for Naomi. ("Remarks," 18)

What is most significant here with respect to patterns of culture in the Americas is that Walcott could both affirm the core experience of Soul (with its equivalent in other cultures that may cohabit within the same geographical space) and, simultaneously, stress the particularness of that experience without excluding those other cultural particularities. This logic is open and connected to other modes of cultural expression, like Glissant's and Benítez-Rojo's; it presupposes the existence of dialogue and exchange in time and space. In this respect, Walcott establishes considerable distance between himself and the Black Aesthetic of a generation ago, as well as from today's Afrocentrist movement. Neither today's Afrocentrists nor yesterday's proponents of the Black Aesthetic could, or wanted to, make the move from the particular—which is their exclusive interest—to the broader cultural context with its conflictual mix of Others. Is this not what Walcott intended when he said, in his Nobel lecture, "I am only one-eighth the writer I might have been had I contained all the fragmented languages of Trinidad" (Walcott, *Antilles,* 8 [unpag.])?

Monsters, Monkeys, and Tarzan

Marianna Torgovnik, in *Gone Primitive: Savage Intellects, Modern Lives,* devoted her second chapter to "Taking Tarzan Seriously." Her point is to show that Edgar Rice Burroughs' hero of fiction and film, usually dismissed as an insignificant manifestation of popular culture, was in fact the epitome of the racist ideology of empire. The Tarzan films starring Johnny Weismuller were shown throughout the colonial world during the 1930s. In this most ubiquitous and accessible form, the Eurocentric vision of *Tarzan of the Apes* taught colonized people of color to scorn both apes and the African natives in Burroughs' world. More important, they learned scorn for their own color. This self-deprecatory process had become the subject of anticolonial and postcolonial literature a generation before Torgovnik took it up. Walcott confronted this painful self-identification in answer to a question from Tejumola Olaniyan, who had traced a parallel between the monkey-man in Walcott's play *Dream on Monkey Mountain* and the author's own development as a writer: "My question concerns your choice of *Dream on Monkey Mountain* for your presentation and your interpretation of the character Makak. There are so many close parallels between your account—in the introduction to *Dream . . .* —of developing a West Indian theater and the movement of Makak in that play in his quest for his true West Indian self that I am forced to ask: How much of Makak is in the writer?" ("Remarks," 23).

Walcott replied: "If you mean the portrait of the black man as an ape, the black man as a savage, the conventional, very hard-to-break, heraldic, inherited view, which we were taught in the Caribbean about the African—we were taught that—sometimes by black people, that's a punishment of colonialism. That's there . . ." ("Remarks," 24–25).

This exchange came in response to Walcott's description of the character called Makak in *Dream on Monkey Mountain:*

> Makak in the play is based on a man I knew who terrified us when we were very young in Saint Lucia, a man called—and that's the tough thing about this—he was called Makak Roger. Roger was not his name. I think he may have worked for somebody called Roger, so it really was this that people were calling him: "This is Roger's monkey," which is terrible; but that's what he was. He would get very drunk. He was an ugly, short, ferocious man who would be bellowing up the street, and you would hear him coming and everybody was terrified of Makak Roger. . . . But the central thing, of course, is the fig-

> ure of the ape. The African is the ape. The African is the baboon. Tarzan and the apes. It is not only Tarzan and the apes; it's Tarzan and all of the apes, meaning not only Cheeta, but Cheeta's buddies. Meaning those wild guys coming through the jungle screaming. . . . That's the African we were shown in the Caribbean. ("Afterword," 272-73)

The second part of the question was equally interesting and germane to our subject. According to Olaniyan:

> In the beginning, Makak believes in things as they are, in the Eurocentric discourse that constructs him as black and therefore ugly and a monkey. The writer, too, in the beginning, believes in things as they are, that as a writer in English he could unproblematically extend the long line of Marlowe, Milton, and Shakespeare, until he learns that even literary traditions do have their own prejudices. Later, Makak revolts and goes to an Africa of the mind—an Afrocentric baptism that cures him of his inferiority complex. The writer, too, after the scorn from the Great Tradition, tried the "African Dream". . . . Finally, Makak gives up the dream of a glorious imperial Africa and claims his humble West Indian self. The writer, too, insists that the Caribbean exists, and the project is to find it, not necessarily or exclusively in Europe or in Africa, but in all its tributaries and finally in the Caribbean space itself. ("Remarks," 23–24)

This line of questioning clearly parallels the evolution of paradigms of identity in the Americas from the imperial Great Tradition through the taproot metaphor of Afrocentrism to the multirootedness of Glissant's and Benítez-Rojo's postcolonial theory. Indeed, Walcott's own evolution as an artist can be seen to have followed just such a trajectory, as Olaniyan suggested. An examination of Jeremy Poynting's essay "From Ancestral to Creole" demonstrates nicely that a similar evolution is at work in the cultures of Trinidad and Guyana, the region of the greatest postemancipation conflict between descendants of Africans and descendants of Indians in the New World.

Monsters and Gods

The permutations of monstrosity that emerged from our symposium were so varied as to defy easy categorization. In all cases they share certain features, however. The monster occupies a necessary, liminal position at the edges of any culture's conceptual field where alien Others must be dealt with, as Victor Turner demonstrated in *The Forest of Symbols* and *Dramas, Fields, and Metaphors.* In our recent shared past, the monkey-men Derek Walcott described from his own experience were an interiorization of this Otherness by colonized people of color in both the Caribbean and the United States, wherever the plantation system of slavery prevailed in the hemisphere. Within the dominant Eurocentric culture, the construction of black people as somehow lesser creatures can be traced directly to the biblical interpretation according to which Ham, a son of Noah, is the ancestor of all black Africans, as Michael Palencia-Roth points out. But monsters were present in the minds of the earliest explorers and colonizers of the New World well before the institution of African chattel slavery was devised. Monsters lurked in the seas at the edges (liminal sites) of the known world as cartographers conceived them. Moreover, these monsters were logical projections of Otherness, within the discourse of European superiority. When actual monsters were not encountered by the explorers, monstrous traits were attributed to whatever natives were at hand in order to justify branding them enemies of God.

In a fascinating turnabout of this dialectic of Otherness, various Native American and Afro-Amazonian cultures have incorporated the European as monster within their own vision of the world. Three variations on this process are present in the essays by Joanna Overing and Candace Slater, both based on Amazonian research, and by Gossen, based on research conducted in the Mayan cultural region of southern Mexico. The common traits here are the power of the monster, who can do great evil and who must therefore be both incorporated within the culture and somehow restricted to a certain area of activity that the culture can accommodate. In Overing's research, the European in his conquistador's armor is sexually monstrous. The conquistador's wart-covered, monstrous penis is thus a synecdoche for the cultural penetration of the native world that he represents. Slater's research in a community descended from maroons (runaway slaves) in Brazilian Amazonia finds white agents of transformation who can seduce people into joining them in their realm at the bottom of the river, from whence local folk never return. The Tzotzil-speaking Maya of Chiapas state in Mexico have gone further. They have incorporated Christian saints—Saint Jerome is the prime example—into their cosmogony and have accorded specific and important roles to them.

In a companion piece to the essay published here, Gossen has questioned why it is that none of the divinities in the Tzotzil heavens (which represent creation periods prior to the current, fourth creation) are

Native Americans: "Why should a people so confident in their own identity, as the 'true people,' live in the very center of a cosmos populated by white-skinned deities and adversaries and black-skinned demons and life forces? Where is the 'Indian' in their cosmological, spiritual, and historical landscape? Why is everything that creates, sustains, and threatens the Tzotzil world ultimately attributed to non-Indians?" (Gossen, "Cosmology," 462). He examines and then discards the postcolonial hypothesis that the Tzotzils, in a reactive posture, have simply banished all threatening Others to an otherworldly domain. His conclusion is based on the cyclical notion of time characteristic of Mayan culture.

> One solution to this puzzle appears to lie in the power of Maya-derived cyclical time-reckoning to absorb otherness in an ever-evolving historical matrix that consistently yields new end points and renewed identities. In the case of Chamula, this process constantly yields a new set of Chamula communities—a renewed home community and many recently founded immigrant colonies. Cyclical time-reckoning allows for selective accommodation and comprehension of new actors and new ideas by placing them morally in past time. . . . This logic creates a continually evolving present in which "Indianness" is logically foregrounded at the expense of new waves of others who are systematically relegated to a newly reconfigured past. New Others merge with morally equivalent antecedent beings who populated and changed the cosmos over the three historical epochs leading to the present, fourth, epoch. ("Cosmology," 466)

Coyotes and Other Tricksters

"Animal Souls and Human Destiny in Mesoamerica" begins with a Tzotzil Indian assimilating Gossen to Coyote, who is his presumed co-essence, and concludes with the ethnographer's supposition that the culture of nagualism may be evolving toward an African-American version of Soul. Midway through his analysis, Gossen divulges that there may be as many different variations on the precise function of Coyote—or any other animal co-essence of humans—as there are villages in the region Mayan culture occupies, not to mention its diaspora in wider Mexico and the U.S. Gossen acknowledges that he initially sought to represent "a coherent theory of selfhood" in his published research, but that he has come to the realization that "the concept of animal souls . . . bears more resemblance to a fluid metalanguage of discourse and practice for dealing with self, Other, and human destiny than it does to any rigid system of belief."

The distinction is of capital importance. Versions of it also come through in the contributions by Hymes and by Jay Miller and Vi Hilbert. To the extent that the dominant culture has successfully reduced Native American cultural systems to a "rigid system of belief," it has been able to use this presumed scientific knowledge to marginalize, trivialize, and, finally, to restrict them to ethnographic reservations. To acknowledge that the belief systems of Native Americans anywhere in the New World may be evolving and may, in fact, have been involved for centuries with mediating between the past and the presence of Europeans and their descendants is to acknowledge that these same native peoples are also actors in their own contemporary history. The ramifications of this acknowledgment would take us well beyond the scope of this book into areas where postimperial theory overlaps with government policy, as it does in Chiapas, Mexico, today.

Hymes takes a more literary approach to Coyote narratives from the Pacific Northwest. By focusing on the telling of Coyote stories, he has drawn out of them aesthetic qualities that belong ultimately to the individual storytellers whose versions he has studied. Thus, Coyote stories become more modern in the sense that they do not represent, any more than do the animal co-essences of the Tzotzils, an immutable indigenous reality fixed in a distant, precontact past. In Miller's preliminary remarks to the story of Starchild, as told by Hilbert, he too insists on the variations in tellings of the cosmogonic narratives of origin that belong to the Lushootseed cultural heritage. Far from a rigid, unchanging system that would relegate Native Americans to an irretrievable past, the Lushootseed stories of the beginnings of the world represent a continuing mediation between past and present.

This aesthetic dimension of Native American Coyote stories links up with observations made by both Dramé and Walcott at the symposium. Dramé pointed out that in one traditional society of West Africa certain features of an Anancy story must be attributed to the genius of the adolescent storyteller. Walcott related a version of a West Indian folktale featuring the hero Ti-Jean as it had been told by his school friend Mock. In retelling the tale, the new Nobel laureate retained the inventive Creole elements that give a particular flavor to this body of tales common to the African diaspora in the Caribbean. Thinking I would find the text in Walcott's published play *Ti-Jean and His Brothers,* I discovered that the most characteristic creole elements had been written out of the published play, which corresponds to a different literary model. This example, and those adduced by Dramé and Hymes as well, demonstrate that wherever we turn in the vast body of animal tales in the New World—even in their presumed transatlantic origins—we find not an unchanging root of identity but a richly patterned corpus existing in relation to other texts and the density of their cultural contexts.

Sacred Cows and Imagined Communities

Brinsley Samaroo ends his essay on "Animal Images in Caribbean Hindu Mythology" with an observation on the invention of tradition, a term he borrows from Eric Hobsbawn and Terence Ranger. It is especially interesting that Samaroo has found this process at work in a New World Hindu community. Anthropologists and philosophers in the West long vied with one another in demonstrating the degree to which Hinduism was immemorial and fixed in a distant past. Their theses provided ample justification for the necessity of Western imperial domination to bring Indian society into the modern world. To the extent that Hindus in significant overseas communities like those in Trinidad could be tied to that same vision of changelessness, they could be marginalized within modern postcolonial states. In Trinidad and Tobago, where Indo-Tobagonians today constitute roughly one-half of the total population, it was possible until a few years ago for black Creoles to dominate the political scene and ignore the *Indians*, a term that can still be found in some social-science writing that purports to describe the region.

In the late 1970s, the black Creole novelist Earl Lovelace published a novel entitled *The Dragon Can't Dance*. The plot uses the central Caribbean festival of Carnival and the traditional dragon mask that the protagonist has redesigned year after year to trace the evolution of the urban poor of Port-of-Spain in the late 1960s and early 1970s. The novel's climax corresponds in historical time with the spread of the Black Power movement in the Caribbean.

Lovelace's novel has an important subtext concerning the arrival of rural Hindus (Indians) in one of the typical Creole yards (neighborhoods) of the Trinidadian capital. The reader who attends only to the principal plot line may well conclude that the novel is pessimistic about Carnival. The protagonist, whose identification with the threatening Carnival dragon connects him to the presumed origins of the Afro-Trinidadian Carnival in a creole culture of resistance to slavery and oppression, participates in a spontaneous hijacking of a police jeep, spends several years in prison, and emerges with a new consciousness of his Trinidadian identity. The traditional Carnival with its taproot concept of black Creole identity has to die (in fact, it is appropriated by the new commercial sponsors, who commodify the old *authentic* cultural ritual) so that a new, more inclusive national identity may emerge. The Indian characters, Boya and Dolly Pariag, are at first scapegoated by the black Creoles of Calvary Hill (Boya's shiny new bicycle, the means by which he is beginning to accumulate capital through commerce, is destroyed by unknown individuals with universal community approval); but at the end of the novel, they begin to give a new meaning to the old, shallow, and mendacious Carnival slogan: "All o'we is one."

The dragon of the novel is a densely coded figure that Lovelace uses to mediate ethnic and political conflict in contemporary Port-of-Spain. He has understood that Indo-Tobagonians are not monolithic cultural *Indians.* Lovelace's genius was to be able to imagine a community, in Benedict Anderson's sense of the term, that could transcend the old, inherited hostilities that the dragon symbolizes in the first part of the novel. When Aldrick, the protagonist, emerges from prison, he understands Pariag; but he can no longer play the dragon, whence the novel's title. Thus the dragon, formerly Aldrick's essence in the symbolic economy of the text, has become the site of a sociopolitical struggle over the changing identity of Trinidad. Aldrick has had to sacrifice his identification with a mythological beast that tied him to an exclusive Afro-Caribbean past in order to forge a more inclusive, more humane Trinidadian identity. It is to Lovelace's credit that he represents this change as difficult, sometimes violent, and incomplete in the fictional present. In the decade following the publication of *The Dragon Can't Dance,* Trinidadians brought to power a mixed-race political party with numerous Indo- and Sino-Tobagonians at the ministerial level, among whom was Minister of Agriculture and Marine Exploitation Samaroo.

Not all contemporary societies in the Americas have been able to redefine and broaden their idea of *communitas* through a similar act of imagination. In the same year when *The Dragon Can't Dance* sketched in elements of a new cultural identity in Trinidad and Tobago, one corresponding to the rhizome model, Antonine Maillet published a novel that quite self-consciously attempted to revive the historical memory of a dispersed and partially deculturated minority, the Acadians of New Brunswick and Nova Scotia, Canada. The Acadians had been dispersed *manu militari* by the British in 1755 to make way for a new English-speaking population in the disputed area. Highland Scots, driven from their homeland by the British, were resettled in what would become New Scotland (Nova Scotia), with many New England colonists joining them even before the American Revolution. All but a few French-speaking Acadians were transported by British ships and dumped along the Atlantic coast of the future United States. A large population became the Southern Acadians (Cajuns) of Louisiana. Smaller populations eventually were absorbed into the thirteen original colonies of the future United States and Florida. The overland trek from coastal Georgia by small groups of dispersed Acadians between 1772 and 1780 resulted in a return to the land of their birth by the ancestors of Maillet, who commemorates this heroic exploit in *Pélagie-la-charrette,* published in 1979.

Rather than allow the dispersed elements of the Acadian nation to "little by little sink their floating roots in foreign soil" (Maillet, *Pélagie,* 16), the heroine of *Pélagie-la-charrette* opts for an arduous journey, fraught with perils, of the sort culture heroes typically endure. In this narrative, it is a collective journey, both back to a point of physical origin and forward to found the nation of today. In the course of their journey, the past and future Acadians collect two interesting specimens who, for a time, appear destined to join the collectivity. Catoune, a half-breed girl who had been reared by Indians (*savages,* in the text) contributes to the survival and even to the salvation of members of the Acadian group. In the Carolinas, a misadventure results in a black slave being added to the wagon (*charrette*). His blackness caused the deliverers of Catoune, who was about to be sold as a slave, to mistake him for a log (mahogany?) to which they thought she was chained. Despite the black man's talents—he devises a novel way to grease the wagon's wheels, a critical skill under such conditions—he is dismissed by the group as someone who does not, could not possibly, belong: "The Negro, the slave from Charleston, a man Black both of skin and origin could not [bear the name Théotiste, Pélagie's father's name]. . . . He was black in a white land, and furthermore he owed his life and his freedom to Pélagie" (*Pélagie,* 129). A bit later on, he "already speaks our language, practically rolling the r's and, true as I'm standing here, he's even begun to whiten" (*Pélagie,* 135). Neither cultural assimilation (speaking Acadian French) nor the whitening that the reader takes as a comic touch, will do the trick.

Without further explanation, the narrator gets rid of the black man just before the group reaches Acadian soil, telling the reader that he went off to join the savages. Catoune simply disappears into the forests. One might assume that she, too, joined the "savages"; but "three generations swore later on that from Pélagie's grave [in Tintamarre, the cradle of the nation] she responded to Acadia's call. For a century after that Catoune's voice could be heard in the Tintamarre swamps on nights when the wind howled" (*Pélagie,* 281).

The logic of the narration is clear: Impure and alien racial elements must be expelled from the stock of the new Acadian nation. The Micmac Indians of old Acadia are destined to disappear from their homeland in this view, since they are already in the eighteenth century "half-breeds, sold out to the Whites, living in wooden cabins like Europeans" (*Pélagie,* 181), thus justifying their eventual displacement by the returned Acadians. Conversely, the frequent references to genealogy by two narrator-characters, Pélagie and Bélonie, her male counterpart, guarantee the purity of Acadian bloodlines and reassure the reader of the biological homogeneity of the group.

These are the narrative elements that point most clearly to Maillet's taproot model of cultural identity. Moreover, it is clear that, for her, language (Acadian, not Quebecois French or English), religion (Roman Catholic), and race (blue-eyed blonds) are coterminus.[6] Black French-speaking Acadians have existed since the eighteenth century in New Brunswick,[7] but the narrative logic of *Pélagie-la-charrette* treats them as an imaginative impossibility. These, then, are the elements relating to cultural identity that contextualize the animal tales included in *Pélagie-la-charrette* and provide them with density and meaning.

Two tales are told, early and late in the narrative, that reinforce the theme of the national quest for the homeland. They are structurally similar. With respect to the details of Acadian identity that I have just adduced, the tales are a literary *mise en abyme,* that is, they replicate the structure of the national quest while simplifying it for comprehensibility. The tale of the white whale is told by the narrator-character Bélonie at precisely the moment when Catoune and the black slave are "saved" in Charleston, South Carolina. The hero, who is of low birth (*vilain,* or "peasant"), must free the magic gold ring from the belly of the white whale, which has swallowed a bear, which has swallowed a fox, which has swallowed a chicken. The ring is to be found in the chicken's innards. Rather than kill the animals in succession, the hero in Bélonie's version travels ever farther into the innards of the whale (and, eventually, into the guts of the other animals) to find the ring. Allegorically, the white whale is the North American continent, which, in the late eighteenth century, incorporates a host of nonhomogeneous elements that have recently swallowed up the remnants of the Acadian nation who must be saved by a heroic quest. Maillet's omniscient narrator assures us (*Pélagie,* 70) that the tale of the white whale belongs to Bélonie's repertoire but that in this telling it has a different ending, which is precisely that of her novel.

The second tale is told near the end of *Pélagie-la-charrette.* It is taken from the stock of Ti-Jean stories that are shared by white Creole populations of North America (Acadians and Cajuns) and black Creole populations from Louisiana to the southeastern Caribbean. In *Pélagie-la-charrette,* the version given involves Tit-Jean's plans to marry.[8] He has a boat built as his wedding gift for his bride; but to complete it successfully he must acquire three magic words from a sorcerer. The sorcerer tells Tit-Jean that he can get the three magic words only from the Great Lady of the Night, who lives in a distant place. Tit-Jean receives directions for a one-way trip, but none for the return.

The relationship of this story to the preceding one, and the function of both as narrative *mises en abyme,* begins to emerge. Once again, the narrator is Bélonie, who "kept it for great occasions. A story unlike any other" (*Pélagie,* 248). Before the story begins, the omniscient narrator assures the listeners or readers that "this is the story of one of [Bélonie's] ancestors, one of the first of the race, who lived before the tower of Babel, when all men spoke the same language" (*Pélagie,* 248). Identical race, lineage, and language (the foundations of nationalism posited on the taproot model) are established in the narrative frame. Thus the one-way ticket, so to speak, that the sorcerer provides Tit-Jean replicates the boat trips the English "provided" the Acadians in 1755, with no hope of any return. Insofar as this story replicates the structure of the earlier one about the white whale (*baleine* is feminine in French), the white whale and the Great Lady of the Night seem to have an analogous function. The story about the white whale is located near the beginning of the long trek back to Acadia, a narrative strategy that suggests that the white whale is the North American continent itself. But the Great Lady of the Night is further identified as Tit-Jean's "distant ancestor" (*Pélagie,* 249) in a phrase where *distant* can refer to both genealogy and geography, and it may be that Maillet has another function in mind for her, despite the structural analogy.

As in the earlier story, the hero must enter into the monstrous figure through its mouth and descend into its guts in search of the treasure. This time, however, Tit-Jean encounters a dragon in the intestines, and he must slay it in time-honored tradition. After slaying the dragon, Tit-Jean disdains the diamonds and pearls that pour from its stomach, "the treasure that men have sought since the beginning of time" (*Pélagie,* 251), taking only the three magic words, which are never identified in the text. Since this tale is located strategically near the end of a novel that concerns itself with the (re)foundation of a nation, we can take the unidentified magic words to be the gift of the national language that is also the vehicle for the telling of Maillet's own novel. In this respect, they meet the fundamental test of the *mise en abyme* technique.

As an allegory of the nationalist quest, Bélonie's tale of Tit-Jean and the Great Lady of the Night does not have an unambiguously happy ending. On leaving the body of his distant ancestor, Tit-Jean makes the mistake of exiting feet first. Birds see his posterior, twitter at the comical sight, and awaken the sleeping giant, who inadvertently closes her jaws and cuts Tit-Jean in two. The distant ancestor now appears to be the original homeland of Acadia, which exists only in historical time since its loss to the British in the eighteenth century. The homeland, founded by a culturally homogeneous group of French colonists in the seventeenth century, has left nothing to her children other than their language, the symbol and vehicle of their culture.

In his discussion of *Nationalism and the Politics of Culture in Quebec,* Richard Handler has described "images of the nation as a living individual—a tree, a friend, a creature with a soul—[that] convey . . . a sense of wholeness and boundedness" (Handler, *Quebec,* 40). Both the allegorical whale and the Great Lady of the Night clearly represent the wholeness and boundedness of a nation. The whale, however, has ingested foreign elements and is not, therefore, a proper home for Acadians. The Great Lady of the Night episode, with its dragon and Tit-Jean's dangerous emergence—the hero is cut in two, as new Acadia was when Cajun society was founded in Louisiana—allegorizes the dangers facing the new nation in the narrative present, which can be read as either the time of the late-eighteenth-century return or the late-twentieth-century writing of the novel. In both cases, danger lurks: in the form of the British dragon that had colonized the vital space of historical Acadia or in the form of the Anglo-Canadians, whose culture threatens to annihilate the Acadians in the present. The fact that the sorcerer in Antonine Maillet's Tit-Jean tale did not provide a map for the return both allegorizes the difficulties of the eighteenth-century trek led by Pélagie in the novel and signifies to its readers that today Acadians can survive only by use of their wits. Therefore, the Acadian culture hero must be a trickster. The Great Lady of the Night exists currently as the bounded, protective figure of the nation only in Acadian memory. She can no longer protect her descendants in the way a nation such as Quebec does, for instance.

We are now in a better position to understand the full import of the white-whale story told by Bélonie early in Maillet's novel. Its relationship to the eventual disappearance of the liberated black slave and the mixed-race character Catoune is fundamental. Just as the heroic Acadians must trek up the Atlantic coast of the future United States without being corrupted by its alien culture, so the founders of a renewed Acadia on native soil must arrive unsullied by foreign blood. This is the allegorical import of the multiple animals, swallowed by the whale, which the hero simply passes through, but does not kill, in order to reach the treasure. Alien Others are not to be disturbed—like Catoune and the liberated black slave from South Carolina, they should even be respected and assisted where possible—but neither may they enter into the definition of the nation. These are the limits of the imagined community of Acadians. *Pélagie-la-charrette* uses animal tales basically to reinforce an ideology of the nation that is restrictive and negative.

Richard Handler has analyzed similar elements in the twentieth-century ideology of Quebec nationalism. Abbé Lionel Groulx's fear of miscegenation, exemplified in his 1922 novel *L'appel de la race* (The Call of the Race), provides many of Handler's examples in his discussion of "The Negative Vision: Pollution and Death" (*Quebec,* 47–50). For Groulx, intermarriage with "not-Quebec" (Handler's term for the several threatening Others that have surrounded Quebec from the eighteenth century into the present) could only lead to miscegenation, loss of cultural identity, and eventual cultural death. The characters Catoune and the freed black slave in *Pélagie-la-charrette* have an identical function. Taken together, they represent the threat of not-Acadia, which must be eliminated from the new nation. As an example of cultural nation-building, Antonine Maillet's *Pélagie-la-charrette* stands at the opposite extreme from Earl Lovelace's *The Dragon Can't Dance.*

These two recent literary examples open onto diametrically opposed ideologies of the nation and its culture. The animal tales or their literary equivalent are finally understood in terms of their function and setting within a larger cultural whole that provides a frame of reference for the hermeneutic process of establishing meaning. Far from being fixed in some legendary past, they continue into the present (and surely will continue into the future as well) to serve as a locus for debate, conflict, and, ultimately, the resolution of conflict in the collective imaginings of peoples of the Americas.

NOTES

1. An excellent outline of the Manichaean view of black and white aesthetics in the United States can be found in Addison Gayle, Jr., "Cultural Strangulation: Black Literature and the White Aesthetic," *The Black Aesthetic,* ed. by Addison Gayle, Jr. (New York: Anchor, 1972), pp. 38–45.

2. Alex Haley's *Roots* (New York: Doubleday, 1976) is, of course, a result of the taproot model of identity and an illustration of the sentimental version of its aesthetic. The popular wave of roots culture that it stimulated later in the decade, in the U.S. and abroad, would be followed by the more aggressive, politically committed ideology of Afrocentrism, which stems from the same ideological source.

3. A sketch of the rhizome model of culture can be found in Deleuze and Guattari's *Kafka: For a Minor Literature* (1975). The model was made more explicit the following year in *Rhizome: An Introduction.*

4. Our use of *creole culture* here is fundamentally different from that of Benedict Anderson in *Imagined Communities,* where he follows the Spanish-language tradition of identifying *criollo* with New World descendants of (pure) European stock. (See his chapter 4: "Creole Pioneers.") Like much else in the New World, the term *creole* has undergone a transformation. We use it, as do Creole people of color, to identify individuals and societies (including their languages) that result from a process of syncretism. To understand even a central concept like *creole,* one must know whether the utterance stems from a taproot or a rhizomous model of culture.

5. See Ron Wellburn, "The Black Aesthetic Imperative," *The Black Aesthetic,* ed. Addison Gayle, Jr. (New York: Anchor, 1972), pp. 126–42. In this article, the music of Soul is described as fighting a pitched battle with (white) rock music that has incorporated (read: stolen) elements of jazz. The taproot metaphor of culture as a racial imperative informs the entire argument.

6. In television interviews I have seen, Antonine Maillet has insisted on the blond, blue-eyed characteristics of true Acadians. They are thus differentiated ethnically from Quebecois, who are said to have originated in different regions of France.

7. As I was preparing this introduction, I chanced upon a television program called *Visions d'Amérique,* which originates in Quebec. A local interviewer talked to several residents of Montreal who belong to what Canadians

call visible minorities. One of the interviewees described himself as a "black Francophone Acadian, born in Cap au Sable, New Brunswick." In Maillet's fictional Acadia, Paul H. Brown, for that is his name, could not exist.

8. Maillet uses the variant spelling *Tit-Jean,* presumably to render an approximation of Acadian pronunciation. Both *Ti-* and Tit- derive from the French word *petit* (little), as in Littlejohn of Robin Hood fame. In the Ti-Jean cycle of stories, however, it is important that the hero be small, relatively lacking in strength or defenses, whereas the Littlejohn of the English tradition was quite large. Ti(t)-Jean is clearly a trickster figure himself, for he must use his wiles to escape from apparently impossible situations.

REFERENCES

Anderson, Benedict. *Imagined Communities: Reflections on the Origin and Spread of Nationalism.* London; New York: Verso, 1991 [1983].

Asante, Molefi Kete. "Putting Africa at the Center." *Newsweek* (23 September 1991): 46. (This is a succinct formulation of the position to which Arthur M. Schlesinger, Jr., took such strong exception in the pages of *Partisan Review.*)

Benítez-Rojo, Antonio. *The Repeating Island: The Caribbean and the Postmodern Perspective.* Post-Contemporary Interventions. Durham, N.C.: Duke University Press, 1992.

Clifford, James. *The Predicament of Culture: Twentieth-Century Ethnography, Literature, and Art.* Cambridge: Harvard University Press, 1988.

Deleuze, Gilles, and Félix Guattari. *Kafka: Pour une littérature mineure.* Paris: Minuit, 1975. English-language edition Minneapolis: University of Minnesota Press, 1986.

———. *Rhizome: An Introduction.* Paris: Minuit, 1976. Translated as "Rhizome" in *I and C,* no. 8 (1981): 49–71.

Gates, Henry Louis, Jr. "Beware of the New Pharaohs." *Newsweek* (23 September 1991): 47.

Gayle, Addison, Jr. "Cultural Strangulation: Black Literature and the White Aesthetic." In *The Black Aesthetic,* ed. Addison Gayle, Jr., 38–45. New York: Anchor, 1972.

Glissant, Edouard. *Poétique de la relation.* Paris: Gallimard, 1990.

Gossen, Gary H. "The Other in Chamula Tzotzil Cosmology and History: Reflections of a Kansan in Chiapas." *Cultural Anthropology* 8, no. 4 (1993): 443–75.

Groulx, Lionel, abbé. *L'appel de la race.* Montreal: Fides, 1956 [1922].

Haley, Alex. *Roots.* New York: Doubleday, 1976.

Handler, Richard. *Nationalism and the Politics of Culture in Quebec.* Madison: University of Wisconsin Press, 1988.

Hill, Errol. *The Trinidad Carnival.* Austin: University of Texas Press, 1972.

Hobsbawn, Eric, and Terence Ranger, eds. *The Invention of Tradition*. New York: Cambridge University Press, 1983.

Jay, Gregory. "The End of 'American' Literature: Toward a Multicultural Paradigm." Unpublished typescript dated 9 October 1989. (This paper was read at the fall 1989 Rutgers-Camden conference of the New Jersey Department of Higher Education as part of the Multicultural Studies Project.)

Lovelace, Earl. *The Dragon Can't Dance*. London: Deutsch, 1979.

Maillet, Antonine. *Pélagie-la-charrette*. Paris: Grasset, 1979. (All translations are my own.)

Rosaldo, Renato. *Culture and Truth: The Remaking of Social Analysis*. Boston: Beacon, 1989.

Schlesinger, Arthur (M.), Jr. "A Dissent on Multicultural Education." *Partisan Review* 58, no. 4 (1991): 630–34.

———. *The Disuniting of America: Reflections on a Multicultural Society*. New York: Whittle Direct Books, 1991. (A more complete version of the *Partisan Review* extract cited in my text.)

Todorov, Tzvetan. *On Human Diversity: Nationalism, Racism, and Exoticism in French Thought*. Cambridge: Harvard University Press, 1993. (Orig. ed. Paris: Seuil, 1989.)

Torgovnik, Marianna. *Gone Primitive: Savage Intellects, Modern Lives*. Chicago: University of Chicago Press, 1990.

Turner, Victor. *The Forest of Symbols: Aspects of Ndembu Ritual*. Ithaca, N.Y.: Cornell University Press, 1967.

———. *Dramas, Fields, and Metaphors: Symbolic Action in Human Society*. Ithaca, N. Y.: Cornell University Press, 1974.

Voldeng, Evelyne. *Les mémoires de Ti-Jean*. Vanier, Ontario: L'Interligne, 1994.

Walcott, Derek. *Ti-Jean and His Brothers*. In *Dream on Monkey Mountain and Other Plays*. New York: Farrar, Straus & Giroux, [1970].

———. *Omeros*. New York: Farrar, Straus & Giroux, 1990.

———. "The Odyssey." First performed in Stratford-upon-Avon, 24 June 1992.

———. "Remarks" following delivery of "Animals, Elemental Tales, and the Theater," at the University of Virginia on 8 October 1992. Unpublished typescript prepared by A. James Arnold from an audio tape and reviewed by the author.

———. *The Antilles: Fragments of Epic Memory*. The Nobel Lecture. New York: Farrar, Straus & Giroux, 1992 (1993).

Wellburn, Ron. "The Black Aesthetic Imperative." In *The Black Aesthetic*, ed. Addison Gayle, Jr., 126–42. New York: Anchor, 1972.

Michael Palencia-Roth

Enemies of God: Monsters and the Theology of Conquest

Christopher Columbus's letter of 1493 to Sánchez, which brought to Europe the first news of the discovery of new islands in the Atlantic, is notable for what he said he did *not* find, as well as what he said he did. He "did not find," he said, "as many had expected, any monsters among [New World people], but rather men of great deference and kindness. . . . Thus [he] saw no monsters, nor did [he] hear of any, except those . . . people who are considered by the [other] islanders as most ferocious: and these feed on human flesh" (Major, *Columbus,* 13–14).[1] In the more private diary of the first voyage, monstrous men became an obsession for Columbus.[2] Although on first seeing Native Americans he marveled at their strong and handsome bodies and their lack of shame at their nakedness, he soon began to write of hearing about people like "one-eyed men and other men with dog-heads, who ate men," men who decapitated their captives, drank their blood, and cut off their genitals (Varela, *Colón,* 51). One-eyed men appear several more times in the diary, as do dog-headed men (for example, 23 November 1492; 26 November 1492) and other mythical creatures. But they *all* appear as absences; they are not there.

The present essay explores the following issues and problems. When Native Americans turned out not to have monstrous or inhuman features, monstrous or inhuman behavior was attributed to them by Europeans, truthfully or not, in order to redefine their nature, and this in turn often in order to justify European actions in the Americas. Moreover, these attributions became part of the cultural allegorization of the New World. Their effectiveness as justifications and allegorizations depended on the belief in a complex duality between the human and the nonhuman. The expression of that duality was influenced by the Western tradition of the monster, or teratology, a tradition articulated primarily through two discourses: one, biological or physiological; the other, behavioral and moral or theological. Eventually, as will be seen, New World people who were defined as monstrous came to be considered "enemies of God."

The biological and theological discourses cannot and should not be kept ever isolated and distinct from each other, for historically they met and mingled with some frequency. The biological discourse on monstrosity originates with Aristotle, almost two millenia before the discovery of America. In *Generation of Animals* (IV.iv.770b, 5–6), Aristotle wrote: "The first characteristic of the monster is to be different." He also said (*Generation of Animals*, IV.iv.769b, 30): "For the monster is a sort of deformity."[3] Although the context of Aristotle's argument here is biological, these and related Aristotelian ideas influenced Western conceptions of the monstrous in disciplines other than biology, for instance, anthropology, ethnography, iconography, geography, and even theology. The monster—*teras* in Greek, *monstrum* in Latin—generally is a creature similar to yet different from human beings. Both the similarity and the difference are important in the term's semantic field. A monster deviates from an accepted norm of humanity. This may be a simple thought, but it has enormous consequences.

The term *teras* or *monstrum* has religious connotations as a sign of some sort from the gods or from God. Other related senses of the term include: serpent, abortion, monstrous birth. *Teratuomai* is to speak of marvels, or to talk nonsense. *Teratologia* is a tale of monsters or of marvels. Here, in exploring teratological discourse, I shall emphasize a perspective that Aristotle influenced but did not develop himself: the theological one. I am particularly interested in the implications of teratology for the history of moral thought in relation to a central activity of Western societies and nation-states: conquest and colonization, both before and during the early European history of the New World.

Classical Teratology

As he does in so many subjects, it is Homer who establishes the paradigm for many subsequent Western writers and thinkers on teratology.[4] I have discussed Homer in an essay entitled "Mapping the Caribbean" and so here should like only to mention him. The most paradigmatic encounter between the civilized Greek and the barbarian Other is narrated, as Derek Walcott has noted, in the episode of the Cyclops in *The Odyssey.* The Cyclops, or Polyphemus, is a "monstrous man" (*Odyssey* 9:187) both biologically and morally: biologically, through his gigantic size and his single eye, and morally, through barbarous practices and attitudes.[5] These include, for instance, an utter indifference toward the rules of hospitality, a disregard for law, an ignorance of agriculture, and a scorn for social traditions, as well as a dislike for living in communities.

The Cyclopean people live somewhere in the Mediterranean. It is probably no accident that such concerns about encountering and defeating strange beings should have informed a poem composed during the Greek colonization of the Mediterranean when parts of it were still unfamiliar. Monsters generally are creatures of hearsay and are encountered—supposedly—beyond the borders of the known world. By the time Herodotus began to travel and to write in the fifth century B.C., the *terrae incognitae* had been pushed back from the Mediterranean and to the South, the North, or the East. Significantly, in this kind of writing, Europe was placed at the geographical center of the world and of civilized life. The concept of such a center is a normative one and has historical consequences. For instance, the placement of Europe, or "the West," at the geographical and moral center of the world gave rise to a Western tradition of core-periphery thought that changed cardinal directions into geographical locations and attributed cultural values to those locations.[6]

The work of Herodotus contributed greatly to the history of the geography of cultural values. Repeatedly, in his *Histories,* Herodotus transmitted stories that were more extreme in their description of "uncivilized" peoples' social practices, attitudes, and appearances the more distant from his home the peoples' lands were. Thus, certain "Indians to the East" of the Persians habitually kill old people and then feast on the remains (3.99). Beyond them live tribes of goat-footed people (4.25); beyond them is a country of people who sleep six months a year (4.25); beyond them live the one-eyed people (4.27). But the "most savage" of all are the "androphagoi," or man-eating people, who "acknowledge no right or wrong, nor have any laws or customs," and are nomads (4.18, 106).

Ktésias the Knidian (fl. 400 B.C.) called Herodotus a liar but then went on to describe a few "monsters" of his own at the edges of his world: man-eating manticores; pygmies; cynocephali, or dog-heads, who bark and possess enormous canine teeth; people born with white hair that turns black by age sixty; people with ears so large that they use them as blankets when they sleep at night; and the usual spate of sciapodes, or shadow-footed people, and acephali, or no-headed people (Photius, "Ctésias le Cnide," 135–47). This style of ethnographic typologizing, widespread from this point on, became even more popular in the Middle Ages, especially in geographical and travel literature, and in cartography.

All these descriptions have several points in common. First, they are based on hearsay and concern people who live far away. Second, each monstrous race has recognizably human features: The manticores have human faces; the dog-heads have human bodies; and so on. Third, the descriptions utilize negations or reversals, which may be either physical or social. Thus in some people, the usual signs of aging are reversed; others have no moral system and no laws, or no fixed abodes.

Augustine and Isidore of Seville

These characterizations do not yet add up to a *theology* of the monstrous. That is, monsters in these texts are not viewed as occupying an assigned place in an order totally created by God with them and others in mind. In the West, that kind of thinking comes to the fore with the desire of Christian writers to understand the world as the creation of God in every detail.[7]

As far as I have been able to determine, the first descriptions prefiguring a Christian theology of the monstrous may be found in the pseudepigrapha of the Old Testament. Let me cite two of them, the earlier one being the *First (Ethiopian Apocalypse of) Enoch*, a text written in the second century B.C.:

> And [angels] took wives unto themselves, and everyone (respectively) chose one woman for himself, and they began to go unto them. . . . And the women became pregnant and gave birth to great giants whose heights were three hundred cubits. These [giants] consumed the produce of all the people until the people detested feeding them. So the giants turned against [the people] in order to eat them. And they began to sin against birds, wild beasts, reptiles, and fish. And their flesh was devoured the one by the other, and they drank blood. And then the earth brought an accusation against the oppressors. (*Old Testament Pseudepigrapha,* 1:16)

Cannibalism, gigantism, bestiality, civil disorder: All are indices of the monstrous. Moreover, in *First Enoch,* monstrous acts and monstrous appearances are linked. The second example comes from the pseudepigraphical life of Adam and Eve:

> For Eve later conceived and bore a son, whose name was Abel. And Cain and Abel used to stay together. And Eve said to Adam, "My lord, while I was sleeping I saw a vision—as if the blood of our son Abel was in the hand of Cain [who was] gulping it down in his mouth. That is why I am sad." And Adam said, "God forbid that Cain would kill Abel! But let us separate them from each other and make separate places for them." And they made Cain a farmer and Abel a shepherd, and in this way they might be separated from each other. (*Old Testament Pseudepigrapha,* 2:266)

Important here is the fact that the very human Cain is not monstrous in appearance but in behavior, that the behavior most feared is that of cannibalism, and that the evil person has to be physically separated from the good one. Eventually, of course, Cain was banished by God for his murder of Abel and was branded with a sign of difference, the "mark" of Cain (*Genesis* 4:15). God intended this mark to protect Cain from being killed by others during his exile, but it also isolated him from other human beings, wherever he might go.

Most medieval Christian writers on teratology depended on Pliny's *Natural History* (A.D. 77) for their source material. Pliny, like Ktésias and Megasthenes, described different sorts of monsters but did not place them, as Aristotle had, in a scientific biology or, indeed, in any kind of systematically comprehensive theory of human nature.[8] In contrast, both Saint Augustine and Isidore of Seville, for instance, although they relied on Pliny, did discuss their notions of monstrosity within a comprehensive and coherent world view. Augustine issued what might be called a Christian apology of the monstrous, and Isidore, a Christian taxonomy and etymology of the monstrous.

For Augustine, nothing in God's world can be accidental, however bizarre it may appear. Therefore, in chapter 8 of book 16 of *The City of God,* Augustine asked himself where monstrous races came from and who fathered them (2:116). After enumerating a stock Plinian catalog, Augustine said that "whoever is anywhere born a man, that is, a rational mortal animal, no matter what unusual appearance he presents in colour, movement, sound, nor how peculiar he is in some power, part, or quality of his nature, no Christian can doubt that he springs from that one protoplast": Adam and, from him, Noah and his sons, the progenitors of all the world's people in the postdiluvian age (*City of God* 2:117). Augustine did not specify here which of Noah's sons he considered to have fathered the monsters of the world, but earlier, in chapters 1 through 3 of the same book, he suggested that it was Ham, the middle son who sinned against his father by not covering his nakedness.[9] As descendants of Ham, monstrous races are evil. The implication is that, although all races are part of God's creation, some are worse and more sinful than others. Sinful races are seen as deformations of God's plan, just as the actions of Cain and Ham are considered deformations of the actions of good human beings. The continent of Africa was considered to be populated by the descendants of Ham, as can be seen in the T-O Map based on the theories of Isidore of Seville, the seventh-century Spanish bishop who authored a compendium of Western knowledge then currently accepted as true (fig. 1.1). Not coincidentally, the kind of thinking evidenced in this T-O Map is one of the sources of Western racism against blacks. Europe and Asia were thought to be the homes of the descendants of Noah's good sons, Japheth and Shem. In this way, the history of monsters and the history of cartography are related to the development of racism in the West.

As befitting a work entitled *Etymologies,* Isidore analyzed and presented the world through language. The first of his twenty "books" in this magnum opus deals with grammar, and a number of the rest treat the etymological roots of certain disciplines and subjects. In book 11, Isidore treated "monsters" in detail. After discussing the parts of the body and the "ages of man," Isidore stated that monsters are, in fact, not *contra naturam* because everything created by God is part of nature and a product of his divine will (Isidore, *Etimologías,* 2:46).

Fig. 1.1. T-O Map, Isidore of Seville, *Etymologiae.* Augsburg, 1472. (Courtesy of the University of Illinois at Urbana-Champaign Library)

Isidore then proceeded to catalog the Plinian races (*Etimologías* 2: 48–55). He thus advanced a conception of the monstrous not very different from that of Augustine, though more ethnographic and taxonomic. Neither Augustine nor Isidore, however, discussed what one was supposed to do if one came upon such monstrous races or what the position of the Christian West toward them should be.

Alexander the Great, Gog, and Magog

As the Christian West became increasingly confident of what it considered to be its rights and responsibilities as a civilized and Christian culture, its position toward so-called monsters became more sharply defined and more critical. The West saw itself as the agent of the civilizing and Christianizing process. In the Middle Ages, among the figures who symbolized that process is Alexander the Great.[10]

A. R. Anderson begins his book on Alexander the Great with the following observation: "The union established between Greece and the Near East by Alexander's conquests brought into being a new conception, that of *oikumene,* the civilized world of common interests [from which term *ecumenical* derives]. Of this New World Alexander was the creator, of it he became the guardian genius to protect its civilization and to keep its frontiers inviolate against the barbarian dwelling outside" (Anderson, *Alexander's Gate,* 3). The idea of the need to separate civilized from uncivilized nations is neither new with Alexander the Great nor unique to Western culture. This, for example, was the intention of the Chinese when they built the Great Wall in order to keep out the northern barbarians. Keeping the barbarians out or defeating them in battle has generally been viewed by "more civilized" nations as morally necessary for the preservation of the civilizing process itself and of the civilization under siege.[11] How this moral imperative was expressed in the case of Alexander the Great was through legends that transformed him into a Christian warrior hero and barbarians into enemies of God.

The legendary Alexander became the hero of Greek romances such as that by Pseudo-Callisthenes and of popular medieval retellings of his life. This legendary Alexander was identified as the author of widely circulated letters about his exploits: for instance, the letters to his teacher, Aristotle, and to his mother, Olympias, both of which deal with his march to the East, his exploits in India and beyond. On this march, according to the letters, Alexander meets and defeats creatures like giant savages and acephali (see Lecouteux, *Monstres,* 1:85). Particularly relevant to the ideology of conquest is Alexander's letter to his mother, Olympias, part of which deals with his encountering the peoples generally associated with Gog and Magog (I cite from the version found in *The Byzantine Life of Alexander*):

> To another place I came, sweetest mother, with all my armed hosts; and there I found nations that ate the flesh of human beings and drank their blood like water and that of all animals that creep. For they buried not their dead, but rather ate them. And when I had beheld their polluted ways, in fear I besought Providence that I might use force against them, lest with their lawless, godless deeds they pollute the earth. We routed them in full force, slaying most of them and taking the rest captive. . . . Fear took possession [of them]. For all having heard that Alexander, king of the Macedonians, was present among them sacking their cities and slaying all their people, . . . at God's command they fled with all their might, pursuing each other, the first the second, and the second fleeing pursuing the third. Thus indeed these dread, polluted nations were most wretchedly ravaged to the end, and I fearlessly pursuing them in their flight. At any rate their

> kings in all were two-and-twenty, and by the mountains—the two great mountains called by the ancients Breasts of the North—here were they shut in with all their kind. For the aforesaid heights had no other entrance or exit than that one alone into which they entered and became confined. . . . When accordingly I beheld these marvellous and most rugged places, with all my heart I earnestly importuned the power of Providence above, that with divine might he bar the entrance to the mountains. What then doth God himself the great and mighty? He commanded the great mountains, "Leap ye," and it happened. . . . And I commanded that brazen gates be built with dispatch, in width twenty cubits, their height two-and-sixty; and the whole entrance to the mountain I closed. . . . Outside of these huge gates I commanded that a structure forthwith be built of stones exceeding marvellous. . . . And having done these things thus I fenced the entrance and plated all the stones. . . . And I set up in addition a column bearing my name. And the kings then inclosed within the mountains [were] Og and Magog with Xaneth himself three-headed; another was Kynokephalos [and so on] . . . these were the peoples most foul and full of ungodliness that I fearfully shut in in the regions mentioned, thereby ridding the whole land of the North of their wantoness. (*Alexander's Gate,* 39–41)[12]

Gog and Magog are mentioned in the book of *Ezekiel* (38:1–3). And in *Revelation* (20:7–8), we read that, after the end of the thousand years, "Satan shall be loosed out of his prison, and shall come forth to deceive the nations which are in the four corners of the earth, Gog and Magog, to gather them together to war; the number of whom is as the sand of the sea" (fig. 1.2).

Alexander enclosed Gog and Magog for several reasons: to make the world safe; to punish sinners and to separate them from good people; to carry out the will of Providence; to achieve what some today, in the new world disorder affecting parts of the planet, might call "ethnic cleansing." In effect, by justifying the use of force through a condemnation of certain cultural practices and of certain races as "polluted," "lawless," and "godless" and subsequently by confining these races within controlled and restricted spaces far away from the centers of "civilized" life, the legendary Alexander the Great created in the Middle Ages what scholars of American history can readily identify as "reservations."

Fig. 1.2. Gog and Magog, in the last days of the world, break through Alexander's Gate. Pseudo-Methodius, *Revelationes* (fifteenth century). From Cary, *The Medieval Alexander,* 131. (Reprinted with permission of Cambridge University Press)

As the European geographical knowledge of the world became more accurate, the location of the enclosure of Gog and Magog shifted farther to the North and beyond the Caucasus (*Alexander's Gate,* 87), moving in a pattern of continuing remoteness and inaccessibility resembling what we find in descriptions concerning, say, the Earthly Paradise and the Kingdom of Prester John. Almost always, we find Gog and Magog in unknown lands or at the edges of the world. A case in point is the Ebstorf World Map (fig. 1.3), which I have commented upon elsewhere. This circular map describes the world as physically identified with and defined by the body of Christ. Symbolically, therefore, many areas or peoples on the map are commented on—interpreted—simply by virtue of their placement on or near Christ's body. Thus the Garden of Eden is near Christ's head, the entire map being

Fig. 1.3. Ebstorf World Map (thirteenth century). From Rosien, *Die Ebstorfer Weltkarte.* (Courtesy of the Newberry Library, Chicago)

oriented toward the East. Most of the monstrous races may be found on Christ's left hand, the sinister side of the body, an association of monstrosity with left-handedness that will be echoed in the sixteenth century. These panels of monsters are outside Europe, not only on this map but on other famous maps like the Hereford World Map (fig. 1.4). Moreover, Africa is identified as the continent of Ham, announcing a connection not lost on medieval viewers. Jerusalem in the Ebstorf map is in the center of the world and at Christ's navel. The Kingdom of Gog and Magog may be found in an isolated panel on the right-hand side of Christ, in the distant North and far away from civil societies (fig. 1.5). The Latin legend states that these impure people, Gog and Magog, have been enclosed by Alexander, that they are allies of the Antichrist, and that they live on human flesh and drink human

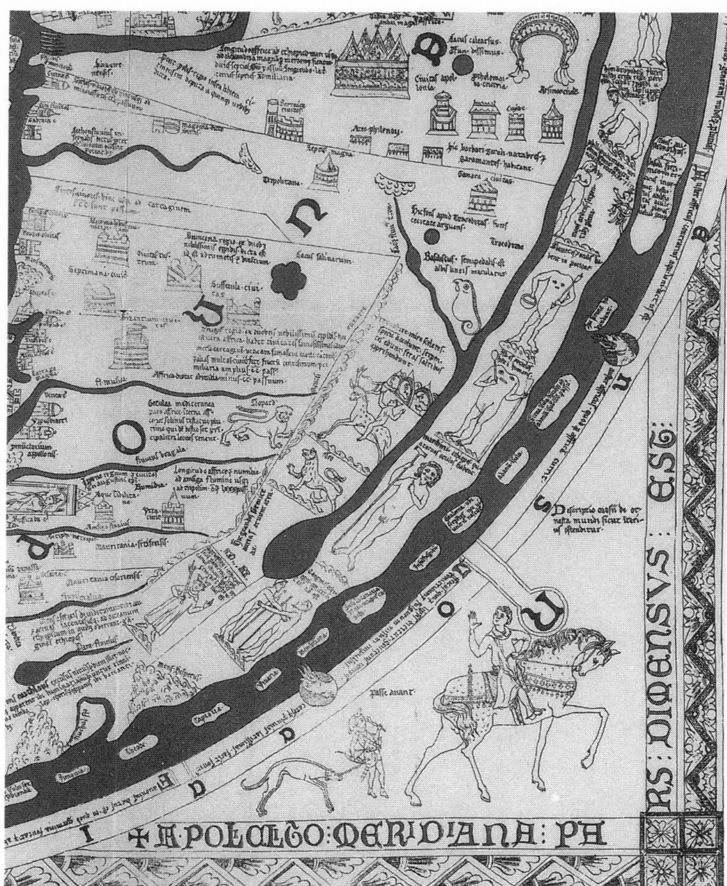

Fig. 1.4. Detail from the Hereford World Map (thirteenth century). From Miller, *Mappaemundi: Di ältesten Weltkarten.* Vol. 4 (Courtesy of the Map and Geography Library, the University of Illinois at Urbana-Champaign)

Fig. 1.5. Detail (Gog and Magog) from Ebstorf World Map (thirteenth century). From Rosien, *Die Ebstorfer Weltkarte.* (Courtesy of the Newberry Library, Chicago)

blood (Miller, *Mappaemundi,* 5:32–33). Such a marginalization foreshadows legal and theological ones in the New World in the sixteenth century and reinforces the idea that monstrosity need not be overtly physiological; it may be moral, behavioral, or social.

Columbus Revisited

Sailing west in order to arrive at the East, Columbus expected to come upon monsters and barbarous people like Scythians, Amazons, Gog, and Magog, whom he had read about in cosmographies such as those of Pierre d'Ailly or in travel accounts such as those of Mandeville (see Zacher, "Mandeville's Travels," passim) or of Marco Polo, who located the Kingdom of Gog and Magog in "Tenduc" beyond the Great Wall of China (Polo, bk. 1, ch. 59).[13] Columbus's attitudes toward these New World people resembled, in part, those of the legendary Alexander in his letter to Olympias or those of the crusaders. Columbus considered himself to be on a messianic mission that was intensified by the fact that it succeeded the seven-century *reconquista* in Spain itself.[14] Acting in this spirit, Columbus saw a landscape waiting only to be claimed for his king and queen and for the glory of his church. The people he viewed either as noble savages living in a golden age of innocence (and ignorance) or as barbarous enemies of the Crown, of man, and of God. In Columbus's opinion, the noble savages, like docile and intelligent children, would happily become subjects of the Crown and convert to Christianity. The fate of the bellicose savages, whom he identified and classified as enemies, Caribs, cannibals, or man-eaters (all four terms became synonymous in his mind), he discussed in a document that is important in setting the stage for what followed in the next two decades.

This document, known as the "Memorandum to Torres" and written in Santo Domingo on 30 January 1494, contains two items relevant to the present analysis. Both concern cannibals. In the first, Columbus wrote his sovereigns that he had sent several cannibals to Spain with Antonio Torres so that they might learn Spanish and be used as translators in subsequent voyages; they were also to be baptized. In the second item, Columbus recommended that these cannibal Indians be converted and enslaved for "the good of [their] souls" (*Colón,* 154). Rather than devastate people by the swift cruelty of battle, slavery defeats them by the slower process of daily degradation. Slavery also generally involves the physical removal of people from their native lands. It creates walls—visible or invisible—around people that turn them into the Other. By thus imprisoning people within the dominant culture, slavery, too, is a kind of enclosure.

The response of the Crown was to postpone discussion of slavery and also to tell Columbus that it would be better to baptize Native Americans and convert them *over there,* in the New World, rather than in Spain (*Colón,* 153). This response shows how the Crown simultaneously incorporated Native Americans within their empire and marginalized them. The double movement of incorporation and marginalization is central to the process of colonization and found expression in the sixteenth century in a number of texts and forums. It became part of the debate on the humanity—or on the monstrosity—of the Indians.

Theological Teratology

Lack of space prevents a detailed analysis of the dynamics of incorporation-marginalization in the policies of the *reducción* or the *encomienda* or, indeed, in the Laws of Burgos (1512), policies that effectively isolated and controlled Indians in the New World. I would like to comment, however, on a set of issues behind the question most vigorously debated in Spain in the sixteenth century. Was the conquest of the New World justified? Answers to this question in turn depended on how other questions were addressed. Were the Indians civilized or barbarous, and how was the extent of their civility or barbarism to be determined? Were they rational beings? Did they possess souls? What was their "nature?" Were they natural owners, natural slaves, or natural children? Indeed, were they even human? Among historians of the early New World, the generally accepted view is that these questions were framed for the Spaniards by two traditions: one, a tradition of political thinking that originated with Aristotle; and, two, a tradition of canon law heavily dependent upon the thought of Augustine and Aquinas. I do not dispute this view. But I would like to suggest here that the tradition of teratology also framed these questions and influenced the discourse. In effect, the New World barbarian was defined in the sixteenth century as morally so monstrous—as a *teras*—that for some Europeans he was not human.

Such a definition of the Indians' monstrosity depended on defining—through a kind of circular reasoning—their "nature" as inhuman. Here, as Anthony Pagden has pointed out (*Fall,* 38–39), the work of an early sixteenth-century Scottish theologian, John Mair, is representative of a tactic taken by several Spanish writers of his time and subsequently. In discussing whether or not Christians could legitimately rule over the pagans of the New World, Mair wrote:

> These people [the inhabitants of the Antilles] live like beasts on either side of the equator; and beneath the poles there are wild men as Ptolemy says in his *Tetrabiblos*. And this has now been demonstrated by experience, wherefore the first person to conquer them, justly rules over them because they are by nature slaves. As the Philosopher [Aristotle] says, . . . it is clear that some men are by nature slaves, others by nature free. . . . And it is just that one man should be a slave and another free, and it is fitting that one man should rule and another obey. . . . [T]his is the reason why the Greeks should be masters over

> the barbarians because, by nature, the barbarians and slaves are the same. (*Fall,* 38–39, quoting Mair, f. clxxxvijr)

It was of course not unusual for a Christian theologian to cite a pagan philosopher in support of an argument. Saint Thomas Aquinas built a career on the practice. What is important here is a series of equivalences that, as Pagden has recognized (*Fall,* 39), went more or less like this: Men like beasts = wild men = slaves = barbarians. Furthermore, these men were this way *by nature.* This kind of conception does not have Augustine's generosity toward difference.

Between 1512 and 1516, also in pursuit of the question of whether or not Christians could legitimately have dominion over these "barbarous oceanic islands" (Palacios Rubios, *Islas,* 3), Juan López de Palacios Rubios, who had read Mair (*Islas,* 15), also sought an answer in the nature of the Indians themselves. In *De las islas del mar océano,* Palacios Rubios made observations that were rhetorically so balanced that he could be cited approvingly by people on both sides of the question. On one hand, for Palacios Rubios the Indians were "rational beings, peaceful, and capable of understanding Christianity" (*Islas,* 9). On the other hand, Indians were sexually charged people who engaged in promiscuous sex and did not have a concept of the family (*Islas,* 9–11). These and other negative qualities defined them for Palacios Rubios as primitive by nature, a primitiveness further proved by the fact that, "seduced by devils," they practiced idolatry, praying to a god they called Cemi (*Islas,* 11). Even the fact that Indians seemed to live, like the pagan Greeks and Romans, according to "natural law" and were worthy of salvation (*Islas,* 15) could not obscure the more fundamental fact of their natural primitiveness.

Other writers did not attempt the rhetorical balance of Palacios Rubios concerning the Indians. For instance, for Friar Tomás Ortiz Indians were irredeemably bestial and inhuman. There was no question of their following any kind of natural law or of their resembling in any way the pagan but noble Greeks and Romans. Here is what Ortiz reported in about 1524 concerning his experience of Indians on Terra Firme:

> These are the characteristics of the Indians which show that they do not deserve to have [civil] liberties: They eat human flesh on Terra Firme; they are sodomites, more than any previous generation of men; they have no sense of justice: they go about naked; they have no sense of love or shame. . . . They are bestial and they pride themselves in

> having abominable vices; the young people do not respect their elders, nor sons their fathers. . . . They are traitorous, cruel, vengeful . . . [and] most inimical to religion. They are thieves. . . . Husbands are not faithful to wives, nor wives to husbands. . . . They are cowardly like hares. They are dirty: they eat lice and spiders and raw worms wherever they find them: they possess neither the arts nor the skills of men. . . .
>
> Until they're about ten or twelve years old it seems that they might turn into well-mannered and virtuous adults; but after [ten or twelve] they turn into brutal beasts. In sum, God has never created a people so steeped in vices and bestialities, without any admixture of goodness or civility. . . .
>
> We are speaking from our own experience of seeing these things. These people are as stupid as donkeys and they think nothing of killing each other. (Translation mine, from Martyr, *Décadas,* 440–41)

Equally negative, but more measured in its rhetoric is the "memorial" written about the same time (1524–25) by "el Bachiller Enciso," as he is known in the documents. In seeking to justify the conquest of the Indies, Enciso alleged (1) that Indians are polytheistic; (2) that they eat human flesh, which is against natural law; (3) that they sin against nature [sodomy; in Spanish: *el pecado contra natura*]; (4) that, on killing each other, they say that they are going to live with the Cemy, the devil. All these things, said Enciso, are against both natural and divine law, and for any one of these sins the pope had the authority to give these people and their lands to the Catholic king (*Colección,* 1:44–50).

Cannibalism, sodomy, bestiality were among the practices that were said to prove that Indians were "unnatural men," even though in appearance they might resemble other human beings. For Europeans, such practices dehumanized a culture like that of the Aztecs, which in some respects rivaled and even surpassed European cultures. Francisco de Vitoria, who was one of the most reasonable of the more liberal voices in Spain during the first half of the sixteenth century, considered Indians also to have sinned "against human nature"—especially through sodomy and cannibalism—and therefore to be deserving of punishment (Vitoria, *Relectio,* 116).

Juan Ginés de Sepúlveda, as Pagden has pointed out, deemphasized Aristotle and brought Augustine to the fore (*Fall,* 112), describing actions of the Indians as sins against nature and against God. For Sepúlveda, the Indians' depravity classified them as inhuman and bestial. He compared them to monkeys, bees, spiders, and pigs. He even called them *homunculi,* those "unnatural" and "monstrous" beings that, according to medieval medicine, were created by magic or by other nefarious means. Sepúlveda's kind of thinking may be called metaphorical teratology. Unable to assert a physical monstrosity, Sepúlveda, through the use of simile and metaphor, concocted a verbal one.

Scholars have considered Sepúlveda's an exaggerated and eccentric voice in the sixteenth century. Exaggerated it may have been; but eccentric it was not. Sepúlveda's attitudes—despite the presence and force of the arguments of Bartolomé de las Casas against them—were common enough in the sixteenth century in Europe. These were given their most revealing and interesting symbolic expression in the iconography of the time.

Iconographical Teratology

Conventional teratological representations of New World people continued well into the seventeenth century. These representations largely repeat the tradition rather than alter it or comment on it in a significant way. Therefore, other than noting their presence and frequency, I think it more fruitful for elucidating the history I am tracing to focus on certain examples that show New World people very much resembling Europeans. Here, despite an obvious figural identification of Europeans and Indians in terms of appearance, a rather intricate symbolic battle of differentiation is being waged that both exploits and undermines surface similarities. In the following examples, that battle centers around the particular New World signifier for monstrosity: cannibalism.

The first is an allegorization of America by Philippe Galle in a work entitled *Prosopographia* (1579–1600) or "figured personifications" (fig. 1.6). In it, he depicts America as an Amazon warrior woman, carrying the head of one of her male victims and stepping over a severed arm. It is not the image of "America" that identifies her with cannibalism but the legend underneath. She is "America, an ogresse who devours men, who is rich in gold, and who is skilled and powerful in the use of her bow . . ." (Galle, *Prosopographia*). The verbal description of her as a man-eating "ogresse" recalls Polyphemus, the man-eating ogre of *The Odyssey,* while the figural identification with the Amazons goes back to Herodotus and others. Here, a pagan and classical content has been set in a different geographical, historical, and moral con-

Fig. 1.6. Philippe Galle, "America" (1580). (Courtesy of the New-York Historical Society, New York, N.Y.)

Fig. 1.7. Paolo Farinati, "America" (1595). (Courtesy of Villa della Torre, Verona, Italy)

text. That context, however, is civilizational rather than explicitly Christian. At this point, the allegorized "America" may be an "enemy of civilization." But in this depiction, "America" is not defined as an enemy of God.

The more religious allegorization of America as a monstrous cannibal is evident in two other illustrations. The first of these is Paolo Farinati's "America," a lunette allegorizing the New World that was painted for a villa in Verona, Italy, in 1595 (fig. 1.7). Here we see a cannibal occupied in roasting a human arm and shoulder. He has turned away from this act on his left, however, away from the evil and sinister side of the body and toward the right side of the body, toward the crucifix. Symbolically, by turning away from his monstrous cultural practices and toward Christianity, the New World Indian will be saved, will enter the family of man and become civilized. Iconographically, Farinati represents what had been present in New World history as early as Columbus's memorandum to Torres, perhaps even as early as his first observations on the Indians during his first voyage. For Farinati, then, the process of evangelization was a process of incorporation within the family of man and the Christian church; colonization and conquest promised eternal salvation.

But the dynamics of these processes are not so unambiguous as these remarks might make them appear. A more complex and problematic vision is evident in an engraving that was published in 1592 in the de Bry brothers' multivolumed series entitled *Great Voyages* (1590–1634). This engraving illustrated Hans Staden's *True History*, originally published in 1557, which narrated his adventures as a captive of cannibals in Brazil (fig. 1.8). In this engraving—which I analyzed in

Fig. 1.8. Untitled illustration of Hans Staden's *True History.* From de Bry, *Dritte Buch Americae* 3:155. (Courtesy of the University of Illinois at Urbana-Champaign Library)

an earlier essay entitled "Cannibalism and the New Man of Latin America in the 15th- and 16th-century European Imagination"—we see incorporation and marginalization at work at the same time. The simultaneous movement of these two processes may be noted in the four women on the left. The three who have sagging breasts are eating human flesh *and* sucking on their fingers. As Bernadette Bucher has remarked, in sixteenth-century European iconography the old woman or the hag was associated with witchcraft and with evil (Bucher, *Icon,* 48). Moreover, also according to Bucher (*Icon,* 49–50), finger sucking was a well-known iconographic tactic for alluding to gluttony. Why is this important? Gluttony, of course, is one of the seven capital sins; cannibalism has never been part of any Western list of capital or deadly sins. Here, the cannibal is made into a glutton, thus making possible a moral incorporation within the Christian community and at the same time an exclusion from it. That is, the cannibal is defined as a sinner, an unredeemable Other, and exiled to the margins of Christian culture, much like Gog and Magog were on the Ebstorf World Map. The fact that this very same engraving depicts a young and beautiful female cannibal who is also eating human flesh but *not* sucking on her fingers indicates the ambivalence in Europe toward New World Indians.

The link between cannibalism and gluttony is explicit in the first confessional published in the New World, *Confesionario breve, en lengua Mexicana y Castellana* (Short Confessional in Mexican and Castillian), which was printed in Mexico in 1565. One of the main groups of questions that the priest was supposed to ask each Indian in the confessional concerns gluttony (folio 82r–83v). Two of the ten questions in this group have to do with eating meat and read as follows: (1) "Did you by chance eat meat during the time of fasting?" (2) "Did you eat human flesh at some time, or the corn meal that is cooked with it? Because this is a very great and terrible sin" (Medina, *Confesionario,* 82r–83v).

As these examples from iconography and a sixteenth-century confessional demonstrate, Indians may not be physically deformed, but the message is clear: Cultural practices like cannibalism are considered to be deformations of human nature, *contra naturam,* or monstrous; they will be condemned, controlled, corrected, or eliminated by any means necessary. This is symbolized in the first example by verbally defining New World Indians as pagan and monstrous, in the second, through a symbolic positioning of the body of the cannibal. In the third instance, the condemnation of monstrous Indians involves both incorporation and marginalization by associating cannibalism with gluttony. The fourth example explicitly brings cannibalism within the order of sins governed by the confessional.

We have followed a long and winding path in identifying the new enemies of God for the European imagination, the newest incarnations of Gog and Magog. One of several possible guides on this path and a hitherto unexplored link between the classical and the Christian—as well as between evangelization and conquest in a New World setting—is the legendary figure of Alexander the Great. That I am not so far off is evident in a comment by the sixteenth-century Dominican theologian Melchior Cano. Do not suppose, he wrote sarcastically in 1546 in "De dominio indorum," that the Spaniards in the New World were anything other than conquerors. After all, he continued, we would not be prepared to describe Alexander the Great as a simple "traveller" (cited by Pagden, *Spanish,* 34).

The theology of conquest in New World history is in some respects, though not in all, a teratological theology. When no physically monstrous Indians were discovered, the physiological or the biological notions of monstrosity were deemphasized. Behavioral, moral, and theological conceptions of monstrosity then came to the fore. Yet both the biological and the behavioral notions of monstrosity depend, as Aristotle wrote, on difference and on deformity. In search of justifications for the conquest and colonization of the New World, Europeans overlooked the similarities between the races and defined the Indians of the New World as different, deformed, monstrous, and inhuman. These definitions had profound consequences for the subsequent treatment of Native Americans, even up to the present day. Europeans were not the first to have so dehumanized another people, nor will they be the last.

NOTES

1. My English revises Major's translation slightly and follows the Latin a bit more closely, particularly in translating the term *monstrum* as monster rather than as *cannibal.* It is too early in the European history of the New World for the term *cannibal* to be used as the equivalent of *monster.* That comes later. The Spanish original also uses the word *monstruo* rather than *caníbal* (see Varela, *Colón,* 144–45).

2. I have explored Columbus's obsession with monsters and man-eaters in other essays, one of them to appear in *Cross-Cultural Studies,* volume three of *A History of Literature in the Caribbean,* currently being edited by A. James Arnold for the International Comparative Literature Association. My essay here is intended especially to complement that essay, entitled "Mapping the Caribbean."

3. The word I have rendered as *different* is *anomoion* in the Greek; likewise *deformity* is *anateria* in the Greek.

4. The first speaker in the Virginia conference and its most distinguished guest was Derek Walcott. In his wide-ranging opening address, some of it occasioned by the news that morning that he had won the Nobel Prize for Literature for 1992, Walcott remarked on the importance of animals as symbols in Caribbean literature, one of the central themes of both the conference and its projected book, and reminded the audience of the presence of animal metaphors in Western literature itself as early as *The Odyssey.* In that work, the confrontation between the civilized and the noncivilized was seen metaphorically, Walcott said, as the paradigmatic confrontation between a small, cunning animal (Odysseus) and a large, stupid one (Polyphemus, or the Cyclops). He also went on to say that the use of animal imagery to describe human beings in the New World sometimes depended on the following set of terms, which are considered to be intimately related: "animals, beasts, savages, cannibals, niggers." My essay on the "Enemies of God" is in some senses also an

exploration of this set of relationships, especially how it evolved historically and what its effects were on the history of the New World.

5. These two physical characteristics immediately identify him as a different order of being; later in history, each characteristic will identify a separate race of men.

6. Although core-periphery analysis is usually considered part of world-system theory, which focuses on the transformations of the world through capitalism from the beginnings of the global age (1500) to the present, in fact world-system theory can be used to analyze any interdependent and cross-cultural network of exchanges. Scholars like Janet Abu-Lughod have applied world-system theory to European and Asian economic and cultural networks in the Middle Ages. And Barry Cunliffe uses world-system terminology to analyze Greek and Roman relationships with the "barbarians" who surrounded them.

7. This is not to say that only Christianity among the world's religions has a theology of hybrid and strange creatures. Other cultures may have such theologies, and quite different ones at that. For example, in our own hemisphere, Native American cosmologies often place monsters in their pantheons. Or, in India, beings that would be considered monstrous in the West—those with elephant heads like Ganesh or those with multiple arms like Shiva—are viewed by Hinduism to be manifestations of the Divine. *The Mahabharata* has many such examples. (See Samaroo below on the effect of contact between the Indian cosmogony and the Christian one in Trinidad. Ed.)

8. Wendy Reid Morgan makes this general point in her excellent dissertation for Deakin University (Australia, 1984).

9. Augustine concluded this chapter thus: "Accordingly, it ought not to seem absurd to us, that as in individual races there are monstrous births, so in the whole race there are monstrous races. Wherefore, to conclude this question cautiously and guardedly, either these things which have been told of some races have no existence at all; or if they do exist, they are not human races; or if they are human, they are descended from Adam" (*City of God* 2:118).

10. The lack of space obliges me to leave to one side analysis of a fascinating series of primarily Ethiopian texts, written between the sixth and the fourteenth centuries, known as *The Contendings of the Apostles*. In some of those texts, monsters are both Christianized and are themselves evangelists. The most prominent of these was Saint Christopher, called by scholars of teratology "the cynocephalic saint" (see Friedman, passim; White, passim, but especially 22–46). Saint Christopher was a dog-headed man who, on being "saved," lost his dog-head and then, in the service of the Christianizing mission, regained it in order to terrorize barbarians into accepting Christ, eating those who did not convert.

11. In his study of *Tragedy and Civilization*, Charles Segal writes that

the great civilizing heroes of Greece—for instance, Theseus, Oedipus, and Odysseus—defeated "monstrous deformations of humanity like the Cyclops" (3). Any defeat of a monster implies that order has been restored to the world. The monstrous barbarian, of course, need not be defeated in battle; he may be excluded from the start.

12. Interestingly, this entire episode—since it was not in the manuscript he was directly translating from—is missing from B. P. Reardon's magnificent collection of ancient Greek novels. The Gog and Magog adventure is narrated in chapter 29 of book 3 of *The Alexander Romance* by Pseudo-Callisthenes. (See Reardon, *Collected Ancient Greek Novels,* 731.)

13. Columbus read and commented upon the *Imago Mundi* by Pierre d'Ailly. Both author and reader connected the Scythians with the kingdom of Gog and Magog, located it in Asia (the continent of the sons of Japheth), and spoke of people who live on human flesh and drink the blood of human beings.

14. See, for instance, the work of Alain Milhou and Pauline Watts, both of whom have studied Columbus's messianism.

REFERENCES

Abu-Lughod, Janet. *Before European Hegemony: The World-System, A.D. 1250–1350.* Oxford: Oxford University Press, 1989.

Anderson, Andrew Runni. *Alexander's Gate, Gog and Magog, and the Inclosed Nations.* Cambridge: The Medieval Academy of America, 1932.

Aristotle. *Generation of Animals.* Ed. and trans. A. L. Peck. The Loeb Classical Library. Cambridge: Harvard University Press, 1953.

Augustine. *The City of God.* Ed. and trans. Marcus Dods. 2 vols. New York: Hafner, 1948.

Bry, Theodor de. *Dritte Buch Americae darinn Brasilia durch Johann Staden von Homberg auss Hessen / auss eigener erfahrung in Teutsch beschrieben. Item historia der Schiffart Ioannis Lerij in Brasilien / welche er selbst publiciert hat / jetzt von Newem verteutscht.* Frankfurt am Main: Theodor de Bry, 1593.

Bucher, Bernadette. *Icon and Conquest: A Structural Analysis of the Illustrations of de Bry's* Great Voyages. Trans. Basia Miller Gulati. Chicago: University of Chicago Press, 1981.

Cano, Melchior. "De dominio indorum (1546)." *Biblioteca Vaticana MS.* Lat. 4648. Cited in Pagden, *Spanish Imperialism and the Political Imagination,* 34.

Cary, George. *The Medieval Alexander.* Ed. D. J. A. Ross. Cambridge: Cambridge University Press, 1956.

Colección de documentos inéditos relativos al descubrimiento, conquista y colonización del las posesiones españolas en América y Oceanía. Ed. Pacheco, Cárdenas, Torres de Mendoza, et al. 42 vols. Madrid, 1864–84.

Cunliffe, Barry. *Greeks, Romans and Barbarians: Spheres of Interaction*. London: B. T. Batsford, 1988.

Friedman, John Block. *The Monstrous Races in Medieval Art and Thought*. Cambridge: Harvard University Press, 1981.

Galle, Philippe. *Prosopographia*. N.p.; ca. 1580. Paris, Bibliothèque Nationale (Department of Engravings).

Herodotus. *Histories*. Ed. and trans. A. D. Godley. Loeb Classical Library. 4 vols. Cambridge: Harvard University Press, 1946.

Homer. *The Odyssey*. Ed. and trans. A. T. Murray. Loeb Classical Library. 2 vols. Cambridge: Harvard University Press, 1984.

Isidoro de Sevilla. *Etimologías*. 2 vols. Ed. and trans. José Oroz Reta and Manuel-A. Marcos Casquero. Madrid: Biblioteca de Autores Cristianos, 1982.

Lecouteux, Claude. *Les monstres dans la littérature allemande du moyen âge: Contribution à l'étude du merveilleux médiéval*. Vol. 1. Stuttgart: Kümmerle Verlag, 1982.

Mair, John (Johannes Major). *In secundum sententiarum*. Paris, 1519.

Major, R. H., trans. and ed. *Christopher Columbus: Four Voyages to the New World: Letters and Selected Documents*. Intro. John E. Fagg. 1961; Reprint, Gloucester, Mass.: Peter Smith, 1978.

Martyr, Peter (Pedro Mártir de Anglería). *Décadas del Nuevo Mundo*. Madrid: Ediciones Polifemo, 1989.

Medina, Alonso de. *Confesionario breve, en lengua Mexicana y Castellana*. Mexico: Antonio de Espinosa, 1565.

Milhou, Alain. *Colón y su mentalidad mesiánica en el ambiente franciscanista español*. Valladolid: Casa-Museo de Colón, 1983.

Miller, Konrad. *Mappaemundi: Die ältesten Weltkarten*. Vol. 4: *Die Herefordkarte*. Vol. 5: *Die Ebstorfkarte*. Stuttgart: Jos. Roth'sche Verlagshandlung, 1896.

Morgan, Wendy Reid. *Constructing the Monster: Notions of the Monstrous in Classical Antiquity*. Ph.D. Dissertation, Deakin University, 1984.

The Old Testament Pseudepigrapha. 2 vols. (Apocalyptic Literature and Testaments). Ed. James H. Charlesworth. Garden City, N.Y.: Doubleday, 1983; 1985.

Pagden, Anthony. *The Fall of Natural Man: The American Indian and the Origins of Comparative Ethnology*. Cambridge: Cambridge University Press, 1982; 1989.

———. *Spanish Imperialism and the Political Imagination: Studies in European and Spanish-American Social and Political Theory 1513–1830*. New Haven: Yale University Press, 1990.

Palacios Rubios, Juan López de. *De las islas del mar Océano*. Written between

1512 and 1514. Trans. Agustín Millares Cano. México: Fondo de Cultura Económica, 1954.

Palencia-Roth, Michael. "Cannibalism and the New Man of Latin America in the 15th- and 16th-century European Imagination." *Comparative Civilizations Review* 12 (1985): 1–27.

———. "Mapping the Caribbean." In *Cross-Cultural Studies*. Vol. 3 of *A History of Literature in the Caribbean*. Ed. A. James Arnold. Amsterdam; Philadelphia: John Benjamins, [forthcoming].

Photius. "Ctésias le Cnide." In *Bibliothèque,* vol. 1 (codices 1–84). Texte établi et traduit par René Henry. Paris: Société d'Editions Les Belles Lettres, 1959.

Pliny. *Natural History*. Ed. and trans. H. Rackham. Loeb Classical Library. 10 vols. Cambridge: Harvard University Press, 1957.

Polo, Marco. *The Travels of Marco Polo*. The Marsden trans.; rev. and ed. Manuel Komroff. New York: Boni and Liveright, 1926.

Raccolta di documenti e studi pubblicati dalla R. Commissione colombiana pel quarto centenario dalla scoperta dell'America. Ed. Cesare de Lollis. 6 parts, in 14 volumes. Rome: Ministerio della pubblica istruzione, 1892–96.

Reardon, B. P., ed. *Collected Ancient Greek Novels*. Berkeley: University of California Press, 1989.

Rosien, Walter. *Die Ebstorfer Weltkarte*. Hannover: Niedersächsisches Amt für Landesplannung und Statistik, 1952.

Segal, Charles. *Tragedy and Civilization: An Interpretation of Sophocles*. Cambridge: Harvard University Press, 1981.

Varela, Consuelo, ed. *Cristóbal Colón: Textos y documentos completos*. Madrid: Alianza, 1982.

Watts, Pauline. "Prophecy and Discovery: On the Spiritual Origins of Christopher Columbus's 'Enterprise of the Indies.'" *American Historical Review* 90, no. 1 (1985): 73–102.

White, David Gordon. *Myths of the Dog-Man*. Chicago: University of Chicago Press, 1991.

Zacher, Cris. "How Columbus Read Mandeville's Travels." *Actas del primer encuentro internacional colombino*. Ed. Consuelo Varela, 155–60. Madrid: Turner Libros, 1990.

Joanna Overing

Who Is the Mightiest of Them All? Jaguar and Conquistador in Piaroa Images of Alterity and Identity

In recent years, with such works as Tzvetan Todorov's *La conquête de l'Amérique: La question de l'autre* and Peter Mason's *Deconstructing America: Representations of the Other,* as well as with new contributions by Anthony Pagden and Peter Hulme, we have been presented with highly interesting discussions of the development during the conquest of the Americas of European imagery of, and discourse on, the "radical Otherness" of the New World's indigenous peoples. The populations of the Americas appeared for the most part as the exotic and pathological antithesis of what the conquerors thought themselves to be. Thus the cultures of America became defined as an ensemble of negations to be contrasted with the civilized and cultured society of the developing ruling classes of Europe (Mason, *Other,* 43–44; Kohl, *Abwehr,* 69). One of the most interesting observations made by Mason in his analysis of Eurocentrism with respect to the New World was that the Europeans, in conquering the Americas, fixed the status of Native Americans at the level of the lower echelons of their own society, placing them alongside the mad, the wild, the child, the lower classes (Mason, *Other,* chapter 2).

Incorporated into the language of alterity used to characterize both domestic and foreign European Others was the rich imagery of the

Guianese ethnocentrisms; for the discovery itself of both the comparable and the incomparable carries its own powerful implications, which allows us then to continue a conversation, both academically and with the indigenous people, regarding the question of *why* the difference (which in many ways is a matter that is less complex than the one of similarity).

Mine will be the simple answer, that of the contrast between hierarchical and relatively egalitarian political strategies and between social philosophies that stress social asymmetry rather than social symmetry. As already noted, Mason makes the significant point that the Native Americans were identified with Europe's subaltern classes. The root metaphor for Otherness in Eurocentrism, certainly as it was elaborated as political and colonial discourse, was first and foremost that of inferiority. The gaze was that of the conqueror who took for granted a natural order premised upon conquest and the relations of superordination and subordination that might emerge from it. So extreme was the strength of this notion of the inferiority of the Other that the divide between self and Other easily slipped into the opposition of the human and the nonhuman (see Todorov and Mason, *Other,* passim).

The cultures of Amazonia have no subaltern classes, and for most of its indigenous societies, certainly those of the Guianas, where the persistent destabilization of hierarchy in personal relations is the norm, it would be a misconstruction to identify specific social divisions or whole categories of people within them as inferior or subordinate to others (Overing, "Anarchy," and Thomas, *Order,* passim). So while it is the case that the Piaroa may associate certain characteristics of White people with those of affines (the in-law being their archetypical category of internal Other), affinity is a complicated matter and does not carry with it the idea of stable relations of subordination and domination, as say holds for the Western notion of class relations. Since the *right* to domination is alien to the Piaroa understanding of proper social relationships, they would not judge external Others, even if monstrous, as *inferior* beings who were therefore rightfully subject to Piaroa domination. Judgments carrying connotations of inferiority tend to have as little relevance to their logic of exteriority as to that of interiority. The idea of inferiority, normal to Eurocentrism, is a much less pervasive element within the Piaroa system of alterity, which manifests instead a certain tolerance of difference (as well as a fascination and fear of it and a strong desire for it).

Such an attitude toward difference that tends to lean more toward its acceptance than is true for the Eurocentric vision does not signify that the Piaroa discourse on alterity is not as well a discourse upon relations of power. But it is the potency, not the inferiority, of the Other that is most cogent to many Native South American classifications, and thus for the Piaroa the state of difference tends not to carry with it an automatic value judgment of inferiority. On the contrary, often as precious as it might be dangerous, difference is understood to be highly necessary, if not always desirable, to their own material existence. Here we are faced with the widespread Amazonian message that alterity is the hallmark of this-worldly social living: The achievement of the social state itself, and hence of the world of the interior, requires the force and creative powers of those different from self; and without the benefit of such alterity, there can be no fertility and no productive capacity (Overing Kaplan, "Amazonian" and "Dualisms"; Overing, "Market," 182–202). As will be shown below, he who is sometimes monster may also be a privileged being. Within such a system, identity and difference are not absolute categories, and in practice the classification of another as belonging to either the world of inside or outside tends to slip and slide. The illusive inclusiveness of the Piaroa classification of alterity will be one main theme of my discussion.

Such relative inclusivity is relevant to understanding the difference between the Piaroa classification of alterity and the Eurocentric one. One salient reason for the incommensurability that Mason unfolded between particular European and Native American discourses of alterity can be found in the contrast between the hegemonic and totalizing rhetorics of inequality, which are highly *exclusive* in their views of humanity, and the rhetorics of equality, which are much more *inclusive* and less totalizing or absolute in their categorizations of humankind.

The Question of White People: Their Knives and Their Perfume

As is true for the European discourse upon Native Americans, the Piaroa discourse upon White people and their images of them can only be comprehended when placed within the broader framework of their constructions of alterity in general. Consequently, to interpret adequately their treatment of White people, whether in mythic images and the exegesis of cosmology or in daily talk, it is necessary to know as well their language of alterity in a multiplicity of contexts where self and Other are distinguished. For example, there is the context of the interior Other where affinity, gender (Overing, "Gender," 135–56), shamanism (Overing, "Evil," 244–78), leadership, and exchange (Overing, "Market") all play a role; and although it is often difficult to define in any absolute sense the boundary between the internal and exterior Other, we can tentatively categorize as the external Other the spirit guardians of land and water, the gods of both mythic and present-day time, the animals and fish, and the peoples who are not Piaroa. There is no room to explicate fully such a complex of alterity for the obvious reason that agency and its variation within the Piaroa universe is an immense topic inclusive of all the beings of their universe. Nevertheless, certain dominant principles related to the Piaroa classification of agency are important to the interpretation of their discourse on White people.

For instance, when analyzing the Piaroa classification of agency in the universe, it became clear to me that it was very difficult indeed to delineate the boundaries between the human and the nonhuman in this system. Animals are human when dwelling beneath the earth in the primordial homes of their parents, and the "fathers" of these humans-animals can still today with their gigantic penises impregnate sleeping Piaroa women. Likewise, plants, fish, and some artifacts and stars are still human in the ever-present "before time" of mythic times. Also, the present-day gods of the Piaroa, though not ancestors, are said to be human, and they are named as The Human (Tüha) Tianawa. Thus it is not surprising that, unlike many European representations of Native Americans (at least during the conquest of the Americas), the Piaroa images of White people are ones that clearly incorporate them within the general category of humanity.

The Piaroa creator god, Wahari, created White people *as people* in the same manner that he earlier created the Piaroa, from fish of the same lake of origin. Wahari then created in similar manner all the indigenous peoples who neighbor the Piaroa. Indeed, my initial response to the Piaroa treatment of White people in both mythology and everyday talk was to note their apparent relative lack of interest in the topic. Mason has also noted that other ethnographers have remarked on the fact that indigenous peoples "do not seem unduly preoccupied with the Whites" (*Other,* 162–63). Given the extreme violence of the early centuries of conquest in the region of the Middle Orinoco, I wondered about the Piaroa lack of rancor or antagonism. In the Piaroa epics of creation time, "the Whites" (D'ea'tu) wandered in and out of events seemingly at the whim of the myth teller; it was almost as a literary flourish that they would take their place alongside other peoples. As a cohesive series, all the peoples would be listed: the Piaroa, the Whites, the Ghahibos, the Yanomami, the Piapoco, the Yaruro, the Cuiva, the Baniva, the Yabarana, the Waicuri, the Yekuana.

Upon closer inspection, it became evident that there was a difference, for "Whites" would sometimes enter mythic time alone, rather than as one among many peoples. They tended to do so, but by no means always, when certain themes were being stressed, especially those pertaining to violence, coercion, sexual perversity, and cannibalism—all topics particularly relevant to Piaroa constructions of alterity. Other peoples, for example their neighbors, the Waica (the Yanomami), the Makiratare (the Yekuana), and the Pemon, were neither so isolated nor so strikingly "good to think through" in the elaboration of such excessive behavior. The symbols repeatedly used to express the excessiveness of the Whites tended to be gender-linked, for mentioned time and again were the weaponry of the Spanish soldier, his sword and his knife, and the perfumes of the Spanish woman, —the representations respectively of male violence and female promiscuity. The following episodes about Wahari and his family include portrayals of White people typical of the mythic cycles:

1. Buok'a was jealous of his brother, Wahari, who had just completed his creation of the Piaroa. Out of spite, Buok'a proclaimed, and thereby created, all the dangers that the Piaroa would thereafter experience that would lead them to early deaths. Buo'ka seized all types of Piaroa food—cassava, maize, and pineapple—and ground it up to work magic against them. He announced that these people must not live. They would die from sorcery and jaguar attack and from the cannibalistic raids of dead souls. It would be dangerous for them to hunt alone, and they would die by falling from trees. Buok'a did these things against the family of his younger brother, Wahari. If he had not made such pronouncements, only very old people would die, while children and young adults would not. The Piaroa would have been as plentiful as the Spanish.

In retaliation, Wahari made dangers for the Whites, the family of Buok'a (and Paruna, see 4. below). Wahari created the Whites for his older brother to mollify him, but then proceeded to pronounce the future of their deaths. He said that the sword and the knife would be dangerous for the Whites. They would kill their friends and families with these weapons. They would cook their friends and family. They would imprison them, members of their own family. Wahari then said to Buok'a: "Now your family is the same as you made mine!" Buok'a replied: "Yes, many of the Whites will die, but the Spanish will create more people than your people." Buok'a said this.

2. After Wahari had created the Piaroa and they were multiplying, as too was their food, he decided to pay his people a visit. To visit them, he disguised himself as a Spaniard with black hair and Spanish clothes—trousers, shirt, and shoes—and he carried a knife. But the Piaroa were frightened by this disguise, so he decided to disguise himself in Piaroa garb, wearing a loincloth and many splendid ornaments. He wore beads, face paint, and leg and arm bands. Then he realized that the Piaroa would be afraid of his ornaments because in Piaroa theory ornamentation is the outward manifestation of powerful predator forces contained within the body. Wahari understood the symbolic homology of Piaroa ornamentation and the Western knife and sword: In both cases a man in full dress is displaying his capacities as a (cannibal) warrior. Thus Wahari approached the Piaroa without ornamentation, and they were not afraid.

3. Along the rapids of the Orinoco, Wahari came upon the son whom he had fathered through an incestuous union with his sister, Cheheru. His son pestered him to claim him as his son and to teach him to hunt. Annoyed, Wahari threatened him with the violence of the Whites. He said, "Here comes a boat filled with White men. These men kill us, eat us, and put us in jail. I am going to give you to these people if you do not leave me alone!"

4. Cheheru was angry with her brother, Wahari, because he had exchanged her for six boxes of Paruna's White people's goods, which included matches, fishhooks, and machetes. Instead of staying with Paruna as his wife, Cheheru became a promiscuous wanderer. She followed handsome men of every group, creating perfumes as she made love; and when she wandered among the White people she created perfumes in bottle form. The use of these perfumes transforms women into crazy wanderers, to suffer the illness of "monkey urine madness" just like the illness Cheheru had. If Cheheru had stayed with Paruna, the owner of "White people's goods," the Piaroa would have been able to marry White people, have many children by them, and be as plentiful as the Whites.

5. Wahari, poisoned into madness by the forces of his father-in-law (Kuemoi, the mad devourer of jungle beings who was also the creator god of the culinary arts), was arrogant with his sister's sons and accused them of cowardice for desiring water when working in the hot

sun. Soon after, Wahari, poisoned further by the forces of the sun from which the powers of Kuemoi were derived, lost his reason and wandered for years living a violent, mad, and promiscuous life among other peoples. Cheheru, his sister, joined him when he lived with White people. Wahari played with the White women, and Cheheru with the White men. But at each place they visited, they soon had to move on because the Whites would become angry with Wahari for his play and jail him.

Typical of many of the peoples of Amazonia, the Piaroa make a distinction of identity and difference that strongly opposes the inside and the outside, safety and danger, friend and foe (Rivière, *Marriage*; Lizot, *Yanomami*). It is an image of alterity that always carries with it at the very least the potentiality of "the cannibal Other." Thus violence is understood to be immanent within all relations of alterity, and the White people who carry knives and swords and who sway so far with their casual physical violence and use of coercive institutions from Piaroa ideas of proper sociality become especially apt symbols for the monstrous in social behavior. As Mason comments when he observes that Europeans were in turn the Other in the eyes of the Native Americans, "It is the excessiveness of the European presence which explains its monstrous forms" (*Other,* 160). It is certainly the Piaroa point of view that Whites treat each other as insiders in ways that should only be possible between strangers. Because they are understood to be people who "cannibalize" themselves, White people are used in Piaroa myth as a highly suitable exemplification of the monster and cannibal Other. Such an image is given literal weight, as can be seen by the ways in which past and present events and facts become interpreted and (re)contextualized through mythic discourse: The tinned meat in the stores of the towns and in the anthropologist's knapsack was believed to contain the flesh of people; in the Piaroa legends of the Kerinya (Carib) slave raids of the seventeenth and eighteenth centuries, the cannibal raiders who stole victims for their anthropophagous rites were said to be White people. Those who cannibalize themselves certainly cannibalize others (see also *Other,* 159; Guss, "Yekuana," esp. 417–18).

Yet there is another side of the coin to the episodes depicting the violent or promiscuous Whites (Wahari and Cheheru did find White partners in abundance with whom to play), which leads us away from the idea that the Whites as monstrous are but an inverse image of the virtuous Piaroa. In the mythic cycles, Whites who cook and eat people do not appear fortuitously, for it is the *domestic argument,* the breakdown of *internal* relations within the families of the Piaroa creator gods, that leads to the introduction of the excessive Whites. As Mason notes, there is a link in Native American mythology between internal conflict and the arrival of the external stranger (*Other,* 156–60; "Yekuana," 427, n. 9). In Piaroa myth, it is with the father's denial of his son and his desire to kill him that the cannibal Whites appear in their boat to be usefully used as a threat. And it is a brother's violent jealousy, along with his sibling's retaliation, that leads to the creation of the violent Whites. Similarly, it is the arrogance of a mother's brother toward his sister's sons that leads the former to live a life of wildness among the promiscuous White people.

Mason suggests further that such domestic conflict provides the operator for reducing difference between the inside and the outside, and with the decrease of distance, the stranger becomes not so strange—and therefore more similar to self. As Mason so aptly puts it, "The narratives begin, not from a unity which is subjected to violence from outside, but from a totality that is itself already fractured. This fracture is an initial lack which calls for a supplement to supplete it" (*Other,* 159). It can be said that, as a structure of alterity, the path sought by the Piaroa was assimilation; but the desire was only for *partial* incorporation, one that could be achieved through the establishment of particular types of social relations. The wish was not for the totalizing reduction of the Other to self as when the Europeans insisted upon the Christianization of the Native Americans. Rather, the Piaroa stress was upon their social need for difference; if the Other was to be reduced totally to self, then all benefits to self of the Other's potent foreign powers would be lost.

The specific desire (as will be unfolded below) was to establish *symmetrical* relations with the Whites through the process of trade and marriage. But as Mason notes, symmetry was precisely what was not reciprocated by the Whites (*Other,* 160). The supplement was too excessive and not commensurable with the initial domestic rift that it came to fill. It is this excessiveness in the reactions of Whites, he argues, that prevents a sufficient reduction of difference to allow for symmetrical assimilation and for the relation of Native American and European to emerge as a reversible one. His judgment is undoubtedly correct. The violence of the Whites was much more than was bargained for, but it is another train of thought that I wish now to follow. This is to address the significance of a Piaroa egocentrism that is associated with the idea that the monster characteristics of the Whites were created in the first instance through the *intent* of Piaroa creator gods. In the remainder of the paper, it will be my object to unfold the idea that although the Piaroa are obviously concerned about their own asymmetrical relationship with the Whites, their most immediate focus in their constructions of alterity, and of identity and difference, is upon the complexity of the human condition itself and upon the exploration of all its possibilities—not only its virtues but its frailties and monstrosities as well. The Piaroa stress is upon the human predicament itself, and thus upon the absurdities and evil as well as the positive strengths of human power, whereas in the European imagery, the emphasis is upon inversion and upon the right of Europeans as superior human beings to subjugate the inferior Other. In the latter vision, evil and danger are assumed to come from without, not also from within.

Although in the present-day world Whites are best construed as exterior to the Piaroa, it is the ethnocentric gaze of the Piaroa that makes the history of Spanish origin a solely internal matter. They did not come from outside, but from within, and therefore the very location and monstrosity of the Whites as external Other is understood to be a Piaroa matter and as such a product of indigenous history. It was the creator god Wahari who initially determined the location of Whites as elsewhere when he placed a barrier in the lake of origin for the Piaroa and the Whites in order to separate the jungle Piaroa from the non-jungle Whites. It was likewise Wahari who in the heat of a domestic argument made violence the mode of life for his brother's people, the Whites. It was the fault of both Wahari and his sister, Cheheru—not that of the Whites—that the Piaroa today cannot establish reciprocal relations with the Whites: Paruna, who was the original owner of White peoples' goods, expressed his desire to intermarry with Wahari's family and to establish *social* relations of exchange with its members. It was the profligate acts of Cheheru and Wahari that sabotaged all possibility for Wahari's family to form any sort of unity with Paruna or his family and, according to Piaroa exegesis, for the Piaroa themselves later to unite with the Whites. Cheheru refused her marriage with Paruna to become a promiscuous wanderer; Wahari visited Paruna not with the intention of establishing a friendship bond but only for the purpose of exchange; he also committed incest with Cheheru, an incident that resulted in the two brothers-in-law, Wahari and Paruna, quarreling together for eternity on the edge of the world; and finally, the only consistent relations that Wahari and Cheheru managed to establish with the Whites were escapades of short-term carnality. In this series of events, while the intentions of Paruna, the master of the Whites, was to behave in a civilized way, those of the mighty creator gods of the Piaroa were not so honorable.

It was also due to the excessive behavior of Wahari that at the end of mythic time he lost his guardianship of the jungle to be replaced in this role by Re'yo, the giant spirit of the jungle who is clothed in Spanish conquistador armor. From the beginning of time on earth, Wahari was the master of the jungle, and as such his duty was the protection of the people of the jungle. He also acquired for them the gifts of the culinary arts and taught them how to live in a peaceful and social manner. However, toward the end of mythic time, Wahari betrayed his own people by transforming many of them into animals to be hunted and devoured at a great feast that he gave to display his powers to Cheheru. It was then that all the remaining peoples of the jungle (including the Whites) chased him down to kill him. Wahari was replaced as master of the jungle by the great conquistador spirit, Re'yo.

It should now be clear that there exists an ambiguity in Piaroa portrayals of White people. On the one hand, they are often envisioned as coercive cannibals and sexual miscreants, and the Piaroa, who abhor violence and stress the danger to social life of all excessive action, view such behavior on the part of Whites as monstrous. Yet at the same time, Whites are consistently categorized as people, and so they have an identity with the Piaroa, as beings created in the same lake of origin by the same powerful mythic god. Moreover, it is not just the disaster of the violent Whites with which the Piaroa must contend as a result of the profligate behavior of their creator gods, for the Whites' excessive and immoral behavior served as an operator throughout the mythic cycles for the creation of all types of dangers particular to Piaroa human existence. The violence of the Whites takes its place alongside other tribulations, such as disease, menstruation, snakebite, work, affines, exchange partners, foreign sorcerers, and vengeful gods of the mythic past (Overing, "Cannibalism," 86–102). Finally, Whites can also have their honorable side, as the mythic episodes about Paruna indicate.

What is more, the qualities of Re'yo (the giant, conquistador master of the jungle) introduce yet another ambiguity, the possibility that the Piaroa might positively value and not just denigrate the White people's capabilities for violence. In Piaroa imagery, the mighty powers of the Whites have become further monsterized in the figure of Re'yo, but it is an exaggeration that has transformed them not into a more negative force but into a (more or less) positive one at *the service of their own protection.* It becomes clear that the Piaroa perspective on the dangerous does not carry with it an absolute either/or valuation: Context is essential, for it is their understanding that power which may be disastrous when acted out within a social setting has positive virtue in the role of the guardian warrior. His service is not without its perils, but that is to be expected with the monstrous—and with warriors.

Re'yo, the Master of the Jungle, and Ahe Itamu, the Master of Water: The Puzzle of Western Dress

During the time of mythic history, the two creator gods, Wahari and Kuemoi, were the "before time" guardians of the jungle and the rivers and were thus responsible for the well-being of the members of their domains, as well as for their health and their fertility. When these two creator gods became transformed toward the end of mythic time into Tapir and Anaconda, respectively, they lost their powers for such responsibility and therefore their status as masters of these domains. For "today time" (time subsequent to creation events) action, Ahe Itamu replaced Kuemoi as owner of the aquatic domain and became the "master and grandfather of all aquatic beings," while Re'yo assumed the former role of Wahari as master of the jungle. He also became the "master and grandfather of all jungle beings," a category that includes the Piaroa. The Piaroa classify themselves as Dea Ruwa, "beings of the jungle," a category inclusive of all jungle dwellers.

Re'yo and Ahe Itamu played only a small role in creation-time history. Although I was not told the origins of Ahe Itamu, the mythic cycles do depict Wahari creating and giving form to Re'yo, and it seems that he did so in order for Re'yo to perform his future role in "today time" as guardian of jungle beings. Both present-day masters can best be viewed as "of the future" with respect to most action in "before time," although they did occasionally participate in creation-time events. Their behavior, however, was not particularly conducive to the well-being of the Piaroa, for both Re'yo and Ahe Itamu were thieves and seducers of people. In present-day time, they still indulge in such wayward actions, but during creation time, this was the only way they related to people.

Their appearance was, and still is, remarkable, if for no other reason than that they wore European dress. One *ruwang* (the Piaroa shaman-leader) described the master of water as he saw him in a trance: Ahe Itamu, he said, was always a handsome man, dressed in blue-green clothing, standing alone upon clouds of patterned and multicolored air at a great depth beneath the water. The *ruwang* told me that Ahe Itamu also looked like a Piaroa, except that he wore a sombrero, boots, and trousers. As such a handsome man, he was dangerous to people, whom he seduced into his watery domain. Through his beautiful ritual, he would lure young men and women to join him in his river home. Once there, they had no desire to leave and return to the forest.

In contrast to the beauty of Ahe Itamu, Re'yo was the ugly ogre of the forest, a roving "orphan" who never lived a social life. He was a peculiar black giant, clothed with conquistador armor to protect himself. The color of his eyes was "clear," which probably means light blue or gray in the Piaroa classification of colors, the possible color of a Spaniard's eyes. Re'yo took his eyes out and placed them on the ground before he ate. He had ticks attached to his oversize penis. He was also a cannibal and a very dangerous seducer and kidnapper of women. The following tale from creation-time history captures well his monstrosity, as well as the capability of the Piaroa to confront the terrible with play and comedy and by so doing to deflate its danger (Overing, "Evil"). Note that the story also begins with the theme of betrayal and revenge, an operator that should by now be recognized as typical to the structure of Piaroa mythic narrative when violence is being introduced:

A "Before Time" Tale of Re'yo and the Young Girl

A young woman asked a man to marry her, and he agreed. The next day she approached him to say that she had changed her mind: She did not fancy him after all. He then suggests that they go to the mountains to hunt, and she agrees. As he walked through the jungle, he thinks: "I am going to make a trap for her. She is going to know who I am!" After they had walked awhile, they came across the hammock of Re'yo, made of a vine that he had stretched between two trees. The young woman stands transfixed by it, and the man suggests that she sit on it to rest. But the hammock of Re'yo is magnetic, and once she was upon it, she becomes stuck to it. The man, impervious to her cries for help, left her to return to his house.

In the evening, Re'yo returns. "Ah! my hammock is a good fisherman," he exclaims. "It has caught something good, a woman for me!" He took the woman from the hammock to look her over. "What is this?" he asks, looking under her loincloth. "Have you injured yourself?" He looks at her armpits, her breasts, her ears. Soon he had an erection (the penis of Re'yo is very large and has ticks covering its head). But he does not know what to do with it, and he tries to put it into her eyes, ears, nose, mouth, throat, armpits, and breasts—before he finally finds her vagina. He then exclaims, "Oh this is it. I like this. This is my life!" "Your cunt is very tasty," he tells her. Once a day for twenty days he copulates with her and finally impregnates her with his large penis. All the while, he keeps her imprisoned within his magnetic hammock.

When she was nearly ready to deliver her child, the young woman hears Re'yo talking to himself, and she understands that he is planning to cut her open, remove the baby, and then eat her. The next day, before he leaves for the hunt, she convinces him to let her out of the hammock on the excuse that she is much too large to run away. As soon as he leaves, she runs away to the house of her relatives. She tells her older brothers what has happened to her, and she asks them to kill Re'yo for her. They agree and they all return to the house of Re'yo in the evening when he is in the process of eating. When Re'yo eats, he removes his eyes from his head and puts them on the ground. The men surround him and begin to shoot darts into him. "Arghh!" he screams. "What is happening, wife?" he asks. "Nothing," she responds. "It is just that there are many stinging insects about." When Re'yo then reaches for his eyes, the young woman scoops them up out of his reach. Screaming, he finally dies, poisoned by the darts.

Re'yo was not totally inhuman, because he could father a child with a woman. Nevertheless, his humanity was questionable on a number of grounds, the most obvious being his monstrous appearance and actions. More interesting was his status as an "orphan," as "one who lives alone with no family." In the Piaroa view, the conquistadors had also been "orphans," just like Re'yo: neither had families of women and children. The conquistadors lived alone or marched together as single males, and it is significant that Re'yo existed as both one and a multitude. He often acted alone, but a present-day *ruwang* can also call him out of his jungle home to help him to protect his community as a multitude of armored giants—a Spanish army—going into battle for him. Re'yo's lack of sociality and knowledge of normal human familial relations is also made clear through the depictions of his lack of experience with the female anatomy. Because he could not distinguish the proper bodily orifice for sexual intercourse, he conflated all the bodily orifices of the young woman as possibilities for sexual penetration. As a result, before discovering the "tasty" vagina, he tried without satisfaction her eyes, ears, nose, mouth, throat, armpits, and the area between her breasts.

In present-day time, Re'yo would not be portrayed, as he is in the tale above, as a hunter; for as guardian of the jungle the only animal he hunts today is the jaguar, a predator of the animals of the jungle that the Piaroa classify as crossing the zones of mountain and jungle and therefore not belonging to Re'yo's jungle domain. Otherwise, the appearance of Re'yo is the same: Still a giant ogre, he was said to "paint himself with metal" and to wear an enormous hat of metal. He also sports the arms of the Spanish warrior—he always carries knives, rifles, and swords.

Because in "today time" the domains of water and land are controlled and protected by these two powerful spirits, the Piaroa cannot own land or stretches of river, nor can they appropriate these habitats in a territorial manner. Although the Piaroa have important rights of access to both land and water, they never have exclusive rights, those that allow them either as individuals or as a group to exchange or sell parts of these domains. They also cannot treat land and water as property that could be inherited by generations of descendants.[3] Because of the mastery of Re'yo and Ahe Itamu over the land and the water, such control over these resources is not within the scope of either private or political power among the Piaroa. They receive the capabilities to transform and to use the resources of land and water, but they do not have the power or the authority to own them as private property.

In "today time," Re'yo and Ahe Itamu guard their respective habitats, protect them, and punish those who endanger their life forms. They also cooperate as guardians of the gardens that are cleared by the Piaroa. While the land belongs to Re'yo, the master of the jungle, the plants of the garden, which were the children of Kuemoi in mythic time and therefore from the domain of water, belong to Ahe Itamu, its master in "today time." Re'yo and Ahe Itamu hold an ambiguous relation to the Piaroa: Both can be highly dangerous for them; yet they also give their protection, especially Re'yo as the guardian of their own domain.

Because these two mighty spirits are responsible for the resources of the jungle, the rivers, and the gardens, they must be negotiated with on a daily basis by the *ruwang*. From the point of view of Re'yo and Ahe

Itamu, their main duty is to protect their domains and all the inhabitants of them. Re'yo therefore has the obligation to protect not only the Piaroa as beings of his domain but also all other members of the jungle habitat. Wild pigs, armadillos, monkeys, and jungle birds have as much a right to their protection as do Piaroa humans. Thus Re'yo and Ahe Itamu give aid to the Piaroa only when it does not entail harm to the inhabitants of the rivers or to other members of the domain of the jungle.

The Piaroa told me that Re'yo and Ahe Itamu are also responsible for the fertility of their respective domains. Without them, there would be no abundance of plants, animals, and fish. They are, in a sense, earthly gods of fertility, but it is in their general role as guardians with the duty of protecting the lives and health of the members of their domains that the masters of the jungle and water endow fertility. Because of their joint mastery over the gardens, Re'yo and Ahe Itamu work together, bringing sufficient peace between these two antagonistic and competitive elements—the land and the plants growing on it—to allow for the fertility of cultivated plants. They prevent forces of the land from killing the plants of the garden and in turn prevent the plants from making the land infertile. Re'yo and Ahe Itamu are able to cooperate in a task as the creator gods, Wahari and Kuemoi, had never been able to do. They do not confer the capability of fertility, for the forces of Piaroa fertility are a gift from the ethereal Tianawa gods. Rather, Re'yo and Ahe Itamu maintain fertility through protection. They are the warriors who fight for the safety of the residents of water and jungle. Since Re'yo and Ahe Itamu do not give help to beings of their domains in order for them to make a meal of each other, the Piaroa as hunters of jungle animals and fishermen of the rivers are also ripe for their attack. Nonetheless, insofar as the Piaroa need aid in the protection of their lives that will not entail harm to other members of the jungle, the master of the jungle will oblige with the force of his powers.

Some Piaroa split Re'yo into two spirits, or two sets of spirits—one good, one evil—representing the two aspects of Re'yo's relationship with them, as both their protector and the one who punishes them for hurting other jungle beings. A powerful *ruwang* can call upon the more benevolent Re'yo to do battle against the Re'yo intent on harming people. Part of the work of Re'yo is to remind and order the animals to send their diseases to the Piaroa. In their roles as protectors of jungle and aquatic beings, Re'yo and Ahe Itamu are the two most forceful personages guarding the diseases of animals and fish, and in this role they are called "the grandfathers of disease." A word of explanation about the origin of disease is in order. When Wahari, the creation-time master of the jungle, transformed most humans into their present-day form of animal, plant, fish, or fowl, he took away their "thoughts," which had enabled them to live a human cultural life. He then gave them as replacement a new "life of thoughts," which was disease. This disease-knowledge of the animals had its origin in Wahari's previous unsuccessful attempts to create on his own the culinary arts for his jungle beings and as such was the disastrous issue of this creator god's own monstrous and perverted sexuality. The animals themselves do not suffer from this disease-knowledge, but rather pass it on to the Piaroa, who fall victim to it. When the (cultural) "thoughts" of the animals and fish were taken away from them by Wahari, so too was their intentionality: They cannot on their own volition send the disease they possess. Rather it is Re'yo who orders the diseases of the animals to be sent to the Piaroa, while Ahe Itamu directs fish diseases to them. When the Piaroa kill an animal of the jungle, Re'yo might go further to avenge the death: Having sent the animal disease into the body of a Piaroa, he can then as a sensuous force join it there to eat the victim.

Re'yo and Ahe Itamu also steal children from the Piaroa. They do so intentionally in order to replace beings that the Piaroa have hunted and killed in the domains for which they have responsibility. Re'yo takes them to his jungle home in the mountains, and Ahe Itamu draws them down to his water home in the depths of the rivers. To prevent such thefts, the *ruwang* pays the masters of the jungle and rivers to protect the children, particularly each time he teaches them their first *maripa teau,* a dangerous lesson that endows them with the capabilities for using the resources of the forest and the rivers. The *ruwatu* give Re'yo trousers, fishhooks, and other Western implements, which they place in a bundle within the house for him to take. The *ruwatu* also leave similar gifts for Ahe Itamu along the riverbank when they teach the children.

Thus the great spirit guardians in their line of duty also protect the Piaroa. The role in which both Re'yo and Ahe Itamu most frequently help them is that of guarding their children when they walk and play in the jungle. They guard them when they are solicited to do so by the *ruwatu,* who chant daily to the masters to guard the members of their communities. The Piaroa can wear a black face paint when walking in the jungle to protect them against attacks by snakes, jaguars, and sorcerers. This paint, when sung over by the *ruwang,* emits the odors and sounds of Re'yo and Ahe Itamu, which frighten these predators and drive them away from their potential victims. The sounds of the children playing become those of Re'yo walking through the jungle and of Ahe Itamu moving through his river domain. To further frighten off the sorcerers, Re'yo clothes the children in his own suit of armor, his sombrero, his boots; and he gives them his form, that of a fat giant. Only powerful *ruwatu* can use the chants for calling upon the masters of the jungle and river to help them, for to contact them entails great danger to themselves: These spirits can always be unpredictably dangerous, and they can just as well attack as help a Piaroa who deliberately initiates a conversation with them. For a *ruwang* to negotiate with them safely, he has to have considerable knowledge and power himself.

A strong *ruwang* can also ask for Re'yo's aid to guard his community against the dangers of the night. He can call upon Re'yo as a multitude of giants to chase away a jaguar or sorcerer lurking outside the house. One *ruwang* that I knew had a tiny quartz stone within which he could see Re'yo when he took the drug *yopo* at night. This Re'yo dwelt inside the stone and was given the name Re'yo *idoki* (the Re'yo of the stone). He or she could be called forth each night as both a male and a female giant. They would emerge through the smoke of the *ruwang*'s cigar to do battle for him. Yet they too could be dangerous for other Piaroa. The *ruwang* would ask them to attack the sorcerers who wished the Piaroa ill, and they would accommodate him, but they sometimes killed a Piaroa relative as well.

A Dualism: The Power of Might and the Power of Thoughts

The logic for the Western elements of the spirit masters, their dress and the figure of Re'yo as a Spanish conquistador, is best explained in terms of its contrast to the *indigenous* clothing of the mighty Tianawa gods who wear Piaroa loincloths and Piaroa ornamentation: beautiful toucan crowns, necklaces of beads, arm and leg bands. These two sets of images, the Spanish soldier and the "Piaroaized" Tianawa gods, exemplify most sharply two aspects of power upon which the Piaroa endlessly play in their discourse on similarity and difference: On the one hand, there is power's wild, violent, and coercive aspect appropriate to the combative realm of foreign politics where the role of soldier is appropriate, while on the other, there is the productive power of a full "life of thoughts." It is the latter that allows for the creation of community life, or interior space. In the creation of productive power, the transformational forces forthcoming from a "life of thoughts" take precedence over the physical "life of the senses."

The Tianawa gods are not warriors, a role that would at any rate be impossible for them since they live a pure life of "thoughts": They have no sensuous capabilities. They are instead the owners of all forces of thought (*ta'kwarü*), a role they received at the close of mythic time. Highly benevolent gods, they continually give aspects of these forces to the Piaroa. It is these "thoughts" that enable the Piaroa to live both socially and materially in a Piaroa way, for their "life of thoughts" endows them with all their capabilities for hunting, for gardening, for ritual, for reproduction, for living a rational social life. In other language, it can be said that it is their "life of thoughts," given as a gift to them from the Tianawa gods, that affords them the capabilities for transforming and using the resources of the rivers and the jungle toward the end of living a Piaroa life, one of civilized fecundity. The Tianawa gods, who have no "life of the senses" of their own, do not themselves *use* the capabilities they give away. But as owners of all the forces for life enabling the Piaroa to live as they do, it is highly appropriate that these gods wear Piaroa ornaments not only in abundance but also in their most beautified form: Such ornamentation is expressive of their potency as owners of all the forces of thought that together form the source for power that the Piaroa can but tap.

Both sets of beings, the Tianawa gods and the spirit masters, are potently involved in the material well-being of the Piaroa, each in their respective—and very extreme—way. While the gods are guardians of the means that the Piaroa use for transforming the resources of the earth, the spirit guardians of water and jungle are in charge of the resources themselves. It is especially Re'yo, the armored and armed monstrous Spanish soldier, who acts out that reality of power that is on the side of pure might. And just as the gods are incapable of using the forces of thoughts that they own, so too it is the case that the spirit guardians do not *use* the resources of land and water that he guards. Indeed, to do so would work against their role as the protectors of the resources of the jungle and the rivers. There is thus an incongruence to many of the Western items that the Piaroa give to Re'yo. He cannot use fishhooks and matches, for he does not have the transformational capacities (the particular "life of thoughts") to do so. Such tools as payments can best be viewed as a tribute to the transformational powers of White people, in whose image Re'yo acts, to make their tools and to build their cities.

In his role as guardian, Re'yo is primarily a pure "sensual" force: It is physicality and the power of might that he uses to carry out his duty of protecting the resources of the jungle. Nowhere could we find a greater contrast to his violence and forceful actions than in the ethereal imagery of the Tianawa gods. Sitting on their celestial clouds with their crystal boxes of thoughts beside them, they take their hallucinogenic drugs and chant for eternity their songs of productivity. As endowers of fertility through the bestowal of forces of thought, the Tianawa gods are more involved in the protection of the health of the Piaroa than is Re'yo.

As mentioned above, the Tianawa gods are labeled specifically as people (Tüha) and thus are of a class with the Piaroa. It is from them that the Piaroa receive the gift of their *particular* humanity: Each Piaroa is the owner and user of the transformational capabilities given to him or her by the gods, but is never an owner of the resources of land and water, which belong solely to Re'yo and Ahe Itamu. The dichotomy is that of the inside and the outside. The powers of the forces of thought so carefully guarded over by the Tianawa gods pertain most obviously to the internal relations of community life that are built through productive work, cooperation, sharing, and the creation of intimacy and high spirits, while the power of might of the spirit masters belongs to the external relations of foreign politics, which involve the competition of individuals (as in the area of exchange) creating a world ever hovering on the edge of violence, coercion, and predation (Overing, "Market").

It is the Piaroa's view of themselves as users of the forces of thought, not might, that unites them with the Tianawa gods and not with the spirit masters. It is a perspective that also carries with it an image of alterity that opposes safety and danger, moderation and excess, being "of a kind" and being different, being friend and foe. It assumes the Other to be "the cannibal Other." However, as already mentioned and as will be discussed further in the next section, the Piaroa classification of interiority and exteriority is not without its ambiguity, and the states of being to which they refer are rarely absolute ones.

Life as a Predatory Process: The *Ruwang* as the Jaguar "Interior Other"

The imagery for the productive forces of the Tianawa gods is that of ethereal beauty, and their powers are concretized as such. Inside the crystal box of curing chants owned by the fertility goddess are the sublime lights of her songs; there is a long cord of beads that has all the colors of the rainbow; her brilliant crown of toucan feathers lies on a rafter within it. Within her crystal box of hunting prowess are her resplendent amulets and necklace of medallions, and within all her boxes of power dwell many stunning waterfalls. Similarly, the ornamentation that makes a Piaroa person beautiful tells of his or her capabilities for creative abundance and fertility (Overing, "Aesthetics," 159–75). The imagery for the productive powers of the *ruwang*, the shaman-leader, can be as ethereally pleasing as for those of the gods: The clear yet moderate light of the moon that resides within his quartz stones is designated as "the precious light of his wizardry"; the moonlit water within the crystal boxes of the gods is clean, clear, and fresh, and with it, the *ruwang* each night cleanses and beautifies the words of his chants.

On the other hand, the Piaroa view themselves as predators and life as a predatory process (Overing, "Predation," "Evil," and "Cannibalism"). The wonderful forces for production, those attributes for life and creation that allow for the human condition of the Piaroa, are as well the weapons and tools for the cannibalistic process. With their gifts of the culinary arts, the Tianawa gods give to the Piaroa the powers to prey upon the inhabitants of the rivers and the jungle. It is for instance part of the culinary arts to attack, to kill, and to transform into food and artifacts the animals, fish, and plants, all of which once also lived a human life on earth. In general, the Piaroa understand work, upon which the creation of the "inside" is dependent, to be a violent process, for the powers that make production possible are of creation-time wizardry, the original means for predation in the world. In their origin, all productive forces were both evil and ugly, and it is only when they are mastered and cleansed that they can be beautiful—a process that is both social and highly personal. There is no space to expand upon this point, but the social organization and polity of the Piaroa work toward containing the violence of the predatory process through which humans of necessity live. Tamed in this way, ugly productive powers become transformed through civilized predation into beautiful ones ("Aesthetics").

It is the *ruwang*, as the individual who acquires more predatory forces of thought than others from the Tianawa gods, who is the most responsible for the productivity of his community. Because of the powers of his "thoughts," it is he who is also responsible for its protection.

As master and thus protector of his community, and as the one who provides for its fertility, he has a role that is in many ways similar to that of Re'yo, the conquistador spirit of the jungle. The *ruwang* too is the *lone* warrior fighting against the dangerous forces that might affect the community's health and security. The relationship that the *ruwang* has with most agents of the outside world, whether with exchange partners of trading networks or with vengeful spirits from creation time, is one of competition, and as such it is a mutual relationship of force and coercion having to do with the present-day use of the resources on earth ("Cannibalism").

There is nevertheless an essential difference in the respective imagery of Re'yo and the Piaroa leader as warriors. The *ruwang* in protecting *his* domain does not assume the powers of the conquistador soldier; rather he uses the transformational forces of the jaguar warrior—not those of the ordinary jaguar that roams the mountains and forest, but those of the much more dangerous cat who during the mythic time was the original creator of the culinary arts. Kuemoi, the mad creator god during mythic time of "civilized eating" (the human capabilities for hunting, gardening, and the processing of food) also created through the power of his "thoughts" all the great cats as house pets for himself. As a product of Kuemoi's thoughts, the jaguar then became the transformation he assumed for many of his own predatory forays into the jungle. The primordial source for the creator god's culinary creations—of cooking fire, curare, and garden plants—were the poisonous hallucinogens that were his food both prenatally and throughout his life. As owner of all the poisonous knowledge for the culinary arts, he was also a violent and lascivious madman who had the power to satisfy all his (culinary) desires: it is Kuemoi who is portrayed as the archetypical jaguar cannibal of mythic time (Overing, "Evil," 256–59). He stalked all jungle beings as food, and he had two heads, one to eat (jungle) meat raw and the other to eat it cooked. He is also depicted as an evil but mad buffoon who endlessly ran round in circles. Ever poisoned by the drugs he took, he had no sense of propriety, sexual or otherwise. He even raped his own daughter and committed the further outrage of reeling off the names of all the sacred places beneath and above the earth while raping her. The time of creation came to a close when all Kuemoi's poisonous transformational powers for production were thrown out of this world to be housed in safety within the crystal boxes of the celestial Tianawa gods, whose duty then became to guard these dangerous powers for predation.

It is not the *ruwang*'s physical might, but the powerful forces of "thought" originally created by Kuemoi that the *ruwang* draws (carefully) from the crystal boxes of the Tianawa gods; these give him the strength for his own soldier responsibilities. The spirit of songs (*autuisa*) within him is also called the spirit of hunger and the spirit of jaguar's breath; while the spirit of the hallucinogen *yopo* that he inhales each night is labeled as well his spirit of battle (*tekwae*). The power of breath that he uses to sing his chants is called jaguar's roar (*uhuru*), a tribute to his predatory exploits in other worlds. At his death, the predatory powers specific to his warrior duties leave his body as predator animal souls: From his breath emerges a jaguar, from his eyes come bees, while ocelots leave from his hands (Overing, "Predation," 201). The forces of predation that the *ruwang* has collected throughout his life, tamed and beautified through his human consciousness, become transformed at his death into pure animal form. As such, they may kill and devour, but they have lost all capacity for "thought" and thus for the culinary arts.

The power of the *ruwang* clearly has two faces, as indeed in Piaroa theory is true for all power that is human in use: It has its positive productive side, but the very same forces that allow for such productive skill are also rooted in violence and can therefore take a coercive turn. These are the two faces of shamanism, so often noted in the literature. The human predicament, from the Piaroa point of view, is that each individual, as human and not only as shaman, must constantly cope with these two sides of power in order to live a material life that is at the same time social in construction. On the one hand, there is the construction of the peaceful and productive relations of the inside, while on the other, there is the violence of external politics that entails a relationship of reciprocal cannibalism with many of the asocial agents of the universe. The powers of the *ruwang,* as also holds for those of Re'yo, that produce health for his own domain are the same as those he uses in his battles of force against outside agency. Productive power in Piaroa theory always has its destructive side.

Conclusion: Alterity and the Human Condition

This paper began with the problem that Mason introduced in *Deconstructing America* of the incommensurability of European and Native American systems of alterity. However, I also noted that in both the Western and the Amazonian imaginary, the Other is characterized by sexual and culinary incontinence. The complex of anthropophagy, sexual licentiousness, and sexual deviance are stock themes in their respective depictions of each other: Cannibalism and sexual perversity become conjoined in both systems of alterity, and as such operate as but two sides of the same coin (Mason, "Incontinence," 152–90; and *Other,* chapter 4). In Piaroa symbolism, the knife and the sword speak of the monstrous violence of the cannibalistic White men, and it is the perfume of their women that explains their crazed promiscuity. In Mason's scanning of the literature from the sixteenth through the eighteenth centuries, he concludes that, in the Western imaginary, it was usual for Amerindian men to be portrayed as sodomites, homosexuals, transvestites, hermaphrodites, and bisexuals, while their women were seen as lascivious Amazons who render men impotent (Mason, "Incontinence").

Questions can be fruitfully asked about why in both systems of alterity such emphasis is placed upon sexual transgression. First of all, why is sexual (and culinary) perversity such a good way of thinking about difference? Second, are the symbolisms of sexuality really identical? Does the idea of monstrous sexuality play the same role in the two schemes? To a certain extent, we can say that it does, for the Other in both is being characterized as socially beyond the pale. In both, difference in social and political regimes (a complex matter) becomes captured in discourse through a colorful imagery of excessive sex and eating, which I should think might be a widespread strategy within the context of foreign policy where the (possible) violence of enemies must be explained. There is however a critical difference in the political intent of these two discourses, that of the Native American and that of the colonial.

Mason argues convincingly in "Continental Incontinence" that in colonial discourse the excessive sexuality of male Native Americans is a sign of their emasculation and therefore of their lack of power. In this imagery, sexual deviance then becomes a general operator for political impotence ("Incontinence," 152). In contrast, in the Piaroa complex of alterity, males are often depicted with enormous penises, and just as the mythic spirit conquistador, Re'yo, sported with his, so too did other mythic males (Overing, "Cannibalism"). To emasculate males, to render them powerless, would go strongly against the Amazonian logic of sexual excess, which is most notably about power and types of potency. Here, sexual excess speaks of an excess of power, not its lack. Such divergence in the respective treatments of sexual incontinence highlights a conspicuous difference between the Native American and the colonial discourse upon alterity. The Eurocentric discourse, born within a hegemonic and totalizing rhetoric of hierarchy, is highly exclusive in its view of humanity and allows might to the conquerors alone. The ethnocentrism of the Native Amazonian discourse can best be understood as being based upon a rhetoric of equality and in its expressions of alterity is much more inclusive in its categorization of humanity: Power does not accrue to self alone.

I have shown that in Piaroa imagery of the Other an absolute boundary between self and Other is difficult to draw. So, too, is the distinction between the human and the nonhuman. While the root metaphor for alterity in Piaroa discourse is that of "the cannibal Other," such an image can hardly preclude in any absolute manner the Piaroa themselves. For the predatory Piaroa, the boundary between self and Other is not so clear-cut. The reason for such ambiguity is that the language of alterity for the Piaroa is most saliently a means through which the human condition itself can be understood. The Piaroa play upon the complexity of what it means to be human and alive and thereby provide a means for the examination of all aspects of being human. Piaroa discourse upon alterity tends to treat such aspects (the force of thoughts or of the physical) in their most extreme and exaggerated expression. Each aspect is capable of either a highly positive or deadly turn. Thus any valuation of the might of the Whites or the "thoughts" of the Piaroa is a relative, not an absolute, matter. To be sure, the central topic of this discourse is the nature of human power, as is also the case with our European example. But there the commensurability lessens. The Piaroa stress is upon the dilemma of human existence as might generally be the case and therefore upon the absurdities and evil, as well as the positive strengths, of human power. In the European imagery, certainly during the early centuries of the conquest, the emphasis is upon inversion and upon the right of Europeans as superior human beings to subjugate the inferior Other. In this vision, evil and danger are assumed to come from without, not from within.

It is true that in the nineteenth century, many European authors, influenced by the Romantics' rebellion against the rationalism of the Enlightenment, also stressed the nonrational, emotional, and wild aspects of the interior self. For instance, psychoanalytic theory was to be put to the service of taming the neurotic, the uncontrolled, aggressive, and lascivious beast within. But as Raymond Corbey has so convincingly argued in his essay on the role of alterity in the architecture of psychoanalytical theory, Sigmund Freud's understanding of the monstrous primal man within civilized man was in accordance with a nineteenth-century discourse on savagery and civilization and its pervasive association of prehistoric or contemporary "primitives" with the wild, the impulsive, the childish, and the excessive (Corbey, "Phylogenetic," 49). It was a discourse that operated with polar opposites: contemporary and primitive society, culture and nature, man and beast, men and women, white and black, adult and child. These were oppositions used in a *privative* way (see Karstens, "Alterity," 78–81). All of the second pole of opposites essentially lack what is of quality in self: Women, beasts, primitives, and children lack reason, civilization, and control. They are but inversions of self. A convinced Lamarckian, Freud assumed that the nature and experience of prehistoric man were still relevant to the understanding of modern "civilized" man: primitive man still lives within us, internalized, as a sort of lascivious and violent monster that it is the tragedy of modern civilized man to have to control. As Corbey concludes, "The world within as Freud constructed it is intricately related to that of a nineteenth-century civilizatory discourse on races, sexes, classes and empire, and the wild other who inhabits this world within turns out to be an avatar of the colonial and sexual others constructed in this discourse" ("Phylogenetic," 55–56).

A people's understanding of power cannot be detached from its knowledge and creation of a history of power and its contemplations about its development. It is characteristic of both the Enlightenment and the nineteenth-century versions of the history of power for human beings to be understood as having the right of sovereignty over the earth's resources: Power over nature, over the inanimate and the wild, was established as a natural right of humankind. Most such histories of power told of the progress of humankind in its quest for primacy over nature. They began with primordial humankind living in a state of ignorant unity with or bondage to nature and ended with humankind's (usually rational) domination of it. That humans should win this battle to dominate nature through the development of superior knowledge and skills was taken for granted. Humans were placed firmly within nature, but at the same time it was their fate, indeed their obligation and history, to control it. They alone among all beings of nature were given the gift of reason, and it was therefore their responsibility to master the wild, those things and beings without reason.

In Native Amazonian ontology there is no "nature," no inanimate or value-free universe that humans can dominate. The notion of "nature" belongs to the Western paradigm of power, not to the Amazonian one, where other worlds are always filled with agency with whom it is necessary for humans to deal. In Piaroa theory, there is no "natural" order of subjugation between themselves and other agency in the universe. While the Piaroa cannot through domination appropriate for themselves the power of others, they also do not see themselves as dominated by any other agency in the universe. Despite the dependency of the Piaroa upon the Tianawa gods, these gods in no way rule them through relationships of command and obedience. They have no "life of the senses" through which to give commands or to take action upon them if they could do so. From the Piaroa point of view, there can be no stable hierarchy of power in the universe, for each world is immune to any sort of permanent state of affairs where agents from another world could dominate or govern agency within it. No agent in the universe, or group of agents, including humans, can acquire a sufficient means to violence that would allow for the subjugation of others. Thus there can be no victors and vanquished in any absolute sense. The best that humans can do is to achieve equal relations in their often-dangerous dealings with beings of other spaces and other times.

NOTES

I am highly grateful to ESRC and the Leverhulme Foundation, both of which, in awarding me a research grant in recent years, have provided me with the time to work on many of the issues of this article. I also wish to thank warmly participants of the conference "The Anthropology of the Native Caribbean: The View From 1992," held in Leiden, the Netherlands, for their constructive criticism on an earlier version. In particular, I thank Raymond Corbey and Peter Mason.

1. See Pagden, *Fall,* 109–18, on the virulent imagery of inversion, commonly reserved for witches and other deviants, but used by Juan Ginés de Sepúlveda in his debates with Bartolomé de las Casas in 1550–51 on "natural slavery" and the status of Native Americans. See also Mason, *Other,* 52–53.

2. It is relevant that my fieldwork with the Piaroa was carried out in 1968 and in 1977. In 1968, the Piaroa with whom I lived had had minimal direct contact with Whites. By 1977, the process of integration of the Piaroa into the wider Venezuelan society was proceeding through deliberate governmental policy, but they were by no means yet active participants in the market

economy. It is also relevant that most of the data that I present here comes from the 1968 work, rather than from the 1977 material. It was perhaps the case that as the process of contact became more intense, the Piaroa also became more unsure of their responses to White people, and thus their imagery of them became less focused. A research student, Paul Oldham, has recently returned to the London School of Economics after two years with the Piaroa and is now writing about their present responses after some twenty years of experiencing very direct contact with the market society.

3. The lack of property rights over land and water is of course an indigenous understanding. As the Piaroa become increasingly incorporated into the nation-state, their reasoning on such matters will change.

REFERENCES

Corbey, Raymond. "Freud's Phylogenetic Narrative. In *Alterity, Identity, Image: Selves and Others in Society and Scholarship,* ed. R. Corbey and J. Leerssen, 37–56. Amsterdam; Atlanta: Rodopi, 1991.

Corbey, Raymond, and Joep Leerssen. "Studying Alterity: Backgrounds and Perspectives." In *Alterity, Identity, Image: Selves and Others in Society and Scholarship,* ed. R. Corbey and J. Leerssen, vi-xviii. Amsterdam; Atlanta: Rodopi, 1991.

Cortés, Hernán. *Letters From Mexico.* Trans. and ed. Anthony R. Pagden. Oxford: Oxford University Press, 1972.

Guss, David. "Keeping It Oral: A Yejuana Ethnology." *American Ethnologist* 13, no. 3 (1986): 413–29.

Hulme, Peter. *Colonial Encounters: Europe and the Native Caribbean, 1492–1979.* London: Methuen, 1986.

Karstens, Machiel. "Alterity as Defect: On the Logic of the Mechanism of Exclusion." In *Alterity, Identity, Image: Selves and Others in Society and Scholarship,* ed. R. Corbey and J. Leerssen, 75–90. Amsterdam; Atlanta: Rodopi, 1991.

Kohl, K.-H. *Abwehr und Verlangen.* Qumran; Frankfurt: N.p., 1987.

Lizot, Jacques. *Tales of the Yanomami.* Cambridge: Cambridge University Press, 1985.

Mason, Peter. *Deconstructing America: Representations of the Other.* London: Routledge, 1990.

———. "Continental Incontinence: *Horror vacui* and the Colonial Supplement." In *Alterity, Identity, Image: Selves and Others in Society and Scholarship,* ed. R. Corbey and J. Leerssen, 152–90. Amsterdam; Atlanta: Rodopi, 1991.

Overing, Joanna. "There Is No End of Evil: The Guilty Innocents and Their Fallible God." In *The Anthropology of Evil,* ed. D. Parkin, 244–78. Oxford: Blackwell, 1985.

———. "Men Control Women? The 'Catch 22' in Gender Analysis." *International Journal of Moral and Social Studies* 1, no. 2 (1986): 135–56.

———. "Images of Cannibalism, Violence and Domination in a 'Non-Violent' Society." In *The Anthropology of Violence,* ed. by D. Riches, 86–102. Oxford: Blackwell, 1986.

———. "The Aesthetics of Production: The Sense of Community Among the Cubeo and Piaroa." *Dialectical Anthropology* 14 (1989): 159–75. (New York, The New School for Social Research.)

———. "Wandering in the Market and the Forest: An Amazonian Theory of Production and Exchange." In *Contesting Markets: A General Introduction to Market Ideology, Imagery and Discourse,* ed. R. Dilley, 182–202. Edinburgh: Edinburgh University Press, 1992.

———. "The Anarchy and Collectivism of the 'Primitive Other': Marx and Sahlins in the Amazon." In *The Anthropology of Socialism,* ed. C. Hann, 43–58. Association of Social Anthropology Monograph Series 31. London: Routledge, 1993.

———. "Death and the Loss of Civilized Predation Among the Piaroa of the Orinoco Basin." *L'Homme,* nos. 26–28 (1993): 195–215.

Overing Kaplan, Joanna. "Amazonian Anthropology." *Journal of Latin American Studies* 13, no. 1 (1981): 151–65.

———. "Dualisms as an Expression of Difference and Danger: Marriage Exchange and Reciprocity Among the Piaroa of Venezuela." In *Marriage Practices in Lowland South American Societies,* ed. K. Kensinger, 127–55. Urbana: University of Illinois Press, 1984.

Pagden, Anthony. *The Fall of Natural Man: The American Indian and the Origins of Comparative Ethnology.* Cambridge Iberian and Latin American Studies. Cambridge: Cambridge University Press, 1982.

Rivière, Peter. *Marriage Among the Trio.* Oxford: Clarendon Press, 1969.

Said, Edward. *Orientalism.* London: Routledge, 1978.

Thomas, David. *Order Without Government: The Society of the Pemon Indians of Venezuela.* Urbana: University of Illinois Press, 1982.

Todorov, Tzvetan. *La conquête de l'Amérique: La question de l'autre.* Paris: Seuil, 1982.

Gary H. Gossen

Animal Souls, Co-essences, and Human Destiny in Mesoamerica

How a Toyota Wagon Is Like a Coyote

In the spring of 1985, Robert Laughlin of the Smithsonian Institution arranged a U.S. tour for the newly formed puppet theater troupe of Sna Htz'ibahom, the Maya Writers' Cooperative of Chiapas, Mexico. My university was sponsoring one of the performances, and since one of the members of the troupe was a longtime friend and field assistant from San Juan Chamula, where I have done my principal fieldwork, our home in Albany was the logical place for the group to stay. My friend Mariano López Calixto, who has since become the municipal president of his township, felt very much at home with us in Albany, just as he had for several years in Chiapas when we were living there. Worldly and self-confident, he assured us that neither the U.S. nor our home in New York State surprised him very much.

He did, however, surprise me with some unsolicited ethnographic observations about me and my world. Over rum and soda one night, he casually provided a startling assessment of me, based, oddly enough, on our car, a then fairly new 1984 Toyota wagon. It was a strange, long, needle-nosed vehicle that looked rather like a space buggy from a 1950s-vintage science-fiction movie. Moreover, it was pure white.

Amid drinks and laughter, he asserted that our vehicle was a coyote and that our possession of it affirmed his long-standing belief that my animal soul companion was a coyote, an aspect of my persona that he and I had never discussed in Chiapas. Furthermore, he stated that he had often dreamed that my animal soul companion was a coyote and that it really came as no surprise to him that we had such a vehicle. (The link between motor vehicles and animals, by the way, is coded linguistically and perhaps cognitively; the noun classifier for animals (*kot*) applies to cars, trucks, and buses as well, for all of them are non-humans that move about on four feet.) Upon examining the wagon the next morning, Mariano carefully pointed out first the feet (tires and wheel wells), then the nose (the needle-nosed hood), mouth (bumper and small grillwork), eyes (the tapered front-door windows), ears (the two side-view mirrors), and even the anus (tail pipe).

This odd discussion was both funny and serious—also, by the way, strangely flattering to me—for all Tzotzils, indeed the vast majority of over 15,000,000 Indians in Mexico and Central America today, have a private spiritual world of the self that is expressed through the concept of animal souls or other extrasomatic causal forces that influence their destiny. That my friend Mariano chose to speak of the subject with me, even if only in jest, revealed a measure of trust and intimacy, for the nature and identity of one's soul is not a subject for casual conversation in Indian communities; even less is it an appropriate subject for discussion with strangers. Mariano's assessment of me via the concept of my purported animal soul companion was also interesting in another regard. In terms of the ranked world of Tztozil animal souls from jaguars for the rich and powerful to rabbits for the poor and humble, the coyote is vaguely in the upper middle, which is probably close to where I am in the social and economic hierarchy of my nation and my community. It could also be argued that my coyote-mobile had quite a bit to do with my daily destiny.

The concept of animal souls goes well beyond being a mere evaluative vocabulary. These forces matter. They constitute a key node in Indian cosmologies and beliefs about health and general well-being. The individual soul is often revealed to one in dreams and interpreted by diviners, shamans, and other traditional health practitioners. Moreover, Mesoamerican souls are fragile essences that link individuals to the forces of the earth, the cosmos, and the divine. They provide this link because they originate or reside outside the body of their human counterpart, often in the bodies of animals. These alter-ego forces can become lost, afflicted, manipulated by witches, or frightened by sexual excitement or some unexpected event. If these forces are fatally injured, their human counterpart dies. In other words, animal souls and their related individual essences figure prominently in native theories of evil, well-being, fate, and destiny. As such, they are also centrally present in the language, beliefs, practices, and symbols used in traditional health maintenance and curing.

It will be apparent to the reader that this set of beliefs resides at the very core of what might be called a native metaphysics of personhood in Mesoamerica. While I believe this to be so, the challenge of interpreting and understanding this belief is nevertheless formidable. It ranks as perhaps the most intangible and difficult ethnographic subject I have ever encountered. I began, therefore, with the Toyota-as-coyote-as-Gary Gossen anecdote, for it was really only on that occasion that I first experienced a spontaneous exchange on the theme; that is, a conversation that directly involved me as the subject rather than as the observer or interviewer. Through this experience, I was forced to realize that the concept of animal souls, which I have previously attempted to analyze as a coherent theory of selfhood, bears more resemblance to a fluid metalanguage of discourse and practice for dealing with self, Other, and human destiny than it does to any rigid system of belief. Indeed, I have found that several recent studies that comment on my own work in relation to this concept offer compelling evidence to the effect that the belief system is neither as consistent (from one native testimony to the next in the same community and from one Mayan community to the next) nor as stable over time as I had once believed to be the case.[1] All this said, there is equally compelling evidence that the language of souls has fundamentally to do with the Mesoamerican construction of self and social identity, destiny, and power, as much now as has apparently been the case for 2,000 years in Mexico and Central America.

In the text that follows, I will discuss the concept in general terms and then proceed to give examples spanning two millenia that testify to the power of these spiritual ideas over time and space.

Tonalismo and *Nagualismo* in Time and Space

Among the many wonders and enigmas that the Europeans found in the New World, the one that must have confounded them most was the unseen and, for them, unseeable world of the Amerindian human spirit. Although some form of individual and group affiliation with spirits of animals, plants, and other natural and supernatural beings has broad diffusion in virtually all corners of the Americas, these invisible forces have assumed regional characteristics that are highly distinctive. For example, the generic term *totemism,* now common in some cognate form in most Western languages, derives from the Algonquian (Chippewa) *ototeman* (brother-sister kin), a term that, in its original context, refers to the lineal descent of members of a clan from its founding or sponsoring spirits—animal, plant, or other natural or supernatural beings. The term has subsequently been used all over the New World to designate descent lines and spiritual ties between social groups and founding spirits.

The characteristic form of this type of human-animal spiritual affiliation in Mesoamerica does not designate group relationships with spirits, but rather predestined and relatively immutable *individual* relationships with particular supernatural forces. These forces or coessences are called *tonalli* in Central Mexico; *chanuletik* (animal souls) or *ch'uleletik* (souls) in Tzotzil; or cognate terms deriving from the proto-Mayan *way* (sleep or dream) in the Mayan area. These forces are typically identified with animals, but may also, in the same community, take the form of other soul essences. Related to these concepts is the body of beliefs known as *nagualismo,* which generally refers to the transformation of humans into those animals or other spirits with which they have an individual relationship. (Mariano in fact suggested, half seriously, half jokingly, that I became a coyote as I drove my Toyota wagon.) The term *nagualism* is associated particularly with the explanation of how shamans, sorcerers, and witches accomplish their goals for good and ill; the means is through temporary transformation into the animal(s) or other spirit(s) with which they have special supernatural ties (Adams and Rubel, "Sickness," 336).

The thread that unifies these various expressions of the concept focuses on the predestination and life history of the self that lies outside of the self and is thus not subject to individual control. One must live with one's destiny. This destiny is linked to fragile essences that can become lost, frightened, or injured. These afflictions of the soul may cause sickness or misfortune, whereupon one can engage other supernatural forces (often the souls of shamans and witches who are available for hire) to intervene to restore equilibrium to one's charted destiny. The preferred route to spiritual health is propitiation and adherence to normative behavior; that is to say, health maintenance, rather than remedial intervention.

Reports and detailed descriptions of these beliefs are omnipresent in the modern ethnographic literature of Mesoamerica. These concepts have also been extensively described in sources that date from the contact period and the colonial period.[2] Nonanthropologists and Protestant missionaries in our time have also reported these "superstitions" with particular zeal and condescension. For example, Hugh Steven's missionary novel, *They Dared to Be Different,* about the current efforts to convert the Chamula Tzotzil Maya to Protestantism, relates his hero's early experience with paganism: "Mariano's [who later converts] heartbreak would stop, but not his fear and hate. As a child he dreaded his father, stood in awe of the healing powers of the ilol, and felt sprays of ice-cold panic sweep up his back whenever someone talked about the brujo who could change himself into an animal with the power to kill" (Steven, *Dared,* 51).

In the sections that follow, I will present evidence for the antiquity of the concept in Mesoamerica and will proceed to discuss its impressive power in our time as a source of internal social control and social therapy within Indian communities and also, by extension, its strength as a tool of passive resistance to the spiritual and cultural conquest of the region by Western culture. Whatever may have been the public role of these beliefs in the calendrical and dynastic rituals of pre-Columbian state religions, animal soul beliefs have evolved into our time as individual mental artifacts with no attached public cult organization. Today, these beliefs and practices belong to the private, small-scale sphere of spiritual life, whose ritual expression seldom moves beyond the domestic unit and relatively isolated outdoor shrines. Hence, because it does not have a corporate, concrete, public expression, this highly intimate spiritual complex has been difficult to eradicate or change by force. Missionaries and others who have had an interest in planned social change in the area over the centuries have apparently been unable to deal with what they could not see, for *tonalismo* and related beliefs and practices have been, and remain today, largely invisible. Indeed, there is convincing evidence that these beliefs are evolving in the modern era to serve as powerful ethnic markers as Indian communities negotiate relatively esoteric definitions of self and group identity that are not fully apparent, comprehensible, or significant to dominant groups that might seek, by persuasion, conversion, or violence, to "nationalize" or otherwise "neutralize" Indian identity.[3]

Animal Souls in Early Mesoamerican States

The iconography of ancient Mesoamerica is replete with representations of human-animal relationships: transformations, masks, anthropomorphic animals, zoomorphic deities linked with human dynastic leaders, ritual paraphernalia (such as jaguar-skin capes and tunics) that suggest links of ritual practitioners with specific animals, calendar glyphs (day and month signs) as stylized animals, and so forth. Indeed, the motif most fundamentally associated with the rise of the Olmec style, emblematic of Mesoamerica's first great civilization in the Pre-Classic Period (2000 B.C. to A.D. 250), is a were-jaguar creature that has hundreds of variant forms, all of which appear to link human political and religious authority with the supernatural power of jaguars or other jungle cats. Indeed, this iconography merges human and jaguar facial features into a single countenance, delivering the unmistakable message that human, natural, and sacred power somehow come together in this idea (see fig. 3.1).

During what is known as the Mesoamerican Classic Period (A.D. 250 to A.D. 850) the iconographic power of human-animal associations with theocratic statecraft reached new heights with the rise of the great cult of the plumed serpent (associated with the god Quetzalcoatl in the Mexican Central Valley and with Kukulcán in the Mayan area). The plumed serpent developed into what is perhaps the key sacred symbol in the art and architecture of many of the theocratic states that dominated Mesoamerica until the Spanish conquest. Indeed, entire ancient cities, for example Tula (Toltec, eighth century, State of Hidalgo, Mexico), were dedicated to Quetzalcoatl; and the legendary ruler of this state, Topíltzin Quetzalcoatl, was remembered in written and oral traditions of ancient Mesoamerica as the human embodiment of the plumed serpent deity whose name he bore. His cult inspired the rise of subsequent polities, such as the massive Post-Classic urban center of Chichén Itzá (Maya, tenth century, Yucatán). The staying power of this deity and the ideas he embodied is such that it can be credibly argued that shamanic power via co-essences lies at the very root of ancient Mesoamerican civilization (see fig. 3.2).

Until very recently, it was impossible to offer other than speculative interpretations as to the nature of the link between animals, gods, humans, secular power, theory of self, and cosmically ordained destiny in

Fig. 3.1. Jade effigy axe (the "Kunz axe") in the Olmec style. Exact provenance and date unknown, although Central Mexico ca. fifth century B.C. is plausible. (Negative no. 326909; photograph by Rota; courtesy of the Department of Library Services, American Museum of Natural History, New York)

the early Mesoamerican states. However, rapidly unfolding new discoveries in the decipherment of early Mesoamerican writing systems are currently offering testimonies written in Native Mesoamericans' own hand that promise to illuminate the meaning of the iconography. With regard to the animal soul concept, a very early Mesoamerican text about this subject was recently deciphered by John Justeson and Terrence Kaufman. In their presentation of 17 March at the 1992 University of Texas Maya Hieroglyphic Workshop, they analyzed the substance of a brief glyph text that appears on the Tuxtla Statuette (dating from A.D. 162), which places it in the Proto-Classic period in the standard sequence of Mesoamerican culture history). This text is among

Fig. 3.2. Lord Quetzalcoatl. Artist's rendering of a reconstructed bas-relief facade, from the seventh century A.D. Toltec culture. Provenance: Cerro de la Malinche, Tula, Hidalgo, Mexico. From Díaz Infante, *Quetzalcóatl,* 57. (Courtesy of the Universidad Veracruzana, Xalapa, Mexico)

the earliest currently readable written texts in Mesoamerica and is in what is known as the Epi-Olmec style (see fig. 3.3).

Of this statuette, Justeson and Kaufman say that it is probably a representation of a shaman who is calling up an animal soul companion. The figure on the statuette may depict this representation, or the shaman's impersonation of this companion, since it shows a human being in the guise of an animal, wearing a duckbill mask and a cape of bird wings and claws. The lower four glyphs in the column to our left of the figure say: "The animal spirit companion is powerful" (Justeson and Kaufman, "Decipherment," 1703).

In the great florescence of Mayan Classic culture (spanning the period A.D. 250 to A.D. 850), the hieroglyphic inscriptions routinely used

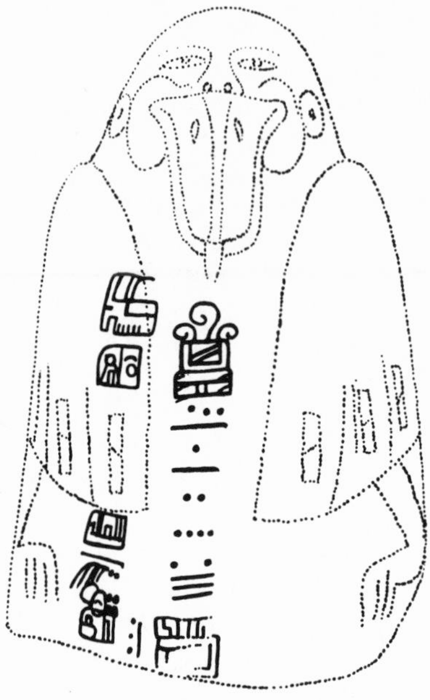

Fig. 3.3. The Tuxtla statuette. Iconography, writing, and Long Count date are in the Epic-Olmec style. Provenance is Vera Cruz, Mexico. Date, as per inscription, is A.D. 162. From Holmes, "Nephrite," 692. (Courtesy of the American Anthropological Association) The lower four glyphs in the column to the left of the figure say: "The animal spirit companion is powerful" (Justeson and Kaufman, "Decipherment," 1703).

the so-called *way* glyph (related to modern Mayan words for *sleep* and *dream*) to signify the link between humans and co-essences, both animal and other. Stephan Houston and David Stuart conclude an important paper on this subject as follows:

> In our judgement, the *way* decipherment fundamentally changes our understanding of Classic Maya iconography and belief. It indicates that many of the supernatural figures, once described as "gods," "underworld denizens," or "deities," are instead co-essences of supernaturals or humans. More than ever, then, Classic Maya beliefs would seem to coincide with general patterns of Mesoamerican thought. . . . Our final point concerns the certainty with which Maya lords identified their co-essences. . . . For the Classic Maya, such self-knowledge may well have been an important marker of elite status. (Houston and Stuart, *Way Glyph,* 13)

Thus, it is now possible to state with a fair degree of certainty that the animal-soul-companion concept and its link with human power and destiny are very ancient and very persistent Mesoamerican ideas that date at least to the time of Christ.

Tonalismo in the Aztec Universe (1550)

Some 1,500 years later, these same ideas—no doubt somewhat transformed by new cultural and linguistic influences and by dozens of generations of theocratic states—found their way to the Aztec empire. Bernardino de Sahagún's Nahuatl-speaking assistants recorded their soul beliefs in the middle of the sixteenth century as follows:

> It was said that in the thirteenth heaven
> [in the uppermost of the heavens]
> our destinies are determined.
> When the child is conceived,
> when he is placed in the womb,
> his destiny (tonalli) comes to him there;
> it is sent by the Lord of Duality.
> (Sahagún, *Florentine Codex,* bk. 6, chap. 22)

In a recent commentary on this text, Miguel León-Portilla writes:

> In several of the books where divine presences are depicted one finds also the hieroglyphs which denote the *tonalli,* the individual human

> destinies which, at given moments and places, are brought by the gods. These *tonalli,* destinies, will determine everything in each human life, from birth to death. The *tonalli* is essentially an individual's *i-macehual,* "that which is granted to one, that which one deserves." Thus, the *tonalli* bears, for all people on earth, the consubstantial origin and imprint of the divine source of life; it is this essence that determines what is going to happen in accordance with prearranged schemes. The unveiling of this predestined plan and propitiation of its divine source are vital to the human condition. (León-Portilla, "Divine Sacrifice," 8)

Concerning this same belief system, Jorge Klor de Alva has recently commented on the fundamental difference between these premises about the Aztec self and the system that the Spanish missionaries sought to impose:

> There was no autonomous will at the core of the [unacculturated Aztec] self since every human being was a microcosm reflecting the forces that made up the cosmos at large. Furthermore, there was no clear boundary between personal will and the supernatural and natural forces that governed the universe. Consequently, *acts* that were believed truly to harmonize the contrary influences of the gods (saints, spirits, "devils"), rather than right *intentions* per se, mapped out the terrain of the ethical individual. Therefore, behavior, performance and punctiliousness, rather than will, contemplation or motivation were the key concerns of the Nahua who strove to be moral. (Klor de Alva, "Aztec Spirituality," 150)

There are many other native testimonies from the contact period that address the complex world of the Mesoamerican soul, although no source, to my knowledge, discusses the subject in such comprehensive detail as Sahagún. Another extremely rich primary source of data on this subject is the famous Quiché Maya epic history known as the *Popol Vuh,* which was apparently originally transcribed in the sixteenth century from a hieroglyphic text that subsequently disappeared. This long account of the "dawn of life" and of the myriad events that lead to the then modern era (early sixteenth century) contains literally hundreds of passages and motifs that can easily be interpreted within the matrix of the Mayan variant of Mesoamerican *tonalismo* and *nagualismo.*[4]

Thus, without belaboring the obvious, it can be stated without exaggeration that Spanish Christians, indoctrinated with the central theological doctrine of free will and choice (as these were given to humanity when God created us "in his own image"), encountered in Mesoamerica a fundamentally different construction of the human condition.

A Soul War from Thomas Gage's *Travels in the New World* (1648)

Although this essay will not consider particulars of impact of the two fundamentally different visions of self and destiny in the collision course of the conquest—a conflict still not resolved to this day—it nevertheless serves my present purposes to provide one rare example of this spiritual encounter from deep in the Spanish colonial era. My goal is to illustrate that the labors of a full century of Christian missionization (1550 to 1650) did not manage to alter this belief system, much less eradicate it. The missionaries did, however, succeed in driving what was once a publicly acknowledged and publicly marked belief system underground, where it would reside relatively untouched into our time.

The text I will use to illustrate this is no ordinary one. It is, by the reckoning of some of us, one of the more colorful documents of colonial Mesoamerica, notable in large part because its author, Thomas Gage, was a turncoat Roman Catholic Franciscan priest who, midway through life, became a Protestant because it was expedient so to do during the Puritan revolution in England, at which time he was obliged to publish his travel journals in a new social and political climate. He brings, thus, both Roman Catholic and Protestant biases to his reporting.

Gage is a marvelous subject unto himself, full of ambiguous personal, religious, and ethnic loyalties. He was a valuable chronicler of Mesoamerican Indian life in the colonial period for several reasons. First, he traveled widely to out-of-the-way places where colonial administration was in its grass-roots mode, that is, where there was considerable slippage between Crown policy and local pragmatics. Second, he spoke not only Spanish but also several Indian languages; yet he did not have a Spanish national identity or the colonial agenda to uphold or defend. Third, his observation of Indian religious and spiritual customs carried an unusual set of biases, reflecting both his newly Protestant and his former Roman Catholic European self. These several unusual aspects of Gage's background may have provided a more objective lens for observing Indian life than one might expect from his Spanish contemporaries within the colonial establishment.

I reproduce the following testimony with only minimal editorial comment, for he writes engagingly and obviously does not need my interpretive assistance. The passages below report an extraordinary episode from daily life among the Pokomchi Maya of Guatemala, among whom he lived and traveled and to whom he provided pastoral care in the middle of the seventeenth century. Gage became involved with the following events through his ministry to a dying Indian named Juan Gómez and through gossip that emerged during the preparations for a proper Christian burial. It turned out, to Gage's horror, that Gómez's death had not been "natural."

> There came unto me at least twenty of the chiefest of the town with the two mayors, jurats and all the officers of justice, who desired me to forbear that day the burying of Juan Gómez, for that they had resolved to call a crown officer to view his corpse and examine his death, lest they all should be troubled for him, and he be exhumed. I made as if I knew nothing, but enquired of them the reason. Then they related to me how there were witnesses in the town who saw a lion and a tiger fighting, and presently lost the sight of the beasts, and saw Juan Gómez and Sebastián López much about the same time parting one from another, and that immediately Juan Gómez came home bruised to his bed, whence he never rose again, and that he declared upon his deathbed unto some of his friends that Sebastián López had killed him. For this reason they had López in safe custody. . . .
>
> The crown officer was sent for and came that night and searched Gómez' body. I was present with him, and found it all bruised, scratched, and in many places bitten and sore wounded. Many evidences and suspicions were brought in against López by the Indians of the town, especially by Gómez' friends, whereupon he was carried away to Guatemala, and there again was tried by the same witnesses, and not much denying the fact himself, was there hanged. And though Gómez' grave was opened in the church, he was not buried in it, but in another made ready for him in a ditch. . . . (Gage, *Travels,* 275–77)

It is evident that Gage had witnessed the tragic aftermath of what, in the view of the Indian community, had been a supernatural battle between the animal soul companions of two powerful shamans. The lion and the tiger (perhaps an English reference to the puma and the jaguar, animals that are native to Guatemala) were the co-essences of

Gómez and López, and hence, their battle in the forest involved both their bodies and those of their human counterparts. Gage's narrative leads us to believe that neither he nor the Crown officials understood what was going on, although ironically all parties—both Indian and Spanish, and even Gage himself—concurred in believing that López was guilty as charged.

Today, one could go to San Juan Chamula or to any of thousands of small communities in Mexico or Guatemala and listen to narratives of events remarkably similar to those reported by Gage in 1648. Although it is obvious, from the tragic consequences that surrounded the public revelation of the Gómez-López encounter, that these belief systems had to move underground into the private spiritual universe of closed Indian communities in order to survive, it is also obvious to any ethnographer with knowledge of Indian languages who works in contemporary Mesoamerican Indian communities that *tonalismo* and *nagualismo* remain vitally alive in the late twentieth century.

Animal Souls in Chamula (1980)

While space limitations do not permit a full discussion of Chamula Tzotzil co-essential soul beliefs, I shall offer a brief synopsis of this spiritual complex as it exists in this contemporary Mayan community. The following is excerpted from a fuller consideration of this subject that is published elsewhere.[5]

San Juan Chamula is watched over and protected today by the sun deity, who is known in Tzotzil as *htotik ta vinahel* (Our Lord in Heaven). I have chosen to refer to this deity as the Sun-Christ, for his current "being" merges the concept of Christ, introduced by the Dominicans in the sixteenth century, with the pre-Columbian sun deity. Central to the Sun-Christ's plan for managing and maintaining order in the universe was a scheme of delegation of powers to his mother (the Moon-Virgin Mary) and to several saints and other supernaturals. He gave to Saint Jerome (known in Tzotzil as *totik bolom,* [Our Lord Jaguar]) the responsibility of individual human destiny. The syncretic link of Saint Jerome with wild animals is probably traceable to the traditional legends wherein he was said to have made friends with a lion while doing penance in the desert. Following this story, popular iconography of Saint Jerome evolved the convention of representing the saint with a docile lion standing or lying at his feet. As Saint Jerome has entered the Chamula Tzotzil pantheon, his senior aspect sits with the Sun-Christ on the third (highest) level of the sky. His junior aspect lives in a sacred mountain called Tzontevitz, which lies in Chamula territory. In both of his aspects, Saint Jerome carries out his mandate for overseeing human destiny through the medium of three types of spirits or souls that are associated with each and every human being.

The first of these is called *ʔora,* meaning "time," "fate," and "destiny." (Perhaps it is analogous to the Nahuatl *tonalli.*) A kind of predestination that is irrevocable from conception onward, the *ʔora* for each person has the form of a multicolored candle that is placed by Saint Jerome in the third level of the heavens at the time of conception. Different lengths and thicknesses represent different lifespans. The longer ones of course have potential for generating greater heat and burning longer than do the shorter candles; hence, the longer candles are associated with longer lifespans. As long as the individual's candle burns in the sky, the associated person and his animal soul companion live. When it goes out—either naturally, by burning up its fuel, or prematurely, through the intervention of a witch (*hʔak'chamel,* or "thrower of sickness")—the person and his soul companion die. Because of its crucial importance to the fate of the individual, the *ʔora* candle is nearly always symbolically present in curing ceremonies.

Related to the *ʔora* is a second type of individual spirit. The *ʔora* is represented in the living human body by the *ch'ulel,* which is an invisible essence located at the tip of the tongue. It is the first spirit to become associated with the body as a foetus—symbolizing the lighting of the *ʔora* candle in the sky—and is the last to depart from the body several days after physical death, symbolizing the total extinction of the *ʔora* candle. It is this essence of the individual that goes to live eternally in the underworld and that returns to visit relatives each year at the Feast of the Dead (31 October-2 November) as long as they put out food for it. The *ch'ulel* has thirteen parts; any or all of the parts may become afflicted. This causes various degrees and kinds of human sickness of a general class of ailments called *ch'ulelal.* A final significant fact about the *ch'ulel* spirit is that it is also present, with all the same attributes, on the tip of the tongue of one's animal soul companion.

This leads to the third type of individual spirit, the animal soul companion itself, called *chanul,* deriving from *chon,* which means "animal." The *chanul* is assigned to the individual at birth by Saint Jerome and the Sun-Christ. This animal shares every stroke of fortune that its human counterpart experiences. It is also of the same sex as its human associate. The *chanul* has two aspects, a junior (*itz'inal*) and a senior (*bankilal*), each of which has thirteen parts. The junior aspect of the *chanul* lives in the sacred mountain named Tzontevitz, located in Chamula municipal territory, where it is tended by the junior aspect of Saint Jerome. The senior aspect of the *chanul* lives on the third level of the sky, where it is tended by the senior aspect of Saint Jerome. During the day, these soul animals roam about the woods and fields of their territories much as an ordinary animal would. However, at night, Saint Jerome, in both his junior and senior aspects, herds them into corrals—the junior one on the sacred mountain, the senior in the third level of the sky. Here they spend the night in relative safety from the perils of darkness—a time when most misfortunes, particularly those caused by witchcraft, occur. It is in order to guarantee this nighttime care that one must make occasional prayers of supplication to Saint Jerome.

By far the most common cause of illness in Chamula is believed to be the loss of or injury inflicted upon one or several of the twenty-six parts of the *chanul* (thirteen for each aspect, junior and senior). Loss can occur during sexual intercourse; during a period of fright, excitement, or anger; or in the course of an accident. Thus human illnesses are typically caused by numerous afflictions of the *chanul* and, somewhat less frequently, by the afflictions of the *ch'ulel,* associated with the candle of destiny in the sky. This makes a total of thirty-nine parts of the human spirit (twenty-six for the double *chanul* and thirteen for the *ch'ulel*) that can be afflicted singly, plus a very large number of combinations of parts that can be jointly afflicted or lost. It is the shaman's role to ascertain, by taking the pulse of the wrist and by observing symptoms, what parts of the soul are afflicted. He or she must then prescribe the necessary candles, herbs, flowers, and foods and say the proper prayers at a formal curing ceremony whose purpose is to restore health and integrity to the soul configuration.[6]

All animal soul companions are wild animals with five digits. Furthermore, all are mammals. It is the sympathetic trait—five digits—that establishes the special tie between humankind and these animals. It is significant to note here that the Tzotzil word for *man* (*vinik*) is the same as the word for *twenty,* indicating that the total of twenty digits is considered to be a striking aspect of human physiology and an important anatomical trait of soul-companion animals as well. (It is relevant to recall that ancient Mesoamerican mathematics and calendrical reckoning were of a base-twenty type, suggesting that time itself was anthropomorphized.) Chamula animal souls are often ranked according to three levels. The third level is the most senior and thus includes those animals associated with rich and powerful individuals; the second level, with moderately successful people; and the first, with the humble and poor. The only animal that all people agree to be a third-level *chanul* is the jaguar. The most powerful shamans and political and religious leaders, therefore, are logically thought to have a jaguar soul companion. In the second level are generally ranked the coyote, the weasel, and the ocelot. The first level (the most junior) includes the rabbit, the opossum, and the skunk. There is general agreement among Chamula people about the jaguar's first-rank position and about the low rank of the opossum, the skunk, and the rabbit. However, the second level is not consistently reported from individual to individual (see fig. 3.4).

These beliefs are related to the reluctance of the Chamulas to kill any of these animals, for they might thereby be killing themselves or a relative. This is said to happen occasionally, and narrative folklore in the community abounds with reports of such misfortunes. A typical story goes like this: "There was a woman who scolded a weasel, not knowing that it was actually her own soul animal. The weasel was angry and decided to eat the woman's baby chicks and eggs that had not yet hatched. The woman saw the weasel go into the hen's nest and ran it off, chased it to its cave. She dug it out and clubbed it to death and then burned it up with fuel oil. She died three days later, for it had been her own soul animal" (Gossen, *Chamulas,* 255–56).

Although normal people should have only one *chanul,* witches are said to have a strong animal soul companion plus an aberrant, anomalous creature that is outside the class of normal animal-soul-companion creatures. It is significant that the type and number of digits, for example, claws and cloven hooves, or too many legs (as in insects), are traits that the Chamulas note as making them *different* from soul-companion animals. Such second animal souls for witches are typically domestic animals and fowl and wild birds. It appears that the anomalous classificatory position of domestic animals—neither wild nor human—gives them important intermediary power both as sacrificial animals (particularly so in the case of chickens and turkeys) and as witches' soul companions. Witches require the power of the strong animal soul companion from the *normal* class of mammals so as to be dominant over all other *chanuletik* in order to do them ill if their clients so desire; they also require the anomalous animal in order

Wild soul companion animals (5 toes, like humans)		*Domestic and other anomalous animals* (Cloven hooves, claws, etc., unlike humans)
Carnivores	Herbivores and Omnivores	Hervibores and Omnivores
Stronger people, rich people and cargo-holders.	Weaker people, ordinary people.	Witches have one of these plus a strong wild animal soul companion.
jaguar ocelot coyote fox weasel	rabbit skunk raccoon opossum squirrel	cattle sheep pigs chickens turkeys wild birds insects
Early creation. Distant habitat (lowlands, hot). Infrequently seen, nocturnal.	Later creation. More frequently seen in highlands. Nocturnal, diurnal and crepuscular.	Recent creation. Seen every day near house compounds. Diurnal.

Fig. 3.4. The logic of the concrete: Chamula animal souls. This table offers a structural examination of the logic of the co-essence concept as represented in the data provided by several Chamula Tzotzils in 1969. Adapted from Gossen, "Souls," 453. I am of course indebted to Lévi-Strauss (*Savage,* 1–34) in my attempt, represented here, to translate the logic of Chamula animal soul classification. (Reprinted with the permission of the Royal Anthropological Institute of Great Britain and Ireland)

to given them access to places such as house compounds, where they will not be noticed. This enables them to do evil things surreptitiously, as in the form of a turkey or chicken, for potential victims would normally not expect a domestic animal or bird to hurt them. In addition, domestic animals are constantly present in and around the living compounds of all families, thus giving them intimate contact with the members of the household. This enables them to harm individuals in the household more easily.

All people, including witches, may learn the identity of their animal soul companion through dreams. Typically, people have the same dream three times. Although an individual's animal soul companion figures prominently in this dream, its meaning is not always clear. In these cases, a shaman must be consulted. While shamans and witches can usually ascertain the meaning of their own and their clients' animal soul dreams, many people are not sure of the identity of their soul animals, even in adulthood. Even if they do know, they are reluctant to discuss the matter publicly.

In summary, then, the factors that determine individual fate and fortune are almost completely beyond the individual's control. They derive primarily from the Sun-Christ, Saint Jerome, the candle of fate, and the junior and senior aspects of the animal soul companion. The healthy body carries this constellation of influences in equilibrium; it is the passive bearer of forces over which it really has no control. The afflicted body suffers from a disequilibrium situation in the whole; a part is missing, injured, or destroyed. As preventive measures, about the only ways people can affect their own destinies are: (1) to pay homage to the deities who are responsible for the soul animals so as to encourage them to continue their vigilance and compassion for humankind, and (2) to be a conservative, conforming, generous individual so as not to attract anger or jealousy, for these emotions could be turned into attacks of witchcraft. As a curative measure, the only traditional way to remedy one's afflicted condition is to hire a shaman to intervene on one's behalf by performing rituals whose primary goal is to restore equilibrium to the several individual spirits that affect the organism.

Truth and Uncertainty in a Changing World

This belief system is not an altogether comforting world view. Many individuals express anxiety over whether or not they are complying with their prescribed destinies. Uncertainty with regard to this matter can easily affect key decisions in one's life and can limit a person's willingness to undertake such risky activities as building a new house or taking a new job. Might one be stretching one's "self?" Might one's neighbors and friends be thinking this? Although this belief system produces occasional private stress, its tendency to encourage social conformity and modesty may help to understand why it continues to occupy an important niche in the life of Indian communities. Proof that it does so lies in the fact that this vision of self and destiny and its associated curing practices compete very successfully with Western medicine and other forms of planned social change, for it is much more than a system of folk medicine. It is, more precisely, a form of thought and reflection about the social reality that surrounds the individual. Remedial rituals that are associated with this belief complex are, in fact, called seeing or watching-over ceremonies. They do not seek to change the preordained path of the soul through the life cycle, but rather to defend it from unforeseen attacks and perils. Curers (seers) seek neither to change nor to circumvent the inevitable, but rather to allow the niche that belongs to the patient to be fully realized according to the will of Our Lord Sun-Christ and Saint Jerome. Obviously, there is present here an enormous latitude for interpretation, a quality that renders this belief system both fluid and adaptable just as it purports to address constant and unchanging truths.

Chamula beliefs in co-essences therefore coexist and compete successfully with Western medicine precisely because they address matters of self and society that are beyond the body; in practice, it is a system of social analysis and social integration. In contrast, Western medicine is pragmatic, individual, and "democratic," in that the same antibiotic accomplishes the same ends for an Indian or a Mexican, a rich person or a poor person. The Chamula system of co-essences seeks, rather, to encourage well-being by means of reintegrating the individual into the cosmos and into the reality of social hierarchy and inequality. The Tzotzils today accept both systems, realizing full well that their own traditional system deals with issues and realities that are beyond the reach of Western medicine.

The Future of an Ancient Idea

As I move this discussion to a conclusion, I want to emphasize that I am dealing with a conceptual universe that is not only very ancient and widespread in contemporary Mesoamerica but also, apparently, highly adaptive to our fast-changing times. It is clear that these beliefs once occupied a central place in the public religious and political life of precontact Mesoamerican societies. It is also clear, for reasons that I have attempted to demonstrate in this essay, that the political realities of the colonial and modern periods have obliged the expression and practice of these beliefs to move out of the public sector into the private, domestic sector, where they have remained—vital, important, but nonetheless discreetly veiled from public view—for centuries.

In her well-known autobiographical commentary *I, Rigoberta Menchú,* the 1992 Mayan Nobel Peace Prize laureate testifies to the reality and to the considerable importance of these ideas in the social fabric of modern Guatemala's Indian community (which is, by the way, the majority ethnic presence in the country):

> Every child is born with a *nahual.* The *nahual* is like a shadow, his protective spirit who will go through life with him. The *nahual* is the representative of the earth, the animal world, the sun and water, and in this way the child communicates with nature. The *nahual* is our double, something very important to us. We conjure up an image of what our *nahual* is like. It is usually an animal. The child is taught that if he kills an animal, that animal's human double will be very angry with him because he is killing his *nahual.* Every animal has its human counterpart and if you hurt him, you hurt the animal too. . . .
>
> We Indians have always hidden our identity and kept our secrets to ourselves. This is why we are discriminated against. We often find it hard to talk about ourselves because we know we must hide so much in order to preserve our Indian culture and prevent it being taken away from us. So I can only tell you very general things about the *nahual.* I can't tell you what my *nahual* is because that is one of our secrets. (Menchú, *I, Rigoberta,* 18–20)

In our time, there is evidence that the commitment of Indian communities to a self-definition of ethnicity and community maintenance, based in part on belief in co-essences, is reemerging in the public arena as Indians in Guatemala and Mexico move to assert their own place in the ethnic mosaic that characterizes both modern nations. No one has stated this "emergent" quality of Mesoamerican soul beliefs more eloquently than John Watanabe, to whom I turn in closing:

> Having a soul means behaving in sensible ways, not just mechanically cleaving to established ways. Soul indeed demands mastery of cultural convention, but this need precludes neither personal opportunism nor

> cultural innovation as long as one has the eloquence to persuade others of one's propriety. Although souls unequivocally situate individuals within a community, they constitute that community more as an inclusive, continually negotiated ground of social interaction than as an exclusive nexus of essential traits or institutions. I would suggest that greater appreciation of these "emergent" qualities of Maya souls might well clarify the tenacity of Maya ethnic identity in the face of rapid, and in Guatemala, increasingly violent, social change. (Watanabe, "Essences," 273)

What, then, is the future of this idea? I know of few features of Mesoamerican life, ancient or modern, that demonstrate more tenacity than this unseen Mesoamerican essence. This tenacity has occurred not through obsessive maintenance of a precious gift from the past but through creative reinterpretation of a distinctively Mesoamerican vision of self, society, and ethnic identity. Perhaps, in the next century, as Watanabe has suggested, the Mesoamerican Indian soul will evolve into something closer to the Afro-American use of *soul* as a generalizing metaphor for the spiritual essence of a historically oppressed people in a pluralistic society.

Postscript (Summer 1994)

The Zapatista rebellion, which began on 1 January 1994 in the state of Chiapas, deep in the Mesoamerican heartland, speaks directly to the open-ended question that I have posed in the concluding section: What is the future of the idea of the Mesoamerican soul? The Zapatista movement may provide an inkling of what is to come.

Although the Mayan Indians who constitute the majority of the small, poorly armed rebel army have yet to see any substantive results in terms of specific political and economic reforms that might improve their lot as impoverished peasant farmers, they have already achieved massive international publicity for their cause as an Indian underclass that has long been largely ignored by the Mexican state. Some observers have asserted that the Zapatistas have achieved that which the Mexico City Olympic riots in 1968 and the passage of NAFTA (The North American Free Trade Agreement) did not: that is, to force the democratization of Mexico's entire political process, which has, for sixty years, functioned as a de facto one-party system. While it is not my present purpose to support or refute these claims, I do want to highlight several aspects of the Zapatista movement that relate directly to the subject matter of this essay.

In spite of its revolutionary posture and its newsworthiness—qualities that might suggest easy access for both reporters and news consumers—the rebellion has an enigmatic, acephalous leadership apparatus that has not been easy for the press, the public, or even the politicians to understand. I refer to the relative invisibility of the Indian directorate, their apparent willingness to allow Subcomandante Marcos—a well-educated, sophisticated, light-eyed, and light-skinned non-Indian from Mexico City—to be their chief spokesperson. How does all this make sense?

The present essay has attempted to interpret the extrasomatic, coessential, nonlocal nexus of causality and destiny in Mesoamerican thought. We have witnessed the studied privacy of discourse and practice involving the co-essences and their identity, as Menchú notes in the quotation cited above. Moreover, we have seen that Mesoamerican Indians are reluctant to act in ways that might be perceived by others as self-serving for fear that this might invite accusations of casting misfortune and sickness on others. As a corollary and counterpoint to this reluctance to engage in instrumental acts that suggest individual volition and exercise of power over others, such assertion of authority is permissible *if* it is mobilized in ways that are credible and legitimate in the eyes of the community and *if* authority so exercised can be viewed as beneficial to the community at large.

In a rather surreal manner, all these traditional Mesoamerican ideas about self and destiny came together in the odd configuration that was witnessed by hundreds of millions around the world in February 1994 at the Cathedral of San Cristóbal de las Casas on the occasion of peace negotiations with the Mexican government. Subcomandante Marcos, wearing a ski mask and flanked by members of the Indian directorate, also masked, met the negotiating team from the Mexican government and the international press to register a list of demands that ranged from nationwide electoral reforms to educational reforms (including a public-school curriculum that would ideally acknowledge Mexico's 10,000,000-strong Indian minorities) to land reform to a charter of women's rights. Why should a blond, European, cosmopolitan Marcos preside over this extraordinary forum on behalf of Indian leaders, male and female, representing at least five of the major linguistic and ethnic groups of Chiapas who constitute almost half the population of the state? Why was there no Indian leader?

Some part of the answer, I believe, lies in the content of this essay. Marcos is utterly plausible as a spokesperson for an Indian cause precisely because he is outside of, extrasomatic to, the Indian community. This *other world* of destiny that is symbolized by Marcos (perhaps also by the emblematic memory of Emiliano Zapata himself, the greatest of all the mestizo peasant warriors of the Mexican Revolution) is the co-essential nonlocal place from which power and causation emanate to start with, whether for individuals or for groups (see Gossen, "Other," 462).

The masked, incognito mode of self-representation of the parties in these events cannot be dismissed as guerrilla theater or merely as a military security measure. It is instead a logical strategy of caution in the arena of instrumentality (read: revolutionary change) whose goals are not yet achieved and whose benefits to the larger Indian community are not yet manifest. Thus individual identities had best be masked lest the leaders be accused of self-aggrandizement and self-gain. If they were so perceived by others—without solid evidence for the overriding legitimacy of their exercise of power—they could easily become potential targets for malevolent supernatural action, as in the casting of sickness discussed above. It is perhaps also for these reasons that the members of the Indian directorate of the Zapatista movement have opted for a lateral organization of coequals rather than for a hierarchical chain of authority.

If the unusual unfolding of the Zapatista rebellion can be partially understood within the matrix of ancient Mesoamerican ideas about self and society, I think these events have another quality that represents something relatively new in the modern era. I refer to the pan-Indian composition of the leadership and constituency of the Zapatistas.

Only on rare occasions in colonial and modern Chiapas history (notably during the Tzeltal Rebellion of 1712 and the War of Santa Rosa from 1867 to 1870) have Indian political and religious movements in Chiapas crossed ethnic and linguistic lines in terms of their constituencies and military mobilization; and when they have done so in such a manner as to become active and visible, these movements have been promptly crushed by the state. Indeed, the Spanish Crown created administrative policies, settlement patterns, and local civil and religious organizations that would, in effect, segregate the Indians from the Spanish and mestizo communities. These same policies also functioned to encourage local identities, languages, customs, and loyalties. These patterns served the Crown's purpose in that they discouraged pan-Indian opposition to state policy. In many respects, this configuration of ethnically and demographically isolated Indian townships has continued largely intact into the late twentieth century.

It is therefore noteworthy that the composition of EZLN (Ejército Zapatista de Liberación Nacional) consists of Chol, Tzotzil, Tzeltal, Zoque, and Tojolabal speakers, as well as Mexican mestizos—ethnically "white" Mexicans—all united in the pursuit of common political and social goals. Additionally, this type of collective action is no longer uncommon, as it certainly was only a decade ago. Such expressions of pan-Indian solidarity are appearing with increasing frequency in our time, both in Mexico and in Guatemala. The nature of these pan-Indian organizations ranges from intellectual, educational, and religious organizations to artists' and writers' cooperatives to crafts guilds (for example, those dedicated to textile and ceramic production) catering to the tourist and export trade.

There is evidence, therefore, that Mesoamerica's "collective Indian soul" has already emerged in the late twentieth century as an active and a public voice in the modern nations of the region.

NOTES

I am extremely grateful to A. James Arnold, to the University of Virginia, and to the Virginia Foundation for the Humanities and Public Policy for the opportunity to try an experiment in what, for me, is a new genre of writing: the archaeology and possible future of an idea. I particularly appreciate Dr. Arnold's encouragement to add the postscript to this essay. This addendum allowed me to consider a dramatic set of current events against the backdrop of the intellectual history that is presented in the body of the essay. A substantially different version of this essay will appear in *American Anthropologist* under the title "From Olmecs to the Zapatistas: A Once and Future History of Souls."

1. The reader may wish to refer to Gossen, "Animal Souls," 1975; Linn, "A Thought on Individuals," 1989; and Watanabe, "Elusive Essences," 1989, for further elaboration of these points.

2. See, for example, Foster, "Nagualism," 1944; Villa Rojas, "Kinship," 1947, and "Nagualismo," 1963; Saler, "Nahual," 1964; and Vogt, "Souls," 1965, and "Spirits," 1970, as well as Sahagún's edition of the *Florentine Codex,* 1969; Ruíz de Alarcón on "Aztec Sorcerers," 1982; and Gage's *Travels,* 1958.

3. See Watanabe's excellent book *Maya Saints and Souls,* 1992, on this subject.

4. See, in particular, Tedlock's edition of the *Popol Vuh,* 1985, 188–93; and Rosenbaum, "Popol Vuh," 1983.

5. See Gossen, "Animal Souls," 1975.

6. See Vogt, *Zinacantan,* 1969, 416–76, for details on curing ceremonies in neighboring Tzotzil-speaking Zinacantán.

REFERENCES

Adams, Richard N., and Arthur J. Rubel. "Sickness and Social Relations." In *Handbook of Middle American Indians,* ed. Manning Nash, *Social Anthropology* 6 (1957): 333–55.

Coe, Michael D. "The Olmec Style and Its Distribution." In *Handbook of Middle American Indians,* ed. Robert Wauchope, 3, no. 2 of *Archaeology of Southern Mesoamerica,* ed. Gordon R. Willey (1965): 739–75.

Díaz Infante, Fernando. *Quetzalcóatl: Ensayo psicoanalítico del mito nahua.* Cuadernos de la Facultad de Filosofía, Letras y Ciencias 18. Xalapa, Mexico: Universidad Veracruzana, 1963.

Foster, George. "Nagualism in Mexico and Central America." *Acta Americana* 2 (1944): 85–103.

Gage, Thomas. *Thomas Gage's Travels in the New World.* Ed. and Intro. J. Eric S. Thompson. Norman: University of Oklahoma Press, 1958 [1648].

Gossen, Gary H. *Chamulas in the World of the Sun: Time and Space in a Maya Oral Tradition.* Cambridge: Harvard University Press, 1974.

———. "Animal Souls and Human Destiny in Chamula." *Man* 10, no. 3 (1975): 448–61.

———. "The Other in Chamula Tzotzil History and Cosmology: Reflections of a Kansan in Chiapas." *Cultural Anthropology* 8, no. 4 (1993): 443–75.

Holmes, W. H. "On a Nephrite Statuette from San Andrés Tuxtla, Vera Cruz, Mexico." *American Anthropologist* 9 (1907): 691–701.

Houston, Stephen, and David Stuart. *The Way Glyph: Evidence for Co-essences among the Classic Maya.* Research Reports on Ancient Maya Writing 30. Washington, D.C.: Center for Maya Research, 1989.

Justeson, John, and Terrence Kaufman. "A Decipherment of Epi-Olmec Hieroglyphic Writing." *Science* 293 (1992): 1703–11.

Klor de Alva, J. Jorge. "Aztec Spirituality and Nahuatized Christianity." In *World Spirituality: An Encyclopedic History of the Religious Quest,* vol. 4 of *South and Meso-American Native Spirituality: From the Cult of the Feathered Serpent to the Theology of Liberation,* ed. Gary H. Gossen, 139–64. New York: Crossroad, 1993.

León-Portilla, Miguel. "Those Made Worthy by Divine Sacrifice: The Faith of Ancient Mexico." In *World Spirituality: An Encyclopedic History of the*

Religious Quest, vol. 4 of *South and Meso-American Native Spirituality: From the Cult of the Feathered Serpent to the Theology of Liberation,* ed. Gary H. Gossen, 3–26. New York: Crossroad, 1993.

Lévi-Strauss, Claude. *The Savage Mind.* London: Weidenfeld and Nicholson, 1966.

Linn, Priscilla Rachun. "A Thought on Individuals, Fatalism and Denial." In *Ethnographic Encounters in Southern Mesoamerica: Essays in Honor of Evon Z. Vogt, Jr.,* ed. Victoria R. Bricker and Gary H. Gossen, 251–62. Albany: Institute for Mesoamerican Studies, University at Albany, State University of New York, 1989.

Menchú, Rigoberta. *I, Rigoberta Menchú: An Indian Woman in Guatemala.* Ed. and Intro. Elisabeth Burgos-Debray. Trans. Ann Wright. New Left Books. London: Verso, 1984.

Rosenbaum, Brenda. "El nagualismo y sus manifestaciones en el Popol Vuh." In *Nuevas Perspectivas sobre el Popol Vuh,* ed. Robert M. Carmack and Francisco Morales Santos, 201–13. Piedra Santa: Guatemala, 1983.

Ruíz de Alarcón, Hernando. *Aztec Sorcerers in Seventeenth Century Mexico: Treatise on Superstitions.* Ed. and trans. Michael D. Coe and Gordon Whittaker. Monograph Series 7. Albany: Institute for Mesoamerican Studies, University at Albany, State University of New York, 1982.

Sahagún, Barnardino de, ed. *Florentine Codex.* In *General History of the Things of New Spain.* Bk. 6 of *Rhetoric and Moral Philosophy.* Salt Lake City: University of Utah Press, 1976 [1969].

Saler, Benson. "Nagual, Witch and Sorcerer in a Quiché Village." *Ethnology* 3 (1964): 305–28.

Satterthwaite, Linton. "Calendrics of the Maya Lowlands." In *Handbook of Middle American Indians,* ed. Robert Wauchope, 3, no. 2 of *Archaeology of Southern Mesoamerica,* ed. Gordon R. Willey (1965): 603–31.

Steven, Hugh. *They Dared to Be Different.* Irvine, Calif: Harvest House, 1976.

Tedlock, Dennis, trans. and ed. *Popol Vuh: The Mayan Book of the Dawn of Life.* New York: Simon and Schuster, 1985.

Villa Rojas, Alfonso. "Kinship and Nahualism in a Tzeltal Community." *American Anthropologist* 49 (1947): 578–87.

———. "El nagualismo como recurso de control social entre les grupos mayances de Chiapas, México." *Estudios de Cultura Maya* 3 (1963): 243–60.

Vogt, Evon Z. "Zinacanteco 'Souls'." *Man* 29 (1965): 33–35.

———. *Zinacantan: A Maya Community in the Highlands of Chiapas.* Cambridge: Harvard University Press, Belknap Press, 1969.

———. "Human Souls and Animal Spirits in Zinacantán." In *Échanges et Communications: Mélanges offerts à Claude Lévi-Strauss à l'occasion de son 60ème anniversaire,* ed. Pierre Maranda and Juan Poullon, 1148–67. The Hague: Mouton, 1970.

Watanabe, John M. "Elusive Essences: Souls and Social Identity in Two Highland Communities." In *Ethnographic Encounters in Southern Mesoamerica: Essays in Honor of Evon Z. Vogt, Jr,* ed. Victoria R. Bricker and Gary H. Gossen, 263–74. Albany: Institute for Mesoamerican Studies, University at Albany, State University of New York, 1989.

———. *Maya Saints and Souls in a Changing World.* Austin: University of Texas Press, 1992.

Dell H. Hymes

Coyote, the Thinking (Wo)man's Trickster

Trickster figures are part of tradition throughout the New World, but for western North America and, increasingly, American literature, the trickster par excellence is Coyote (Bright, *Coyote*). He reaches Virginia both on the ground and in stories and poems.[1]

The first white people to encounter Coyote were often shocked. Since Coyote sometimes made things to be as they would be thereafter, some called him an Indian god. Since he might stop at nothing for the sake of food or sex, such a god symbolized a vulgar way of life that ought to be replaced. (Though a Yahweh who lies in wait for his messenger to kill him because of the state of his penis [Exodus 4:24] might seem a distant relative.)[2]

Today, Coyote has become a favorite symbol, even a patron saint, for a good many writers and artists, admired as a mocking, resourceful outsider, often down but never out. Still, unstinting admiration is as misleading as denigration if the purpose is to understand what Coyote and other tricksters have meant to those who told about them. Evidence will be given below. A relevant observation at this point is that Coyote and other Native American tricksters are almost always unable to learn or remember a song.[3] That mode of power is beyond them.

There is a tendency to take differences in characterization as part of a common essence and to define the trickster as a protean amalgamation of them all. Often the focus is upon what is comic, irresponsible, and unsocialized. There are stories that fit such traits. There are also stories in which the trickster ends in domesticity, matures, shows concern for others, subordinates himself, and goes to the land of the dead rather than be separated from his daughter. There are stories in which the trickster is despised.

Some narrators rank Coyote as the supreme source of a way of the world, as did two Oregon narrators, Stevens Savage (Molale) and Linton Winishut (Sahaptin) of Warm Springs Reservation, while others rank him high, but not highest. Some stories from the Thompson River people of British Columbia show him finding himself less powerful than Old Man. Among the Upper Cowlitz Sahaptin of Washington, Jim Yoke understood Coyote to have ordained all the places in the land, but for Lewy Costima, he acted as the agent of Jesus, and a second choice at that, after Crow was found incompetent. Among the Wishram Chinook of Washington, Louis Simpson had Coyote himself acknowledge at the end of a story that, even though a transformer, he ranked below those with the qualities of a chief.[4] Coyote has just changed Antelope and his sons to how they will be when the Indians have come:

Now then they started to run away, all gray.
Now they had no gold on their bodies.
Now then he told them:
    "You should not be chiefs.
    "I am Coyote.
    "Now this is what people will say:
        'Now these are the ones Coyote transformed,
            Antelope and his two sons.'
    "Indians shall be chiefs;
        you for your part are Antelope.
    "They will say,
        'This Antelope was transformed by Coyote.' "
Coyote said:
    "Salmon is a chief,
        Eagle is a chief,
            and people will be chiefs.
        I am Coyote,
            I am no chief."

The heart of the matter is that a trickster such as Coyote is "good to think" (to apply Claude Lévi-Strauss's phrase about animal figures generally). What is good can differ from one person to another, and even from story to story of the same narrator. It is a mistake to characterize all tricksters, or even the trickster of a particular society, in the same way. If the trickster answers to a Platonic idea, it is an idea that is a starting point, not a realization.

This is not to say that there are no recurrent characteristics associated with cultural areas and evolutionary complexity. It is to say that one must beware what the sociologist W. R. Robinson called the ecological fallacy, which attributes to individuals a property observed across a group. Tricksters and traditions about them were and are resources that reflective people have drawn upon in different ways. We realize that a Shakespearean play, even a canon like the Hebrew Bible, is internally diverse and open to diversity of interpretation. Just so, Native Americans have found in their traditions resources that admit of different interpretations. Their tellings select and group together what is meaningful to them, enacting personal attitudes. In principle, they transmit, but in practice, they may transcend and transform.

The theme of this study, then, is that stories of a trickster must be read, first of all, as the stories of those who told them, not as expressions of a constant culture, let alone as expressions of a single nature. If all trickster stories are thrown into a common pot, it is not surprising that the supposed trickster will taste now of one nature, now of another. But narrators, having relative autonomy of interpretation, can themselves be consistent. Let me illustrate this with a pair of comparisons between two narrators of the Pacific Northwest and then extend the first comparison in terms of other narrators as well.

"The News about Coyote": Simpson versus Smith

"The News about Coyote" was known along the Columbia River, in the Willamette Valley, and perhaps more widely. The premise is that Coyote performs fellatio on himself, seeks to conceal the fact, and fails.

Let me present the story as told by Simpson and Hiram Smith and say something about their versions; compare them further in terms of a continent-wide type of story, "The Bungling Host"; then consider what three other narrators from the same region have made of "The News about Coyote."[5]

Simpson and Smith lived on reservations to which their people had been removed in the nineteenth century, Simpson in Yakima, Washington, Smith in Warm Springs, Oregon. The original communities were almost opposite each other on the Columbia River, the one on the Washington side becoming known as Wishram, the one on the Oregon side as Wasco. The two communities had the same language, and the two men told the story in that language. Yet the Coyote of their stories is different, different in a way consistent with other of their stories.

Here are the tellings. Each is followed by a profile of formal relationships. Chinookan speakers give shape to narratives in terms of successions of three and five, and it is helpful to see them.[6]

The News about Coyote / LOUIS SIMPSON

(A) [Coyote makes news]

Now then he went,
    he went and went,
    he sat down.
Now then Coyote looked all around
Now then Coyote sucked himself.
Now then he did thus:
    he put up his penis,
    he put down his head.
    Someone pushed him down.
Coyote said:
    "You've done me no good."

(B) [The news gets loose]

Now then he locked up the news—
    he did not want it to be made known.
Now then someone made the news loose.
Now then everyone came to know
    what Coyote did to himself.
Now then he had headed the news off.
Now then they made the news break loose.

(C) [The news goes ahead of him]

Now then Coyote became hungry.
Now then he thought:
    "Now I shall eat."

Now then he ran among the people
Now then they said:
"He did badly to himself, Coyote,
"He sucked his own penis."

Now then again Coyote ran.
He thought:
"Over there I am not known.
"Truly now I will not be made known."

He ran again to a house.
Now again they are laughing:
"Now Coyote sucked himself."

The people again are telling one another.
Now then he thought:
"Truly now I am known."

SIMPSON PROFILE

Scene	*Stanza*	*Verse*	*Line*
	A	abcde	1-3, 4, 5, 6-9, 10-11
	B	abcde	12-13, 14, 15-16, 17, 18
	C	ab	19, 20-21
		cd	22, 23-25
		ef	26, 27-29
		gh	30, 31-32
		ij	33, 34-35

The News about Coyote / HIRAM SMITH

He was running along again, *(A)*
then the sun was shining hot.
He was tired,
then he sat down.

He was sitting,
    then he got a hard-on,
        then he sucked himself.

Just got started, *(B)*
    somebody pushed down on his head,
        "Hey, what you doing again?"[7]
He looked all round:
    nobody.
But he heard them.
He thought,
    They'll make news."
Then he did his hands like this: [sweeping gesture]
    it was rimrock straightway to the river,
        this side and that.

He got afraid, *(C)*
    it might make news.
But already it blew the down up over the rocks,
    already the news got ahead of him.
Wherever he goes,
    there at a camp,
        straightway he hears the people.
They're saying,
    "You folks hear now,
    'Coyote sucked himself?' "
Wherever he goes again,
he hears the same thing again,
    then he went off and left.

SMITH PROFILE

Scene	*Stanza*	*Verse*	*Line*
I		A	abc
1–2, 3–4, 5-6-7			
	B	abcde	8–10, 11–12, 13, 14–15, 16–18
	C	abcde	19–20, 21–22, 23–26, 27–29, 30–32

The line-to-line form of the stories manifests their difference. Simpson's Coyote marches to action. Three lines of a common triad of travel (go, continue, arrive) begin a triad of verses (Now then . . . , Now then . . . , Now then . . .). He sits down, he looks around, he sucks himself. Smith uses three verses also, but each step is coupled with an explanatory (exculpatory) detail—he was running along (but) the sun was hot; he was tired (so) he sat down; he was sitting, he got a hard-on, (so) he sucked himself.

Notice the differences in the ending points of the three stanzas. With Simpson, the focus throughout is on the consequence and cost for Coyote. He acknowledges, "You've done me no good" (end of [A]). In (B) the intermediate ending point (third verse of five) has everyone know; the remaining two verses double the opening pair, that Coyote wanted to conceal the news and that it got loose. In (C) both the intermediate and final ending points have Coyote acknowledge that he is known (26, 27–29, 33, 34–35). Twice he has been shamed and denied food. (The story is the second of a set of three in which Coyote fails to obtain food.)

In his middle stanza, Smith dramatizes Coyote's response to the pushing down of his head. In contrast to Simpson's story, the news is not yet loose. Rather, Coyote creates a long ridge of rimrock (still to be seen on the Washington side of the river, across from Mosier). And in Smith's concluding stanza, Coyote is not hungry. True, twice he finds that the news has gotten ahead of him, indeed is all over ("wherever he goes"). But whereas Simpson has the news spoken twice, Smith does so only once. Smith's Coyote does not confess, "I am known." Instead, his last line has the style of the first line of another story.

For Simpson, Coyote is twice-punished, gets his just deserts. For Smith, Coyote is almost a victim of circumstances, embarrassed, but on his way. Nor is the difference between the two tellings accidental. I read Simpson's telling to Smith, asking him to explain bits of it that were unclear (as first published—see pages 134–38 of my "In Vain I Tried to Tell You" on the difference made by restoring the field transcription). I read Simpson's version to him in the Chinookan language. Smith went on to tell it in his own way. That bespeaks a firmly rooted conception of Coyote of his own.

Simpson versus Smith: Providing Food

The same sort of contrast, punitive as against sympathetic, appears in a use by each narrator of one of the most popular themes of Native

American tradition, that of the bungling host. One person provides food by a remarkable feat or power, perhaps by cutting himself or killing a family member; the apparent victim is restored unharmed. The guest invites the host in return, seeks to emulate him, and fails. Simpson tells it in terms of Coyote and Deer, Smith in terms of Coyote and Fish Hawk (Osprey).[8] Here is an English version of Simpson's narrative:

Coyote and Deer / LOUIS SIMPSON

[i] [Coyote visits Deer]

(A) [Coyote comes]

Coyote went on and on.
Straightway he arrived at Deer's house.
Now then the two sit and sit.
Now then Coyote said:
        "Now I'll go home."
[- - -] "All right,"
                Deer said to him.

(B) [Deer gives Coyote food]

Now then he took a knife,
        he just sliced meat from his body.
Now then it was given Coyote.
And he pushed wood up his nose.
Now then his blood flowed out;
        filling a bucket.
Now then Coyote was given it.

(C) [Coyote goes]

Now then he went to the house.

[ii] [Coyote visits Deer again]

(A)

Now again Coyote went;
Straightway now again to Deer.
Now again he cut meat from his body;
Again the meat was given Coyote.
And again he pushed wood into his nose;
        his blood flowed out,
                filling a bucket.

Now again Coyote was given it. *(B)*
Now then Deer told Coyote:
"If you should be hungry,
"You should come to me."
[- - -] "All right,"
agreed Coyote.

Now then Coyote in turn said: *(C)*
"You in turn ought to come to *me*."
[- - -] "All right,"
he said to him.
"Now I shall go in turn to your, Coyote's, house."
That is what he told him.

[iii] [Deer visits Coyote]

Now then Deer in turn went to Coyote's house. *(A)*
Straightway he arrived.
Now there Deer sat *quietly*.

Now then Coyote thought: *(B)*
"Now I shall give Deer a little meat in his turn."
Now then he took the *wife*,
he threw her down on the ground.
Now then he cut her.

Then the woman burst into tears. *(C)*
Then Deer jumped.
Then he told *him*:
"Let that woman alone.
"I shall give you meat."

Now then he just sliced meat from his body; *(D)*
Then meat was given Coyote and his wife.
And he produced blood from his nose;
he gave blood to Coyote and his wife.

Now then Deer went home to his house. *(E)*
Now then he told the two:
"If you two should be hungry,
"You should go to *me*."

Then the woman told him:
"You are bad, Coyote.
"I for my part am not Deer.
"Look at that Deer;
"Everyone will swallow *his* meat.
"I do not have good meat.
"Likewise you, Coyote, are different;
"You are a poor thing, Coyote.
"No one would swallow your meat.
"That is what people will say:
"'Dead things are Coyote's food.'"

SIMPSON PROFILE

Scene	*Stanza*	*Verse*	*Line*
i	A	abcde	1, 2, 3, 4–5, 6–7
	B	abcde	8–9, 10, 11, 12–13, 14
	C	a	15
ii	A	abcde	16, 17, 18, 19, 20–22
	B	abc	23, 24–26, 27–28
	C	abc	29–30, 31–33, 34
iii	A	abc	35, 36, 37
	B	abc	38–39, 40–41, 42
	C	abc	43, 44, 45–47
	D	abc	48, 49, 50–51
	E	abc	52, 53–55, 56–66

In Chinookan myths, a final speech of reproach is always right, and here Coyote's wife is right in her condemnation. Deer has twice enacted the principle of the world as providential. The other beings of the world will provide for those who respect their natures and the ways that govern both. Deer has power to offer himself inexhaustibly; Coyote does not. Coyote, indeed, tries to use, not himself, but his wife. The isolation of Coyote is expressed in verbal choices as well. When Deer and the wife speak, it is to another person; the verb requires or has an object. When Coyote speaks, the verbs used do not. The forms of speaking express the theme of reciprocity. Deer and the wife speak reciprocally, Coyote does not. Coyote's isolation is remarkably expressed in a second way. The terms of the relationship require a "possessive" prefix indicating the other person: not "son," but "my son," "your son," and so forth. The first use of the term for *wife* here is actually ungrammatical; it has no relational prefix.

Coyote and Fish Hawk[9] / HIRAM SMITH

[I] [Coyote seeks food from Fish Hawk][10]

There was a Coyote living. *(A)*
He had six children.
They were starving.

Coyote goes hunting [in vain] *(B)*
He brings nothing.
They're really starving.

He was wandering (was around). *(C)*
Then he thought,
"I'll go see my friend, Fish Hawk."

He went toward him (to visit him).
He saw the Fish Hawk's children.
laughing, raising the dickens (kids usually).

He sat down.
He thought,
"My children will be laughing and doing the same."

He went down the hill to the Fish Hawk's home. *(D)*
He got there.
He went in.

The Fish Hawk asked him *(E)*
"What brings you here?"
But Fish Hawk knew
Coyote was hungry.

Fish Hawk and his wife were eating.
Then they fed the Coyote.

He told them,
"I came to mooch food off of you."
Fish Hawk told him,
"Okay."

[II] [Fish Hawk provides]

Then they went down toward the river. *(A)*
Close to the river bank a big pine tree was standing.
Down in the ice was a big hole.

Fish Hawk he flew up, sprang up, in the tree. *(B)*
He looked down.
[In a little while] he flew down [fast] into the hole in the ice.

Coyote sat there. *(C)*
He thought,
"Gee! I wonder if I risked my partner?"
Coyote thought,
"I might as well go home."
They might think,
he killed his partner.
He was about to go home.

Then Fish Hawk appeared. *(D)*
This side strings of fish,
other side salmon,
he layed up on the ice.
He told Coyote,
"This your children will eat."[11]

He took it, *(E)*
and was on his way.

[III] [Hungry again, Coyote tries]
[i] [He fails]

It lasted them for a while to eat, Coyote's children. *(A)*
Then they started to go hungry again.
The Coyote thought,
"I can do the same as the Fish Hawk did."

He ran down to the river. *(B)*
He climbed up the pine tree.
He sat up there, like the Fish Hawk.

Then he jumped *(C)*
and he missed the hole.[12]
He flopped down on the ice.
Dead.

[ii] [Fish Hawk provides again]

Fish Hawk was watching him.
He went down to the river,
he got there to him:
Coyote, he was dead.
He felt sorry for him.
He dove down, Fish Hawk.
The same as before.
He lay by his side salmon and fish—trout.
Then Fish Hawk went on home.

[iii] [Coyote recovers]

He was dead still for quite a while.
He come to.
He set up.
He looked around:
he saw salmon and fish.
Then he got them.
Then he said,
"That's just what I thought
the Fish Hawk would do for me."
Then he was on his way home.

SMITH PROFILE [13]

Act	*Scene*	*Stanza*	*Verse*	*Line*
I		A	abc	1, 2, 3
		B	abc	4, 5, 6
		C	ab cd ef	7, 8–9; 10, 11–12; 13, 14–15
		D	abc	16, 17, 18
		E	ab cd ef	19–20, 21–22, 23, 24, 25–26, 27–28

II		A	abc	29, 30, 31
		B	abc	32, 33, 34
		C	abcde	35, 36–37, 38–39, 40–41, 42
		D	abc	43, 44–46, 47–48
		E		49
III	i	A	abc	50, 51, 52–53
		B	abc	54, 55, 56
		C	abc	57–58, 59, 60
	ii		aBcDe	61, 62/63/64, 65, 66/67/68, 69
	iii		aBcde	70, 71/72/73–74, 75, 76–78, 79

Both Simpson's Deer and Smith's Fish Hawk are benevolent. Deer offers himself to a vain and thoughtless Coyote, self-isolated from discourse and family. Fish Hawk helps Coyote who considers himself a friend, thinks of how his children will be happy, worries that he may have risked his friend in asking help. Fish Hawk knows without being told that Coyote is hungry; Coyote's characteristic presentation of himself as having known in advance emerges at the end, but is linked to the partnerlike relationship. Whoever told stories to Jeremiah Curtin[14] also saw Coyote and Fish Hawk as partners; but in this story, Coyote is thoughtlessly greedy and, at the end, when he fails, angry. Smith's characterization of Coyote is not collective Wasco, but his own (or in a tradition he adopted as his own).

Stories of a bungling host are a resource that can be put to diverse uses. Conventional scholarship has classified them in terms of the different ways in which the first host produces food.[15] The differences in the relationship between the two hosts have been ignored. Yet as these two narratives indicate, such differences may reveal characteristic differences in the views of the one who bungles. The heart of the story has to do not with magical devices but with reciprocity and solidarity. Sometimes the relationship has to do with the relation between what tricksters are and do and the human community as a whole.

"The News about Coyote": Other Views

"The News about Coyote" was probably known to many communities north and south of the Columbia River.[16] Randy Bouchard has heard a version of it several times from Louis Pichette of Inchelium, both in English and in Colville, a variety of Colville-Okanagon (southern branch of Interior Salishan in northeastern Washington and southeastern British Columbia).[17] Pichette's story has a different frame from those of Simpson and Smith. In theirs, there is no other actor (Lynx) to spread the news; it gets out by itself (as a feather, according to Smith), but as against the Willamette Valley versions, all share having Coyote's head pushed down. One might speak of an Interior Columbia type.

Versions have survived from speakers of the three languages of the Willamette Valley, Clackamas (closely connected to Wishram-Wasco), Santiam Kalapuya, and Molale. All share the feature of Coyote himself asking for news, only to find that the news is about him. This frame of finding that the news is oneself was a resource in the region beyond this story. It is known from the Oregon coast in stories of a young man copulating with his grandmother, knowingly and enthusiastically in Tillamook, just south of the Columbia, deceived and ashamed in Miluk Coos, some distance to the south; and it occurs in a quite uncomic Colville-Okanagon story of Coyote confronted by the wife he has abandoned.[18]

The Clackamas, Kalapuya, and Molale versions might owe their similarity to the fact that all three groups shared the Grande Ronde Reservation in the latter half of the nineteenth century and had interacted with each other before then. Victoria Howard indeed had Molale relatives and knew enough Molale to have understood stories told in it. John B. Hudson remembered Savage and told Melville Jacobs a dream about him. The versions by Howard and Hudson are almost identical in substance, although different in form. They exploit the humor of Coyote finding out that the news he asks for is about him. The discovery is made just once, unlike the other version, in which finding that the news is known happens twice. The focus here is on Coyote's role as an example, learning from his mistake and announcing how things will be.

News about Coyote / VICTORIA HOWARD

He went, *(A)*
    he was going along,
        now he thought:
            "I shall suck myself."

He went on,
off the trail, he covered himself with five rocks,
now *there* he was.
He sucked himself,
he finished,
he came out.

He was going along, *(B)*
he saw a canoe going downriver;
he thought,
"Let me inquire of them.
"Perhaps something is news."

He hallooed to them.
They heard him,
they told him,
"Ehhh what?" }[19]

He told them,
"Isn't something news?"
[- - -] "Indeed! Come a little this way." }

He went close to the river.
[- - -] "Yesss,"
they told him,
"Coyote was coming along,
"Now he covered himself with rocks.
"He sucked himself.
"That's the kind of news that's traveling along." }
He thought,
"Hmmmm! Wonder who saw me?"
He went back *(C)*
where he sucked himself at;
He saw
the rocks are split.
That was where the news had rushed out.
He thought,
now he said:
"Indeed, even though it was I myself,
the news rushed out.

"Now the people are near.
"Whatever they may do,
    should they suppose,
        'No one will ever make me their news,'
    out it will come."

HOWARD PROFILE

Scene/Stanza	*Verse*	*Line*
A	abc	1–4, 5–7, 8–10
B	a	11–15
	bc	16, 17–19
	de	20, 21–22
	fg	23, 24–29
	h	31
C	abcde	32–33, 34–35, 36, 37, 38–46

The News Precedes Coyote / JOHN B. HUDSON

Coyote was going along [down the Willamette River]. *[i] (A)*
    he wanted to go to the falls here [at Oregon City].
Now then he made camp, *(B)*
    now then it became morning,
        now then he went on again.

Now then it became dark, *(C)*
    now then he camped again,
        now then at morning he went on again.
Now then it was dark, *(D)*
    now then he camped again,
        now then at morning he went on again.

Now then at dark he camped again, *(E)*
    now then he slept in a sweathouse,
        now then he turned the sweathouse into rock.

Now then he was licking his penis, *(F)*
now then he came out:
"This sweathouse will be a rock."

Now then he went along, *[ii] (A)*
now then he was going along,
now then he saw a lot of people in a canoe.

Now then Coyote called out, *(B)*
"What's the news?"
Again he called out,
"What's the news?
"What's the news?"

Now then one of those people said, *(C)*
"*What* can be calling out?
"Oh it's that Coyote!"
Now then that person called back to him,
"Hello!"

Coyote said, *(D)*
"*What*'s the news?"
Now then that person said,
"There's no news at all.
"The only news (is) Coyote was sucking his penis."

"Ah! But where was the one who saw me standing?" *(E)*
"Ohhh. I'll go back.
"I'll see where he could have been standing."[20]

Now then he went back, *[iii]*
now then he got to the sweathouse here
Now then he examined his sweathouse,
now then he saw where the rock had been cracked apart.
"Ohhhhh! I suppose this is where the news came out from it.
That is how it is going to be.
That is the way it will always be.
Nothing will ever be hidden.
That is the way it will always be."

HUDSON PROFILE [13]

Scene	*Stanza*	*Verse*	*Line*
i	AB	a abc	1–2; 3, 4, 5
	CD	abc abc	6, 7, 8; 9, 10, 11
	EF	abc abc	12, 13, 14; 15, 16, 17
ii	A	abc	18, 19, 20
	B	ab cd ef	21–22, 23–25; 26–28, 29–30; 31–32, 33–35
	C	a	36–38
iii	A	ab cd e	39, 40; 41, 42; 43–47

As just seen, Hudson elaborates the narrative, marking each line as a verse (with the particle for "Now then") for a very long stretch (3–20). He then turns to three pairs of dialogue (21–35) and one verse of inner speech (36–38) before four lines that again are each a verse (here paired: 39–40, 41–42) and a concluding pronouncement (43–47).

Howard's and Hudson's tellings are alike in that the covering up of the news by rock(s) is in the first of the three parts (stanza A for Howard, scene 1 for Hudson); for Simpson and Smith, the covering up is in the second (stanza B for both). As mentioned, the latter two have Coyote twice discover that the news is out, in a third, last part; Howard and Hudson have it once, in a second, middle part. The Coyote of Simpson and Smith makes the discovery while going on. The Coyote of Howard and Hudson discovers and goes back. He finds how it got out and pronounces a moral. For the Wishram and Wasco narrators, the end is one of going on with personal shame, rubbed in or shrugged off. For Howard and Hudson, it is an occasion to return and point out a moral for everyone.

Savage adds a twist. Like Hudson, he elaborates the form of the story, deploying scenes instead of stanzas. Like Hudson and Howard, the sucking and covering up (in that order now) are in the first of three parts, but so is finding that the news is out. Savage's Coyote goes back to find how it got out in the second of three parts. He finds out from his "lawyers." (That is an original designation, so far as I know, for a narrative device found throughout the Northwest, turds Coyote carries along with him and turns to for advice when he is at a loss. To have Coyote ask them is de rigueur for Savage; it happens in story after story.)

Another small genre on which Savage insists is that Coyote foretell the end of the world (of myth), pronouncing what will be. Savage is so fond of this closing scene that in one story, when the actors are beginning to disband, he has Coyote arrive (out of nowhere, so far as the myth is concerned) and tell them to go back so that he can address the assembly with pronouncement.

Here is Savage's story:

The News about Coyote / STEVENS SAVAGE

[i] [The news gets out]

Coyote . . . *(A)*
After he had gone a little way, he got hungry
He was talking to himself,
"O! I am hungry."

Then he built a house, a rock house. *(B)*
He patched up the walls in the house tight.
Then he went in.
Then he began sucking his penis.

After he sucked it, *(C)*
then he went out.
He was going now.
Then he saw three people drifting downstream in a canoe.
He shouted at them,
"Do you know anything?"

Then they answered him. *(D)*
They said,
"Yes, we know something."
[- - -] "What do you know?"
[- - -] "Coyote has been sucking his penis."

[- - -] "O what do they tell me . . ." *(E)*
They were going, those people,
going down stream in a canoe.

[ii] [Coyote finds out who saw him]

Coyote went back. *(A)*
He went in where he was sucking.
He was looking around after he got in.
Then he saw a hole in the east side.
Then he said,
"There's where the news went out."

Then he began thinking about it *(B)*
and couldn't make (out?) anything.
Then he let out his lawyers.
Then he asked them,
"You tell me."

Then he told them,
"Tell me something."
Then they said,
"Yes, we will tell you.
"A little ways from here people are living.
"Thus we tell you."

Coyote said, *(C)*
"How did they know what they told me about
when I was sucking it?"
Then they said,
"There was a hole in the rock (house).
"There is where they looked in."
Coyote said,
"Who looked in?"
[- - -] "She saw,
Duck saw you,
while you were sucking it.
"Now that's all we tell you.
"Whatsoever you want to do,
do as you please now."
[- - -] "I am satisfied
as you two told me about it."

[iii] [Coyote transforms the informers and pronounces]

Then he put them back in now. *(A)*
Then he started.
Then he came to them, to many people.

While traveling, *(B)*
he was shouted at.
He was shouted at,
"Don't you cross this way."
Coyote kept on going.

Then he arrived there alongside one man. *(C)*
He looked down,
he said,
"What are all these people doing here?"
Then that one began telling him,
he told him,
"They are telling one another about something."
Coyote said, he was told,
'Coyote has been sucking his penis.'
"Now that's what the people are telling one another."
Then he answered, he said,
"Ah, I understand now."

He said, *(D)*
"Now I am glad since you told me about it.
"Now I am going to make an end of this earth.
"Now I am going to kill you all."
To Duck he said,
"Never will you carry news.
"You will (just) be a duck now."
Now he killed them all.

Then he was alone. *(E)*
He said,
"Now people thus will tell this story,
those who will come here."
"Now that's all.
"I am going now East."
That's the end of the history.

SAVAGE PROFILE

Scene	*Stanza*	*Verse*	*Line*
i	ABCDE	abc	1, 2, 3–4
		abc	5–6, 7, 8
		abc	9–11, 12, 13–14
		abc	15–17, 18, 19
		a	20 (21–22)
ii	ABC	abc	23–25, 26, 27–28
		abcde	29–30, 31, 32–33, 34–35, 36–39
		abcde	40–42, 43–45, 46–47, 48–53, 54–55
iii	ABCDE	abc	56, 57, 58
		abc	59–60, 61–62, 63
		abc	64, 65–67, 68–70, 71–73, 74–75
		abc	76–79, 80–82, 83
		abc	84, 85–89, 90

Conclusion

A table may help bring out the similarities and differences among the several tellings. All these narrators share a tradition in which (1) Coyote sucks himself and (2) covers the spot with rock, but (3) the news gets out. Along the middle and upper Columbia (compare the Colville-Okanagon version in note 17), Coyote twice goes on to places that know the news before he gets there (4a) (twice also in Molale; three places in Colville-Okanagon). In the Willamette Valley, Coyote discovers he is the news by asking for news (4b). There he goes back to find out what happened (5) and makes a pronouncement (6) (so too in Colville-Okanagon). In Savage's telling, he also punishes the one responsible (7).

The table uses the narrators' initials and letters and Roman numerals for the stanza or scene in the story, except for Colville-Okanagon, which has not been analyzed ethnopoetically:

	LS	*HS*	*LP*	*VH*	*JH*	*SS*
(1)	A	A	+	Ac	iF	i
(2)	B	B	?	Ab	iEF	i

(3)	B,C	C	+			
(4a)	C	C	+			
(4b)				B	ii	iCDE,iiiABC
(5)				Cabc	iiC,iiiabcd	ii
(6)			+	Cde	iiie	iiiDE

In these versions of a common situation, Coyote is portrayed as a culprit doubly punished by shame and denial of food (Simpson); as one who could plead extenuating circumstances, lightly punished, and continuing along (Smith); as someone caught in public embarrassment, who then takes on the role of transformer, pronouncer of what will be everafter (Howard, Hudson); as someone who takes revenge as well as pronouncing (Savage).

If narrative attitudes toward Coyote lie on a single dimension, indeed, here we have polar ends. Simpson's Coyote is punished; Savage's Coyote punishes others (his is the only version in which Coyote takes revenge). Smith's Coyote performs (creating a landmark) and goes off, Howard and Hudson have Coyote learn from experience and pronounce a useful moral, while Savage, like Winishut of Warm Springs Reservation some sixty years later, has Coyote in charge of a world. For Savage, it is a world that at the end of almost every story is about to be transformed forever. For Winishut, it is a world in which there are precedents for the world that follows as well (for example, jet travel).[21]

Despite all that has happened to suppress their languages, traditions, and original communities, there are Native Americans in the Pacific Northwest who have continued well toward the twenty-first century to interpret and characterize Coyote in distinctive, congenial ways. (Smith and Winishut died only within the last decade.) We honor their thought best not by extravagant generalization but by close attention to the detail of their narrative skill.

NOTES

1. See poems by William Stafford, Wendy Rose, Lance Henson, Joseph Bruchac, Barney Bush, myself, Jim Barnes, Louis Oliver, Joy Harjo, Carroll Arnett, and others in James Koller, et al., *Coyote's Journal* (Berkeley: Wingbow, 1982); see also Peter Blue Cloud/Aroniawenrate, *Elderberry Flute Song: Contemporary Coyote Tales* (Buffalo: White Pine Press, 1989); and Simon J.

Ortiz, *Woven Stone* (Tucson: University of Arizona Press, 1992), especially "The Creation According to Coyote," 41; "The Boy and Coyote," 124–25; "Telling about Coyote," 157–60; and "How Much Coyote Remembered," 224, as well as poems by Gary Snyder, Jarold Ramsey, David Wagoner, and myself in Bright, *Coyote.*

2. More seriously, Ilana Pardes (1992), 87ff, finds traces of polytheism and antipatriarchal bent (for Moses is saved by his wife) in a period of transition.

3. Instances from several Native American traditions are noted in my unpublished "Without a Song" (1983), intended for a sequel to *Coyote's Journal* that was to have been called *Backward Dancer.* For a rare exception, see my "A Coyote Who Can Sing" in Halper (1991), 394–404.

4. Linton Winishut invited Virginia Hymes to record his Coyote cycle in 1975. She translated it in collaboration with the late Hazel Suppah. The Thompson Coyote cycle was obtained by James Teit, *Traditions,* 20–41; and "The Old Man and the Coyote" is on pages 48–49, second of three about Old Man. The rich accounts by Jim Yoke and Lewy Costima were recorded and published by Melville Jacobs, *Sahaptin,* 228–37, 239–46 (these are the English translations in Part 1). Louis Simpson's texts are in Edward Sapir, *Wishram,* reprinted in Bright, *Wishram.* The quoted passage is on page 75.

5. These presentations supersede earlier ones. The stories from Louis Simpson, Hiram Smith, and Victoria Howard have been discussed in some detail in my *Essays,* 91–118, 211–42. The version by John B. Hudson was discussed in my "Comments," 144–50.

The text from Louis Simpson was published in Edward Sapir, *Wishram,* 30–35; the version in my *Essays* and here has been revised in light of Sapir's field notebooks (see Hymes, *Essays,* 134–38). The text from Hiram Smith was first published in my 1981 book; that from Victoria Howard was first published in Melville Jacobs, *Chinook,* Part I and Part II, 95–96; that from John B. Hudson was published in Melville Jacobs, *Kalapuya,* 91; that from Stevens Savage is from the notebooks of Leo J. Frachtenberg, 52–58. Frachtenberg took down these stories in 1910, when Savage may have been fairly old, for he dictated texts to Albert Gatschet at Grand Ronde in December 1877. (Bureau of American Ethnology ms. 2029, "Words, sentences and various texts collected at the Grande Ronde Agency, Northwestern Oregon, in November & Decb., 1877.") "Marriage Ceremonies" is identified as "given by Stephen Savage" at the head of page 37, and "SS did not know his name" on the bottom of the first page of a manuscript identified as "Story of a conflict between the Cayuse and Molala" (or "The Molale Tribe Raided by the Cayuse Indians," Ms. 998, the source cited by Bruce Rigsby, "Waiilatpuan," 141, n. 29). The intervening three pages of "Myth of the Coyote" (overcoming Bear on his way to set up the world) have no legible name but have the ring of the

Savage of 1910. I am indebted to Donald Whereat, of the Confederated Tribes of Coos, Lower Umpqua, and Siuslaw Indians, for xeroxes of these materials. A handwritten copy of Frachtenberg's notebooks was made for Jacobs at the direction of Franz Boas and is in the archives of the University of Washington.

6. The stories here have been analyzed for their intrinsic form and are presented in terms of it. Oral narratives generally, here those of Native Americans, are poetry of a certain kind. They consist of lines organized in certain ways. The ways in which narrators shape their stories are part of what the stories say and mean. I try to show this by the visual relations among lines and groups of lines, indentation, and spacing and by providing for each story a profile that abstracts these relations. In such a profile, lower-case letters indicate verses, upper-case letters indicate stanzas, lower-case Roman numerals indicate scenes, and upper-case Roman numerals indicate acts.

On ethnopoetic analysis further, see Dell H. Hymes, "Fictions," 128–78; "Use," 83–124; and "Ethnopoetics."

7. The English is largely from Hiram Smith. In translating, he partly retold the story as a story in English. In Wasco, line 8 is literally "Just not half"; line 10 has just what was said, as here. In translating, Smith clarified the line by putting before it "someone told him."

8. Louis Simpson's "Coyote and Deer" is in Edward Sapir, *Wishram,* 145–47; compare the analysis in Dell H. Hymes, "Host," 171–98. Hiram Smith's story was told to me in Wasco in 1956 and has not been published.

9. The English is primarily from Hiram Smith. In translating, he would in effect retell the story, keeping closely to the Wasco, but sentence for sentence rather than word for word. Expressions in brackets represent Wasco words that Smith did not translate. His expressions in parentheses elucidate the sense.

10. Note the parallel endings of each group of three lines: "they were starving." The next group of lines also contains a parallel, "he thought," which might be parallel endings, but woven into three pairs of verses (a group of three pairs is a frequent pattern in Chinookan). Each of the three pairs begins with successive steps in Coyote's location: wandering, went toward, sat down. The next group illustrates the common Chinookan triad of three steps in change of location in minimal form: went, got there, went in. The final group of the act again has three pairs. The elaboration of the third and fifth groups fits the frequent role of third and fifth steps in a series as points of culmination.

11. Wasco is literally "These future your children." In English, Hiram Smith explained, "Take this home to feed his children," before saying, "This your children will eat." In lines 49–50, Wasco is literally: "Starting he-took-them Coyote."

12. The Wasco text has simply two verbs in sequence without conjunction

or other marker. Formally, they constitute a single verse. In line 60, Hiram Smith deployed the single word for "dead" with the intonation of a separate sentence.

13. Act III seems clearly to have three parts. Coyote is active alone in the first; Fish Hawk, in the second; Coyote again, in the third.

Scene i has three groups of three verses, fitting neatly into three stanzas. Scenes ii and iii each seem clearly to have five components, but in scene ii, the second and fourth components are themselves composed of components. The same is true of the second component of scene iii. In short, the first scene has two component levels, stanzas and verses, while the second and third scenes have three.

The odd components, of course, are the second and fourth components of scene ii and the second component of scene iii. In this respect, they are equivalent to the stanzas of scene i in having verses as elements, but to consider them stanzas in scenes ii and iii would imply that the other units of these scenes are stanzas as well (lines 60, 64, 69, and lines 70, 75, 76–78, and 79). That seems silly.

The alternative is to consider the three-line components in scenes ii and iii as special cases of expressive elaboration, what I would call amplification within a frame of what are otherwise single verses. See my paper "Performance," 391–434. The special status of these components is indicated in the profile by capital letters (such as stanzas would have).

14. See Jeremiah Curtin, "Wasco Tales and Myths," in Edward Sapir, *Wishram,* 269–70, 287–88, where Fish Hawk is Coyote's son-in-law, of whom he is proud. The latter narrative has Eagle defeat them in diving. Where Coyote would nearly die, striking his head against natural ice, Fish Hawk here nearly dies, striking his head against ice that Eagle has caused (288).

15. Franz Boas, "Tsimshian," 694–702; Stith Thompson, *Tales,* 301–02; Mac Jean Faber, *Host,* passim.

16. No native title is certainly known for any of the five versions. Edward Sapir's "The Story about Coyote" might have been suggested by Louis Simpson, but there is no indication of that in the field notebook; Hiram Smith did not suggest an alternative. Victoria Howard's story is an unnamed part of the longer narrative of how the Coyote named Tənaq'ia went round the world. Melville Jacobs headed John B. Hudson's story with "The News Precedes Coyote"; the Stevens Savage story has no heading in its notebook. I use Jacobs' "News" and Sapir's "about." The story names "news" as its topic and evokes the delight that he and others would take in whatever news might come along. "Precedes" is accurate, but too precise; "about" allows for all the rest of what happens.

17. Here is the story as excerpted from *Ethnogeography of the Franklin D. Roosevelt Lake Area,* an unpublished monograph by Randy Bouchard and Dorothy Kennedy (1979). I am grateful to them for it.

"Some people were gathering eggs at Npak (new Inchelium, not far from the Columbia River) and preparing a pit to cook them in. Once the eggs were being cooked, the people laid down to rest. Coyote came along, saw these people sleeping, and blew on them, causing them to sleep more deeply. Then he dug up their eggs, ate all of them, and piled the shells around each sleeping person. When they woke up, they noticed egg shells around them, even though they had not eaten anything. Also they noticed that Coyote had changed some of their features while they were sleeping—he put tufts on Lynx's ears and twisted Crossbill's beak.

"They knew it must have been Coyote, so they all followed his tracks to try to catch him. But one by one they tired, until only Lynx was left.

"Lynx knew what to do—he caused rain and sleet to fall. Coyote took shelter and Lynx caught up to him, as he knew where Coyote would go. Coyote was sitting under an overhanging rock cliff, amusing himself by swallowing his own penis. Lynx hit Coyote on the back of the head, causing Coyote's penis to stick in his own throat. Then Lynx ran away to tell everyone about Coyote, so that when Coyote reached the nearest camp, people were already laughing at him. He went to another camp, but they had also heard the news and were laughing at him. Coyote went to a third camp, but they were also laughing at him, so he passed judgment. 'News will travel fast, because it has no legs.' This has been true ever since."

18. Tillamook: the opening section of "Wild Woman," told by Clara Pearson to Elizabeth Jacobs, and published in her *Nehalem*, pp. 61–62. Miluk Coos: "The Young Man Lived with His Grandmother," told by Annie Miner Peterson to Melville Jacobs, and published in his, *Coos Myth Texts*, 172–73. Colville-Okanagon: Mourning Dove [Christine Quintasket], *Coyote Stories*, pp. 117–18.

19. Close brackets (}) at the end of lines 19, 22, 29 indicate the close of a pair of verses in a sequence of pairs.

20. "But" (line 36) and "could have been" (line 38) render a Kalapuya particle expressing wonder, čú-nak.

21. I am grateful to William C. Sturtevant of the Smithsonian Institution and to its Department of Anthropology and Archives for the opportunity to read the unpublished notebooks in which the narratives of Stevens Savage are preserved.

REFERENCES

Blue Cloud, Peter/Aroniawenrate. *Elderberry Flute Song: Contemporary Coyote Tales*. Buffalo: White Pine Press, 1989.

Boas, Franz. "Tsimshian Mythology." Bureau of American Ethnology, Annual Report 31 (1909–1910), 694–702. Washington, D.C.: Government Printing Office, 1916.

Bright, William, ed. *Wishram Texts and Ethnography.* Vol. 7 of *The Collected Works of Edward Sapir,* 17–261. Berlin: Mouton, 1990.

———. *A Coyote Reader.* Berkeley and Los Angeles: University of California Press, 1993.

Curtin, Jeremiah. "Wasco Tales and Myths." In *Wishram Texts,* by Edward Sapir, 239–314; in *Wishram Texts,* ed. William Bright, 263–340. Berlin: Mouton, 1990.

Faber, Mac Jean. *The Tale of the Bungling Host: A Historic-Geographic Analysis.* San Francisco State College Master's Thesis, 1970.

Frachtenberg, Leo J. Mss. Archives of the Department of Anthropology, Smithsonian Museum of Natural History. Box 2517, NB 5, 52–58.

Halper, Jon, ed. *Gary Snyder: Dimensions of a Life.* San Francisco: Sierra Club, 1991.

Hymes, Dell H. *"In Vain I Tried to Tell You": Essays in Native American Ethnopoetics.* Philadelphia: University of Pennsylvania Press, 1981.

———. "Comments." *Journal of the Folklore Institute* 18, no. 2–3 (1981): 144–50.

———. "Bungling Host, Benevolent Host: Louis Simpson's 'Deer and Coyote'." *American Indian Quarterly* 8, no. 3 (1984): 171–98.

———. "Language, Memory, and Selective Performance: Cultee's 'Salmon's Myth' as Twice-told to Boas." *Journal of American Folklore* 98 (1985): 391–434.

———. "A Coyote Who Can Sing." In *Gary Snyder: Dimensions of a Life,* ed. Jon Halper, 394–404. San Francisco: Sierra Club, 1991.

———. "Notes Towards (An Understanding of) Supreme Fictions." In *Studies in Historical Change,* ed. Ralph Cohen. Charlottesville: University Press of Virginia, 1992.

———. "Use All There Is to Use." In *On the Translation of Native American Literatures,* ed. Brian Swann, 83–124. Washington, D.C.: Smithsonian Institution, 1992.

———. "Ethnopoetics, Oral Formulaic Theory, and Editing Texts." *Oral Tradition* 9 (1994).

Jacobs, Elizabeth. *Nehalem Tillamook Tales.* Eugene: University of Oregon Press, 1959. Reprint, Corvallis: Oregon State University Press, 1992.

Jacobs, Melville. *Northwest Sahaptin Texts.* Columbia University Contributions to Anthropology, 19 (1, 2). New York: Columbia University Press, 1934.

———. *Coos Myth Texts.* University of Washington Publications in Anthropology. Vol. 8, no. 1. Seattle: University of Washington Press, 1940.

———. *Kalapuya Texts.* University of Washington Publications in Anthropology, 11. Seattle: University of Washington Press, 1945.

———. *Clackamas Chinook Texts.* Part I. Indiana University Research Center in Anthropology, Folklore, and Linguistics Publication 8. *International Journal of American Linguistics* 24, no. 1 (1958): 95–96.

———. *Clackamas Chinook Texts.* Part 2. Indiana University Research Center in Anthropology, Folklore, and Linguistics Publication 11. *International Journal of American Linguistics* 25, no. 2 (1959).

Koller, James, et al. *Coyote's Journal.* Berkeley: Wingbow, 1982.

Ortiz, Simon J. *Woven Stone.* Tucson: University of Arizona Press, 1992.

Pardes, Ilana. *Countertraditions in the Bible: A Feminist Approach.* Cambridge: Harvard University Press, 1992.

Quintasket, Christine/Mourning Dove. *Coyote Stories.* Caldwell, Neb.: Caxton, 1933. Reprint, Lincoln: University of Nebraska Press, 1990.

Rigsby, Bruce. "The Waiilatpuan Problem: More on Cayuse-Molala Relatability." *Northwest Anthropological Research Notes* 3, no. 1 (1969): 141, n. 29.

Sapir, Edward. *Wishram Texts,* together with "Wasco Tales and Myths," collected by Jeremiah Curtin and edited by Edward Sapir, 2–257. Publications of the American Ethnological Society 2. Leiden: E. J. Brill, 1909.

———. *Wishram Texts.* Also in *Wishram Texts and Ethnography,* ed. William Bright, 17–261. Berlin: Mouton, 1990.

Teit, James. *Traditions of the Thompson River Indians of British Columbia.* Memoirs of the American Folk-Lore Society, 6. Boston and New York: Houghton Mifflin (for the American Folk-Lore Society), 1898.

Thompson, Stith. *Tales of the North American Indians.* Cambridge: Harvard University Press, 1929. Reprint, Bloomington: Indiana University Press, 1966.

Jay Miller and Vi Hilbert

Lushootseed Animal People: Mediation and Transformation from Myth to History

The native people along the rivers draining into Puget Sound, the speakers of Lushootseed Salish, have a variety of creation accounts involving Animal People, beings from the dawn of the world "when animals were people" who established the traditions that are still observed in the region around Seattle.

Neither fully animal nor human nor spirit nor fixed in time or space, these Animal People were protean, with many simultaneous attributes that only got sorted out when the world changed or "capsized" in preparation for the arrival of modern humans. As the Epic Age came to a close, each being assumed a single form and became associated with a particular location. Many transformed into particular landmarks where they exist as aspects of geography, unusual acoustics, or appearance. Others became species of plants or animals occupying particular ecological niches. For most natives, the Epic Age continued for countless eons until a sudden flurry of activity prepared for the change, set off by rumors that human people were coming soon. Sometimes, the agent for these events is a being called Changer, who turned Animal People into species, rocks, river rapids, and many other things. For example, he would encounter Deer, who was sharpening stakes to kill Changer before he could transform the world. Changer would ask to examine the slats and suddenly poke them into Deer's head, creating antlers and forever making this animal timid and a prey of hunters.

During this transitional period, everything was in flux. Somehow, every narrative picks up the story in the midst of things. There is no point of beginning for the Lushootseed. Instead, the narrative is continuous and proceeds in terms of connections. Things were already in existence but leading separate lives until a link was made and other events followed in due course. There were so many different origin stories around Puget Sound because there were so many different village, ethnic, and tribal differences to be accounted for. All versions underscored the great language diversity in the area. Some storytellers attributed these differences to Thrush, while others gave it an explanation more like that of the Tower of Babel.

As conditions changed in the region, so did the versions of the epics. Among the most remarkable was that about the heroic figure known as Duwii, who saved most of the Animal People from a flood. Since Lushootseed has regularly shifted the sound of *n* to *d,* it seems likely that Duwii began as a Salishan version of the Noah story. But that is their only point of similarity.

In a nutshell, the story is about competence. It begins with a drought. Duwii asks both River Bullhead and Beaver to bring rain. Now, either one of these people was capable of doing just that, so asking the two of them together was sure to bring trouble. Beaver warned Duwii to be prepared with a large canoe. Duwii was explicitly punished because he doubted the ability of either one of them. Thus not only did it rain but it poured, and the earth flooded. Duwii got males and females of all the Animal People into the canoe. Everyone got on board. In the version told by Susie Sampson Peters, whom all of us at Lushootseed Research know best as Aunt Susie, there is a hilarious moment when Lizard and Snake slither into the canoe and hide in its cracks; they have no confidence in Duwii and are sure he will capsize them before the Flood is over. As an added precaution, the canoe was tied to the top of the only exposed mountain. Other tribes also survived by tying to the peak. After the water crested, one of the seven canoes drifted away from the mountain, eventually landing across the ocean to bring into being the Chinese population. The other six canoes settled along the shores of western Washington State. In the aftermath of the Flood, Thrush gave all these peoples different languages, including the various animals, who were changed permanently into modern species form at that time. Thrush kept for herself the song that makes berries ripen and still uses it to this day.

According to another account, after the Flood, a boy was abandoned by his family because he refused to fast and quest for supernatural help. Starving, he was forced to do so and made contact with God, who instructed the boy to make a special blanket from the skins of many small animals. Then he gathered up all the refuse from the Flood and waved the blanket over it, creating an abundance of food all over. People too were revived, but they had no sense, so the boy made brains for them from the very soil of the place. Waving his blanket over them, he revived these people; but they spoke many languages and therefore were sent to live all over the earth.

While some Animal People were changed on a case-by-case basis, as when Mrs. Grouse left eggs all over the Northwest so that everyone would have grouse to hunt, some transformations were wholesale. In one of the most terrifying of all Skagit stories, Coyote angers his daughter-in-law, Grizzly Bear, by arranging for her to fall into a deep latrine. Already psychotic, Grizzly demands her claws and teeth, kept by her husband, Eagle, for the safety of his family, and goes on a rampage, sadistically killing even her own children. Raging and screaming, various Animal People transform out of fear into modern species.

In this manner, the transformations continue into the present, and the influences of Catholic and other missionaries have become grafted onto native traditions. Changes in history become changes in narrative, but the native voice remains strong.

For the whole region, however, the most important narrative is that of Star Child, the son of a sky father and an earth mother who begins the connection that leads to the present form of the world.

According to Martin Sampson (*Skagit,* 51–55), Aunt Susie's oldest son, the narrative is primarily concerned with the origin of the Nookachamish, a division of the Upper Skagits who lived around Clear Lake. It was there that the noble sisters wished to marry the stars, and it is there that a hill with banded rock is still called Yudwasa (heart) because it marks the place where the escape rope fell to earth and coiled up. The hill is across from a gas station on Highway 9 in the Skagit River valley.

Among the Snoqualmie, who tell a similar story, a small hill near Mount Si also marks the place where their rope ladder fell down. In the Snoqualmie version, the rope hung in the air for some time and the Animal People used it as a swing until Rat, angered that he did not get enough turns, chewed through the rope and it fell to earth. Rat, of course, was condemned to repeat his act forever.

Similar tribes, similar stories, but each was grounded in its lands. That is the point of origins. The more they change, the more they mediate and the more they nevertheless root people in time and place.

To more fully explain the meaning of this, there is no better illustration than the story of Star Child and Diaper Boy, which some of you may also know as "Star Husband." Only here, the focus of action is neither the sky nor the earth, but rather the link between the two created when specific sisters wished to marry particular stars. That link forged the world of the Lushootseed people and continues to define the important aspects of their life and belief.

The following version is based primarily on that of Aunt Susie, but it has also been informed by significant details in a story told by Dora Solomon.[1] Without further ado, let Star Child take over the narrative.

Starchild

1

Two women from the upper class were gathering food. The two were sisters. They were digging for fern roots. They dug for this fern root. Then they dried it. They dug fern roots for four days, these women. Then darkness overcame them. So they lay down, these women.

The oldest one looked up into the night sky and saw two stars. As a halfhearted joke, she said, "Oh, aren't those nice men? Wouldn't they make good husbands for us! Wonder if they would consider taking us? The red one would be yours, and the white one would be mine."

The stars were listening to them, these stars. The red one was young and strong. The white one was old and had pale matter in his eyes.

When the women went to sleep, they were gathered up and taken to the sky. They were there and it became morning. They now see the men. Right away the foolish one rejects the one who became her husband. She says, "I don't want to have to be looking at his face!"

But the husband of the sister is good. Right away the star knew what she felt. "Why do you reject me when you chose at first to admire me. It was your own idea to desire me. Yours!"

She didn't say anything. The sisters settled into their new life. They went on digging. They dug until they had lots of roots. Yet this one remains unhappy about her situation. She is unhappy. She does not like this man. Then she became pregnant.

They are advised by the old one. "Don't you folks go after roots that break off underground." That is where he made his mistake. "Now, why have we been told by this old one not to do that?"

They dug. She, the unhappy wife, broke off a fern root. She dug, and dug, and dug. Finally she dug through. She went and looked. "That is our land down there below!" She immediately covered it over.

They arrived back home. The old man asked right away. "Oh, you folks must have dug a hole through. That's why there was a wind."

The woman replied, "No, it must have been far away. Must have been from a distance. We didn't dig a hole through."

Daybreak. They went again. She went. She said to her sister, "I am going to prepare cedar limbs (for making a rope). "What do you plan to do? You have a good husband."

"I don't like that old one. I don't want to get stuck here when I have a child! I'm going to prepare cedar. Lots of it and I'll break down the fibers and I'll braid it. I'll let myself down."

"It is your decision," her sister said to her. "I'll occupy myself preparing cedar and only you will dig."

She prepared cedar boughs, then she braided until it became night. The braided cedar piled up. Then she made something to sit on. Then she wove, and braided, and wove some more. She made something to hang onto. She took one braided piece and she tied it to a stick that would land first and be ready for her to stand upon. That is how she will know it has reached the earth for her to stand upon. She pulled it until it reached there. It was all right now. She pulled it. She said to her sister. "You will just hold the rope for me. You will hold it while I let myself down." Her sister lowered herself down. "I shall pull it four times, then you let it go and I'll pull it and it will pile up." She went, and arrived. She pulled, and pulled, and pulled. She pulled four times and her sister released it. She pulled it until it piled up. She walked again on the earth.

She looked now for a creek. She walked to the water's edge of Duqwatch. That was its name. Duqwatch. That is its name. She is the one who names it now. She herself names it.

She went. She arrived a long way off. She walked a long way. "What will I use for a baby-sitter? Who will baby-sit?"

Then she saw a good old log. She kicked it, and kicked it, and kicked it. In vain it tried to get up, this old log. It couldn't manage it. It just sat there. She kicked it again and it returned to its original form, as a rotten log. She continued to walk until she came to another one, a log, and she kicked it. It tried in vain to get up. It couldn't become a person! She then kicked it to return it to a log. She went. Again she came to a good log and she kicked it. She would kick it four times. It would try valiantly to get up. It couldn't speak a word. Then she would kick it. She kicked it until it returned to a rotten log. Again she walked until she came to an excellent dry rotten log. It was a good one. She kicked it four times.

Immediately, an old lady got up with a little blanket pinned around her and she spoke in a halting way. "Oh, my granddaughter, I have awakened. I was asleep."

"Get up, grandmother, get up. I am traveling; you will baby-sit for me." She went to another place. There she found four cedars. "Oh, this will be a good place for us to live." She used the four trees as the posts of her house.

So she fixed things for herself. She went and looked at the creek. The salmon must have been running. "I guess I'm to make a fish trap. I'm to trap them, it seems."

So she prepared the cedar to weave the trap. She busied herself splitting them. Then she wove her fish trap. She put it in the water, and she went and made the rest of her trap, a fence and a hole for a long, thin basket trap. (Fish swim into this narrow place and cannot turn around and swim back out.)

She was there and then she gave birth to her child. She said, "You will comfort your grandchild. You will refer to the baby only as a girl child. I hear that there are women from the north looking for males. There are so few people in the world that women are always looking for husbands. Your grandson will get kidnapped. Just call him a girl."

But this silly old women is crazy. The mother of the child goes to get fish from her fish trap, and she sneaks up on the baby-sitter when she returns. Here is what she hears the old women crooning to the baby: "Hush, my grandson, hush, my grandson. Oh! Oh! I mean my granddaughter, I mean my granddaughter!"

"Oh, the crazy good-for-nothing! She calls my baby a boy. He'll get kidnapped." She scolds. "Why do you call your grandchild a grandson?"

"I forgot myself, I forgot myself."

[Aunt Susie instructs her audience, "Say *habuu* or you will get hunchbacked."]

She was there and again she went to her fish trap. She again heard the foolish baby-sitter using boy terms to the child.

"Oh, my child will be kidnapped." She got salmon, salmon, and more salmon. "Why, oh why, do you call your grandchild a grandson? Why don't you call him a girl child? You'll have him kidnapped from you."

"Oh, I forgot myself, I forgot myself." She kind of cries, this old one. Again she went to remove salmon from the trap. But the old one can't seem to comfort the child.

Some women arrived where the old one is. They asked her right away. "What is that you are taking care of?"

"A girl child, ladies, a girl child." As soon as they leave, the foolish old one again croons to the child. "Be still, my grandson. Oh! Oh! I mean my granddaughter!"

"Oh, that old women calls that child a boy!" The youngest one ran and took the child from the old lady, and she examined it all over. Then she found out that it was a boy child. So they kidnapped him.

The old woman sat by herself and the child's mother arrived. "Oh, some women came to your child. I tried in vain to grab onto him, but they kidnapped him away from me!"

"Because you called him a boy child!" The old woman was reminded before she was kicked! "What are you doing to me?" There she was, this old woman. She was kicked. Now again she was a rotten log. Then she was left there.

The mother took the soiled diaper of her stolen child. She took it down to the creek. There she cried aloud. Now she cried. "Here is what I used to do to the clothing of my beloved child. Washing and wringing his diapers. Washing and wringing his diapers." Only to the right does she wring his diaper. Suddenly the diaper cried out! He cried. Cried, this one did. Cried and cried.

She took her child, known as Diaper Child, and wrapped him up. She took her things and her food. She packed them. Downstream she went now and arrived at a place along the shores of Duqwatch.

There she built a fire and lived. She lived there now. She cried. She cried. She cried always for her son. Even though she now had her Diaper Child.

2

Then there is Raven living. He had a big house. A big house Raven had. It was two-fire size. He is high-class, high-class. Raven is full of pretensions that he could never keep up. Raven lived with lots of people around him. Suddenly, Raven said (in nasal Ravenese) "I'm going by water, by water, by water."

So Raven went downstream. Then he saw a little smoke. He landed his canoe and got out. He lifted his pant legs in a very dainty fashion. He went. What is this? A woman sitting. Holding a child. Raven ran after them and pulled them, laughing aloud. He took them waterward. She, the woman, grabbed up things for her child. Its blankets and a little food, and she put them on board the canoe.

So he took his slaves, for so he regarded them, upstream. He named his little slave right away. He named him Drudge.[2] Upstream he went and arrived. Such a high-class slave!

Raven was very mean. Oh, when Raven goes outside he relieves himself on the face of his slave. His feces cover the sides of the boy's head and face, which are all stuck with the excrement of Raven.

So now this one who rejected the star way up there became a slave! Now she became a pitiable slave.

3

Now we deal with the another part of the story. There is her other son [Star Child] with the women from upriver.

He gets older. He walks around. Suddenly, he runs and says, "Mother, there is someone with big eyes over there."

"Where, where?"

"Over there."

"You are our husband and protector." The woman says this to the child. Then she made him a bow. She put a bowstring on it.

He is told. "Everything you shoot is food for us as you grow up." The child went and shot a squirrel and brought it to her. She butchered it and it was food. Time went by and he grew up and he saw another one. His bow is now nearly full size.

"Oh, Mama. There is something I saw with long ears."

"You are our provider. You shoot it! Everything is food for us."

So he shot the rabbit and took it to her. He took it to her and she butchered it and they cooked it. They roasted this rabbit and they ate it.

Again he saw something with staring eyes. "Mama, there is someone with big bugged-out eyes I saw."

"No! No! Don't say that. You are our provider. Do something."

A real bow is now made for him. A big one. Then the child shot a deer. He went after it and pulled it. Then it was butchered. In this manner this fellow grew up. Then he shot an elk. He shot it. Shot it.

4

There is Diaper Child. Slave now of Raven!

Diaper Child gets older, he grows up. Now he is old enough to get the wood supply, and he is taught how to do this. He learns to select a tree with a natural fire hole at the base, then to apply hot stones to this area until the tree is felled in this manner. He is sent toward a mountain across from Sedro Woolley, Washington. He is sent there to burn a fir tree.

5

However, he [Star Child] is forbidden by them. This child is cautioned. But by now he is a grown man, a person with a mind of his own. They caution him, "Do not chase an elk if it goes in that direction. Only if it goes across the river will you chase it." He thinks, "Now, why do they tell me not to chase game over that way? I guess I ought to run and investigate!"

So he ran. This child ran and got to the top. He looked! Oh! There is smoke rising from over there, upstream. And he thought he saw a small creek, but instead it is a big river!

"Oh! That must be where I am from, when I was stolen by those bad people. You folks will find out." He went, sneaking up on these lonely ones. He went and eavesdropped at the side of the building.

"Would she have a husband now if it had not been for my wondering about it, and I ran after the old lady and examined the body of the child she was baby-sitting."

"Oh, so I was stolen, wasn't I. By these no-good people! You folks know about it." Thereupon he returned, making some noise as he approached, and they stopped talking and became quiet. He was curious to learn how he first was taken by these people.

Then his wife asked him, "Did you get any game?" He replied, "There is some! It is laying over there." She went and got it. She took this elk and she pulled it. She backpacked it. Another day came and she went. That is all he can think about, escaping.

He arrives and they, the wives, are still quarreling. "So I was stolen by these dirty things! You'll find out. I'm going to chase that elk. I shall chase it." Then the elk ran. Downhill, upstream from above Sedro Woolley. Until he came to level ground. Then he killed it. Butchered it. He threw the insides out of it. Then he raised it, hung it up. He took the tallow and he put it inside, with his hunting equipment, in his pack, along with his bow and his arrows.

6

Diaper Child's mother advised him. "Oh, I guess your dear relative must be older now. It is not probable that he would still be a child. I suppose by now he is a grown man. You will cry with these words while you are burning down a fir tree, and he will be attracted.

'Oh woe, oh woe, oh woe."
It is said my brother was stolen away by two women who belonged
up river.
I am only the wringings of my mother.
Raven has made me a slave.'

This child makes himself sound very woebegone and sings:

"Oh woe, oh woe, oh woe.
It is said that my brother was stolen by two women from up the river.
I'm from the wringing of my mother.
I've been made a slave by Raven."

Then this one has butchered the elk. And he hung it. He then put the tallow in his pack and he went waterward, drawn to the sound of someone where there is a little smoke rising. He went sneaking up on him. He stood on the other side of the timber that he is working on, it seems. "I'll just listen to him," Star Child thinks.

"Oh woe, oh woe, oh woe.
My brother was stolen, it is said, by two women from up river.
And it is also said that I'm from the diaper wringings of my mother.
I've been made a slave by Raven."

He shows himself a little. He has his face covered with his hands, this child. He is like huddled over as he cries. He is asked, "What are you saying?"

"I am crying. I am drowning my face. I'm crying. I'm crying. It is said, my brother was stolen by two women from up river. They stole him. My mother (it is said) had an old woman for a baby-sitter. She got mad at the old woman and kicked her, and she became a rotten log and Mother walked on after that."

Then that Raven came to her. "Now we are slaves of Raven. We are there upriver. We've been made slaves. We have been made pitiful things by that Raven."

"It is me, maybe! There are two women where I am, but I don't know where they are from. The good-for-nothings quarrel all the time. They quarrel every night, and I listen to them saying what you are saying now!"

"It is only my things now that I will have to go and get. My pants, and my shirt. I guess it will be night before I arrive there, the place of Raven."

"Eat this tallow," said Star Child. He approaches his younger brother and brushes his face. He brushed him. Then he, Diaper Boy, was able to see him, Star Child. Glory! His older brother is a very bright, shiny, handsome young man!

This makes Diaper Child happy. "Oh. I'll load your canoe with wood," Star Child tells his brother. "I'll break it up into pieces for you." He took alder, and pounded it, and broke it in pieces. Then, he loaded the canoe for his brother.

Diaper Boy said, "Oh, that is what Raven beats me about when he examines my feces."

"Right near the door of the house. Near the door of the house is where you will relieve yourself in the evening. And he will gulp it down!" He said that about Raven who thinks he is so smart.

Diaper Child traveled upriver. When he beached himself in the canoe, he threw off all the wood. He threw it. He threw it.

In Raven-talk, his master says, "Real different is Drudge. Real different!" "Why should the good-for-nothing look different?" His mother rushed to his defense by saying, "It is just that he is growing big and strong!"

There he is upland, this one, away from the village. And he sat by his mother and talked to her. "Mother. Someone came to me. A person. I couldn't see him. Then he brushed my face. That made it possible for me to see that he was a nice person. He gave me tallow. I guess he was your son. He said there are two women where he is, and they are always quarreling. He says he is just called 'husband.' It is not said where they are from, and the no-goods are always quarreling. He says he will come here in the morning, your son. I'll bring the canoe down in the morning, to meet him." Overjoyed, the mother thinks, "Oh, you dear one. It is him. Maybe it is him!"

Raven watches them and then says, accusingly, "He talks, that Drudge. He is talking." His mother explains, "About burning down trees is what he speaks of. It will take a long time to fell the tree that burns so slowly."

Diaper Child says, "Eat the tallow, eat it, eat it." Time goes by and Drudge goes to relieve himself, right near the doorway. Raven says, "Look at the feces of Drudge. Mmmmmm." Then he, Raven, gulps it, gulps it, gulps it, gulps it!

Morning comes and he goes downstream. Diaper Child doesn't sleep because he has his older brother on his mind. He goes downriver. He turns the canoe back and forth and puts rocks in to balance his weight, and then he goes downstream.

His brother reaches shore. The elk is put in the middle of the canoe. Over there is some rather good bark and they decide, "We could pry it off and load it on the canoe." So they pried off the bark and loaded it on the canoe, on each end as the elk was in the middle of the canoe.

They sat together and they talked. Star Child asked, "Are there any women where you are? Are there any women?" Diaper Boy responded, "Yes, there are lots. There are four. There are three who are nothing. They don't measure up in any way. But there is one that is a very good, hard-working lady. She works until it becomes night. But the other three are nothing. They just run around all the time and do nothing useful.

"There is Mouse, there is Mole, there is Magpie. They are the three. There isn't a thing that they are good for! The only thing they are good for is running around! But that other one is an exceptionally qualified lady. She can perform all kinds of work."

Star Child decides, "It would be good to have her for a wife. Whoever manages to pack my load is the one I will marry." "That is a good decision," his younger brother says to him. "That is a good idea."

Diaper Child has now grown up. His older brother has brushed him so he is bright. They go upriver. They go upriver after they have discussed it. When they come in view of those living there, they sit facing backward. Raven saw right away and made disparaging reference to his slave, Drudge.

In his own defense, Diaper Boy thought, "Would I be slave to that dirty thing. He'll find out later!" He remarked, "Does he think I'm like the one he has made slave?"

The brothers went and beached. They beached and began packing things up from the river. They took their packs and packed upland. He, Star Child, sat by his mother and brushed her face. He brushed his mother, brushed her. The woman says, "Maybe it was his dear older brother who came down to him yesterday.

Raven, suspicious and weary, asks, "Is it your son? It's your son! It is! It is!" Then he fools the son of the woman. He fools him when he sees them get out of the canoe and tie it. He says. "That is your mother's bed, your mother's bed, your mother's bed."

His mother said, "He is fooling you. The dirty thing is fooling you. Slaves are made to sleep anywhere. They have no bed. When he goes outside, he relieves himself on my face."

Star Child gives her tallow. She eats the tallow given to her by her son, who says, "Eat, mother, eat." Then, they talked together. They conversed. They discussed. He said to his brother [in a stage whisper], "Let Raven hear your plan. He doesn't have good sense. He'll holler it all over!" Sure enough, Diaper Boy whispers, "Whoever can carry my brother's pack is the one that will be his wife. That is the one he will marry!" And Raven immediately hollers, "Fix yourselves, women. Prepare yourselves. Whoever can carry the pack of my stepson will become his wife. Prepare yourselves. Fix yourselves up. Braid your hair."

They got busy, now these women, and braided their hair. Mouse went and dolled herself up. So did Mole. So did Magpie, who was a very handsome woman. When they were all through, they said, "Let Mouse go first." Mouse went to the elk in the canoe and tried to pack it. Mouse took the elk and tried to pack it. No! She just rocked it! Then Mole went. She went. The pack of his just wavered. She wasn't able to pack it. Then Magpie went. She was laughing as she went. He admired her. "Oh, she is the best woman, that one." "No! She is nothing. There is a good woman. She will come later. You'll be seeing her." There is Magpie just straining at the elk and finally let it go. They were all ashamed.

Then there was Mouse going from end to end gnawing at elk, gnawing at the hind end, looking ridiculous. She was nervous and embarrassed before everyone.

Then Little Green Frog is advised by her mother, "Be careful. You will speak last." You will say, humbly, "Would it be me who would be packing the load of such a noble person?" Frog's mother further advised her daughter, "It is against our custom for you to eat what you'll be given to pass around to guests. It is forbidden. You will just lay it down. It will belong to those guests who are seated, those invited by Raven."

Already, things were getting ahead of themselves. Guests were preparing roasting sticks. At the water, still on board the canoe, is the elk, unmoved, and people are being told to make roasting sticks! It was absurd!

Now Little Green Frog shows herself a little, very slowly, moving with grace. "Look at that one coming. Oh, she is the one who will be my wife!" She is blonde, this Little Green Frog, with long hair that falls freely. She deserves praise!

She went and when she came to where people were seated, Little Green Frog spoke, slowly, "Would it be unworthy me who could carry the pack of a high-class person?" She went to the water's edge. There Little Green Frog tossed the elk over her shoulder and carried it upland. She took it to the receptacle inside in the middle of Raven's house. There. Then she invited her mother, "Come on, Mother, come inside."

The rest entered, including the younger brother. Diaper Child is spoken to as a courtesy, but no one recognizes him. No one recognizes Diaper Child.

Then they butchered the elk. As soon as Raven is given the tallow he gulps it, gulps it, gulps it. He gulps it without chewing! As always, he is noted for his gluttony.

Distribution continues. It is cut up. This elk. It is arranged on cooking sticks by the young men, and it is roasted.

Little Green Frog dishes up the tallow, and gives it to her mother, who passes it around. Now the old people eat. They eat this tallow. Green Frog doesn't put anything in her own mouth. She had been advised by her mother.

Suddenly, Raven says, "Uncover the roof, you folks. Uncover the roof. Uncover the roof. Uncover the roof! We are getting too hot." This was happening because someone in the sky was mad at him. The people uncovered the roof. Raven continued to talk. He jabbered. All of a sudden Raven flew! He flew up to the roof. There he was, flapping his wings. Good heavens, what is Raven doing. What is he doing, up on the roof, making such a racket! Suddenly he flew. He was changed. He was changed by the ones from the stars. He flew downriver. He was still squawking. He became a raven forever.

Then the people roasted and cooked and they feasted. Night came, then morning. All these people conversed. Raven however, had been changed. He flew.

The brothers then began to prepare the earth for future generations. They gathered up everything that existed and they burned it. They burned it up. The fur of animals, tools, fishnets, houses, clothes, foods, and canoes they burned. They mashed all the residues to ashes and put them in a bag. They made moccasins, many pairs, to travel the earth. Everywhere they went, they scattered ashes so that all places now have mostly the same things available. Humans sprang from these ashes and began all of the tribes. When their work was finished, they rested.

An old woman speaks. She says to them, this old one. This old woman asked, "What will the coming people use for light? What will be their light? What will they use for light?"

Each of the sons of the star thought, "I guess I had better try my best tomorrow!" They thought about going way up where their father is. Way up in the sky. They would give the earth a soul, and it would be the sun and the moon.

He, Star Child, went in the morning and traveled through the sky. Early he went upriver and it became warm, too warm. It got too hot! He was burning things up. The people got into the water, just to the neck are they showing out in the water. Then, slowly, it became night.

They got themselves out of the water, and they spoke to Diaper Child, "Your older brother is too hot! It is like the heat of summer has become even greater. The people would die.

Instead, they suggested, "If the sun came to that position before it got warm, then got there and got cool, then became night, that would be right!" They discussed it and decided that would be a good way to do it.

"It's too hot! It's too hot!" The people complained about Star Child. When his brother arrived, he asked his brother. "How was it?" Diaper Boy laughed and said, "You were too hot!" His brother said, "I suppose the people died!"

He was told, "As soon as you appeared over there, it got hot. Everyone got into the water. Not one stayed out of the water. Just out from shore over there, out from shore, they put themselves until they were immersed almost completely. They had to hold poles to support themselves!"

"Now it is suggested that you try it. You will try tomorrow."

"Who me? I am to place myself over there and make it warm? Over there, and it will be cool toward evening? That would be good."

When morning came, Diaper Child went. Oh, it is cool while he comes. Just before noon it gets hot. People thought of putting themselves in the water. When he gets over there, it cools off and night comes. Everyone told Star Child, "Oh, your brother is all right. Your brother is satisfactory. He will be the one to light the land."

"Oh, I guess that means I'll go by night," Star Child said. "I'll be going by night." So it was done that way.

Diaper Child asked after he had traveled through the sky, "How was it? How was I? Was I all right?"

"You were all right. When you got there, it was hot. Over there, and it cooled. Your people put themselves in the water until they found out it was all right!" He went!

"I guess I am to go at night," Star Child said, "and I'll just warm my back when the land becomes warm from the sun. My wife will go too." So Star Child prepared himself and so did his wife. He took his wife. That is why there is a little frog on the moon. Her markings are visible when Star Child warms his back.

7

Star Child goes as the moon and the land is lit. After he goes four times, Mink arrives. As usual, Mink lies to his own advantage! He ponders right away, "If Star Child has a wife, what is his wife to me when he marries? Minks considers himself son to this new moon and asks, "Where is Mama? Where is Mama?"

Startled, this woman wonders how can my husband have a child when he had no prior wife? Aloud, she answers, "He is lighting the world!" She waits for her husband to return and explains, "This one came during the night and asked about you. You have a visitor. He says he is your son! The one who came says he is your son."

Star Child replied. "It is that guy, Mink, it is. It is that fellow Mink! Do not trust what he says!"

Mink occupies himself by bringing in wood. He brings in wood and his father goes out. Then, he says, "Mama, I am going along now. I will be the moon." The woman cautions, "Oh, that river is difficult. You'll fall and you would die!"

It is said that he showed himself a little. He showed himself a little, and the sun would look like two. Diaper Child would try to caution him, but to no avail. When he, Diaper Child, arrived at the river, he told Mink. "You hold on tight now. I am going to jump to the other side." So Mink hung on while Diaper Child jumped. He jumped, jumped, this Mink and his father. He hung on making his father look hunchbacked. This one from the stars jumped. It became night. This one is asked, "Why do you become two? Why? You became two before noon and again at noon." "It is this one who keeps showing himself! He is crazy!" Diaper Boy says of Mink. They went home.

After many days, Mink said, "Mama, I am going to light it. It will be me now." She said, "No, you would die. You couldn't jump. You couldn't jump to the other side of the river. You would die!" Mink insisted, "No. I could jump!" She gave in, "Go on then."

He is given some old-time clothing. Mink goes. He arrives at the river, known as the Milky Way, and he hesitates from fear. He stood there daring himself, then he jumped, but just to mid-river he got and he landed! He drifted on the Milky Way. Then it became night. It was early yet but it became dark. This was the first eclipse when Mink died.

On another day, he went again. Diaper Child went again on another day. He went. This one went and Diaper Child came and it was night. When he arrived where his people were, they laughed and said, "What was the matter with you? What was the matter that you made it get dark early?" Diaper Child said, "Ha, it was that no-good Mink who acted up, as usual! And where is he now, in the sky? He was going to light the land and when he jumped, he landed mid-stream and there he drifted. I guess he died!"

His older brother hasn't gone. The moon hasn't gone yet. He keeps coming back to the house where they are gathered. They have a discussion, Diaper Child and his brother. "I guess we had better name the rivers and places. Make things ready for humans." "Yes, they'll have different languages, those other tribes," the oldest one said. "We'll name them all now, from here. We'll start counting them off now."

He named the places known as Point Roberts, Sumas, Nooksack, Lummi, Upper Samish, Bayview, Guemes Island (where the Samish are high-class), Swinomish, Skagit; lower part of Skagit River, Mount Vernon down to Camano City; a branch of the Kikialus people on the northeast end of Camano Island, Snohomish, the Monroe area, Snoqualmie, Duwamish, Puyallup.

These will be kind of alike, but they will call some things differently. They will each be a little different. A branch of the Samish will be similar also, but their speech will be a different one. Named were these: Muckleshoot, Cowichan, Stekine, Alaskans, Haida, Yakulta Kwakwaka'wakw at Cape Mudge, across the channel from Campbell River. These were all named until it was finished.

Yes, that is why storytellers used to kneel, why my grandmother knelt! The Skagit River was named. Right next to the Yudwasa, the heart of the beginning of the earth, where the rope ladder fell from the sky, was the river of the Skagits. They named everything from way over there. At Camano, a creek of some kind. They named lots, but there were many that they didn't name along Camano Island.

What was this one? Browne Point. There is Sqayups. From the water's edge now was where Diaper Child and his brother named places.

They named everything. They named the rivers. Then there were the creeks. These were all named by those ancestors. Mount Vernon, Burlington, Sedro Woolley, Skagit City. Now this Lyman, moving upriver. Channel Gorge, Baker River, Concrete, Sauk River, Illabet, Cascade River. That is going upriver. There are lots of hearts [good-hearted people] at the falls. Then there are those with "people sounding" names. Upriver now, above the falls, is what is named.

Then there are all the lakes. There are many lakes. These were the names that Diaper Child and his brother gave to this land. They said, "Areas from far away will have the same name. Other areas will give the same name to their lands." For example, there is another Slox along the Stillaguamish.

That is the end now.

Conclusions

As "Star Child" and many other stories of the Epic Age make clear to native listeners, things do not just happen. In a sense, people select their own fates. People bring things on themselves by their own actions. Offending spirits cause problems for everyone. Indeed, wishing can make it so, thus everyone has to be very careful what they wish for.

At the start of "Star Child," the sisters wished for husbands and got them. Yet the older sister judged by appearances and did wrong. Her pussy-eyed husband was old, kind, and powerful. He made her pregnant, providing another generation for the world. She did not stop to consider this, but instead made the rope that took her to earth, leaving her husband. This set a precedent, and even now wives will leave husbands. In punishment, she became Raven's slave and his bathroom.

This was the punishment she brought upon herself. Having atoned for her fault, she lived to have her sons reunited and herself freed. Raven, having done his part, became the modern bird.

The lesson that the audience took away was about regard for others, especially mysterious people from faraway who had great power to harm or to help. When Europeans arrived on ships off the Washington coast, they reaped the benefits of this lesson and were treated with more courtesy than their actions merited. Some natives thought that they were Animal People returned, and in a sense, they were, for, like the events of the Epic Age, their arrival made new connections where none had previously existed. Now, centuries later, we are still learning to appreciate these new links in a worldwide change of humanity.

NOTES

1. This "Star Child" is based on a version told by Susie Sampson Peter, Upper Skagit, in 1950, with important details supplied by an account by Dora Solomon, Lummi/Skagit, in 1975, about the creations from ashes; by Charlie Anderson, about Star Child's own brightness eclipsing any view of his wife; and by Martin Sampson (1972), Aunt Susie's son, about geographical details.

2. Raven actually named the boy "person from Clear Lake, Clear Laker" because slaves lost their own identity and were known only by the name of the place or community from where they had been taken. Thus while the label was different in that it was geographical, the sense of it was that someone was ever after to be a lackey or drudge without a personal identity.

REFERENCES

Amoss, Pamela. *Coast Salish Spirit Dancing: The Survival of an Ancestral Religion.* Seattle: University of Washington Press, 1978.

Collins, June McCormick. *Valley of the Spirits: The Upper Skagit Indians of Western Washington.* Seattle: University of Washington Press, 1974.

Hilbert, Vi (Taq^{w}šhəblu). *Haboo: Native American Stories from Puget Sound.* Seattle: University of Washington Press, 1985.

Miller, Jay. *Shamanic Odyssey: The Lushootseed Salish Journey to the Land of the Dead.* Menlo Park, Calif.: Ballena Press, 1988.

Sampson, Martin. *Indians of Skagit County.* Mount Vernon, Wash.: Skagit County Historical Series 2, 1972.

Snyder, Sally. Skagit Society and Its Existential Basis: An Ethnofolkloristic Reconstruction. University of Washington, Ph.D. Dissertation, 1964.

Candace Slater

Breaking the Spell: Accounts of Encantados by Descendants of Runaway Slaves

How do contemporary Amazonian stories of Encantados (Enchanted Beings) mediate both cultural encounter and ongoing change?[1] Two separate yet related accounts of one old woman's abduction and subsequent release by the Encantados suggest a number of preliminary answers to this much larger question. The storytellers whose versions appear in the following pages are descendants of nineteenth-century slaves who fled plantations in western Pará to establish fugitive communities called *quilombos*. This *quilombo* past helps explain some of the striking differences between their tales and the many other stories of enchantment and disenchantment told today throughout much of the Amazon.[2] Clearly part of a much larger narrative tradition, the accounts in question nonetheless are largely unique in their heavy emphasis upon the themes of betrayal, imprisonment, and subsequent escape from captivity. At the same time, divergences in these two versions of the same event underscore the importance of the separate social contexts within which the two storytellers relate the tale.

Although outsiders tend to equate Amazonia with indigenous peoples, the region actually is home to many different social groups including blacks, a particularly high number of whom reside in the

Brazilian state of Pará. Proof of Pará's slave past appears in the several dozen *quilombos* that survive in the Trombetas River and Óbidos-Santarém areas. Despite a long history of multiple contacts with their neighbors, these still largely black communities retain a deep, if often muted, sense of themselves as different from the surrounding world. The recent formation of a pan-*quilombo Raízes Negras* (Black Roots) association to defend residents' rights to the mineral-rich lands that multinational enterprises increasingly covet reflects fears of a new slavery in the form of economic subjugation. Aware that others of their number have ended up as wage laborers on what were once ancestral properties, residents of these communities often evince a new, sometimes defiant interest in their own history and symbolic forms.

Not everyone tells Encantado stories. Nevertheless, they are familiar to a significant portion of the approximately seventeen million people who currently inhabit the Brazilian Amazon (Slater, *Dolphin*). Recounted by Portuguese-speaking, often at least nominally Catholic individuals, they crop up in diverse locations throughout an area roughly two-thirds the size of the continental United States. These stories, which have parallels throughout much of the Spanish-speaking Amazon and some parts of the Caribbean, bring together a number of indigenous, European, and African cultural influences in a hybrid, unmistakably contemporary form.[3]

Particularly common in the countryside, the Encantado stories also appear in various corners of the burgeoning cities, where, today, over half the Amazonian population lives. By no means does everyone who recounts these narratives believe them. "This is a really pretty story that my father used to tell me," or "This is just a tale, but it's a good one," people often say. Opinions on the existence or nonexistence of the Encantados are intimately bound up in attitudes about the regional past and future, and not surprisingly, the same person may recount a single tale quite differently on different occasions. Usually told in the third person, these stories may also be personal-experience narratives. Not infrequently, the protagonist is a friend or relative.

In the simplest terms, the Encantados are supernatural entities in the guise of aquatic animals. Capable of turning themselves into men and women, they may carry off the human objects of their desire to a splendid underwater city, or Encante, from which few ever return. Shamanic healers called *pajés* enjoy special access to these Enchanted Beings, but even they cannot always foresee, let alone control, their actions.[4]

Although the Encantados include various river beings—anacondas, crabs, turtles, certain types of fish—the great majority of transformation narratives feature dolphins. Some of the most familiar Encantado stories concern Dolphin-people (the capitalized form indicates the supernatural being) who show up to dance in the country *festas* that enliven a difficult existence in the Amazonian interior. Dapper in straw hats that hide their blowhole and suits "white as tapioca," Dolphin-men twirl about the floor with the prettiest young women. Later that night, they may show up in one or another dancer's hammock. Sometimes, they whisk away the unsuspecting victim to the river bottom. On other occasions, they leave behind a shoe that turns into a stingray or else a Dolphin baby, who is born nine months to the day. Dolphin-women are often somewhat more reticent than their male counterparts, but they too are wont to carry off the objects of their affection.

The two individuals whose tales we shall now examine were both born in Silêncio do Matar, a *quilombo,* or former runaway-slave community, about two hours by boat from Óbidos, a city of some forty thousand people.[5] The one storyteller, a sixty-eight-year-old tobacco farmer and fisherman named Seu Moreno, still lives in this small rural enclave founded over 150 years ago. The other, his forty-two-year-old niece Dona Dominga, moved to Óbidos almost ten years ago and is presently employed as the bishop's laundress.

A number of the stories told by Seu Moreno and Dona Dominga resemble countless others. Dona Dominga, for instance, describes how her aunt accepts an invitation to a *festa* from a handsome stranger, who she suspects may be a Dolphin. Although greatly attracted to her tall, fair-skinned escort—the only white man for miles around—the aunt nevertheless takes the precaution of filling her pockets with garlic and chili pepper before leaving home. (Both substances are believed to ward off Dolphins.)[6] "So then," Dona Dominga explains:

1. He got a little angry and asked why
        she was loaded down with garlic and chili pepper,
            because she really stank.
    So then, she told him
        there was a Dolphin-man who had a habit
            of appearing in the *festas* around there.
    Then he said,
        Ah, so you're thinking I'm a Dolphin?"
    "I didn't say that!" she exclaimed
        but she didn't throw away the garlic.

Fig. 6.1. Dona Dominga, niece of Seu Moreno; a resident of Óbidos, Pará state, Brazil. (Courtesy of Candace Slater)

So then, when midnight came,
he disappeared,
he went away.
They looked for him everywhere
but they didn't find a thing.
And he never again appeared in those parts,
it was just that once she saw him.
But to this day she tells the story,
yes, she does.[7]

This version of a frequently repeated story reveals a number of individual touches. (The dancers' pockets usually do not bulge with peppers and garlic, for instance.) However, it is definitely in line with the tradition as a whole. So are various tales about entire cities that slip into the river without leaving the slightest trace. "So then," says Seu Moreno at the end of a widely familiar tale of an island that suddenly disappears in the midst of a particularly spirited celebration:

2. I believe this firmly because once
I arrived there in a rural community
and went to sleep.
But look, I couldn't sleep—
I'd drift off
only to awake.
A joyous music
came from the river bottom,
party music, you see?

So then, when morning came,
I asked the people there
what party that had been.
Everyone stared at me
—there had been no party,
no one had heard anything,
only I had heard that music.
But I tell you,
it was a very big party,
and it went on till dawn
—why, who knows if someone there in the Encante
wasn't celebrating a birthday?!

Yet if many of the tales told by Dona Dominga and Seu Moreno draw heavily upon a larger, immediately recognizable narrative tradition, others reveal notable peculiarities. The most striking of those I heard concerns a *caso verídico* (true occurrence) involving an older woman named Dona Claudina, mother to Seu Moreno and grandmother to Dona Dominga. In both accounts, one or more Encantados carry off the old woman against her will. After escaping her abductors with the aid of a Christian holy figure, she recounts her experience to

Fig. 6.2. Seu Moreno, a sixty-eight-year-old resident of the *quilombo* of Silêncio do Matar, Pará state, Brazil. (Courtesy of Candace Slater)

the community, whose worried members had been combing the woods and waters for her.

I was lucky enough to record the first version of the story during the several days I spent as a guest in the bishop's residence in Óbidos in August 1989.[8] Dona Dominga was one of a half-dozen employees—four female, two male, all between the ages of sixteen and sixty-seven—whom I joined around the kitchen table one mid-morning for a snack. When I casually asked the group about the truth of a particular Dolphin story I had heard a few nights before on my boat trip to Óbidos, they responded with a long volley of Encantado tales. While two of the women scoffed at the whole idea of Enchanted Beings, the other members of the group affirmed their existence with varying degrees of conviction. After one woman's flat assertion that the Enchanted Beings were "mere invention," a visibly upset Dona Dominga countered with the following tale:

3. The Encantados exist, *mana,*[9]
    they have carried off
        I don't know how many people.
Now then, grown-ups
    have more of a defense than children
        because they have received
            the priest's oils and holy water. [baptism][10]

Because look here,
    my grandmother was once enchanted, yes,
        but she returned from the Encante.
For this reason I say
    that I believe in the Encante,
        because she returned to tell the story

Look, she used to cure her children
    with a plant called *paracuri,*
        and she insisted on going every day to the river
            where a lot of this plant grew beneath a mango tree.

So then, one fine day when she arrived there,
    it was six in the afternoon,
        and there, beneath the mango tree,
            she saw a little black boy named Firmino,
                a person just like you or me,
                    but very black indeed.

And he said to her,
    "Aunt Clô, what do you want here?"
        She said, "I'm looking for *paracuri*."
    "Come with me then, because I know where there's a lot."
    [he told her]
        "So then, let's go," she said.

At least, that's what she told us
    when she returned.
Because she no longer remembered
    what happened to her at that moment.
When she came to her senses, she was in a city,
    a truly lovely place,
        but she didn't know how she'd arrived.
And look, when the news got out
    that she had not come home,
        everyone turned out to look for her,
            but even though they looked all night,
                they couldn't find her.

So then, they spent all the next day
    and the next,
        looking high and low.
Finally, they decided
    they weren't ever going to see her again.
But just when they had lost hope,
    at the end of the second day,
        she reappeared.
Everybody wept and wept [with joy]
    and she said, "I have returned,
        just to tell you what happened to me."

"Mother, where were you?" asked her son.
"I don't know, I only know that I was in a city,
    and then, a tall white man
        left me at a door.
And when I opened my eyes,
    I was here on earth again.
I had returned home."

[Here one listener clicks her tongue in disbelief. Dona Dominga pointedly ignores her.]

Look, that's all she told them.
And right afterward, she died
        —that very day.
Now then, she used to wear a cord about her neck, you know?,
    with a little image of Christ, like so.
So then, they [the Encantados] decided
    to bring her back to earth
        because she had that Christ about her neck,
            at least that's what I think.

Because the Encante exists,
    there is no doubt about it

[Here two listeners nod while the tongue clicker loudly stirs her coffee with a metal spoon.]

She came back to earth
    just to let us know
        these things are true.

"Why don't you go see my uncle?" Dona Dominga later asked me. "He also tells this story, he can tell you that it's true. Carlinhos [a young pastoral worker from Silêncio do Matar] will be going home for several days tomorrow—you could make the trip with him." As a result of her suggestion, I found myself a few days later seated beside Seu Moreno on the front step of his small straw house framed by orange trees. Pleased at being sought out as a storyteller, Seu Moreno directed his sister to brew coffee for us as well as for the dozen or so curious friends and relatives clustered about the step in the early-morning sun. Although all present listened respectfully to their host, many interjected various details into his accounts or offered similar stories of their own once he had concluded a tale. At the end of Seu Moreno's version of Dona Claudina's escape from the Encante, for instance, one man recalled a similar incident involving a second cousin. ("He now lives in Óbidos, but if you talk with him, he will give you all the details, he tells the story very well.")

4. It was my father who made a *promessa* with Saint Anthony
    to rescue my grandmother from the Encante.
Because she was looking for a remedy
    by the name of *paracuri*
        there by the river
            when she saw two small boys who lived there.

But the boys who appeared to her that day
were not those two,
—they were Encantados in the form of boys.
"Dona Claudina, what are you looking for?" [they asked her]
She said, "I'm looking for *paracuri.*"
"I know where there is a lot," one told her,
and so, they went deeper,
ever deeper into the woods.
Well then, they left her imprisoned
in the hollow trunk of a big tree
and there, she passed the night.

["Poor thing!" one older woman exclaims.]

We looked all over for her,
but even though she heard our shouts,
she couldn't answer.
She spent the whole night there,
a night of heavy rain.
And when she finally managed to get out of there
the next morning, she was dry,
completely dry.

So then, she showed everyone the trunk of the big tree
where she had spent the night.
She had not gone to the river bottom,
but still, it was a thing of the Encante.
The boys were from the Encante,
the Encante of the river bottom.

["That's right," a middle-aged man in a wide-brimmed straw hat interjects.]

Well, after that,
she remained a bit touched in the head,
it wasn't long before she died.
But if my father had not made that *promessa*
with the saint,
she never would have returned.

[Various people nod assent here.]

Ah no, they would have carried her off
right then and there,
you can be sure.

[Here there are more nods and other expressions of agreement.]

At first glance, the two accounts of Dona Claudina's brief sojourn in the Encante do not appear notably different from each other or, for that matter, from the Encantado corpus as a whole. Each builds on the widely familiar idea that the Enchanted Beings can assume the form of particular individuals of the protagonist's acquaintance, and both present the Encante as a physical space ordinarily off-limits to ordinary human beings. Although relatively few non-shamans return to earth after a descent to the Encante, Dona Claudina's partial loss of memory and generalized disorientation are entirely typical of those persons who do manage to escape.

And yet, despite the features that link the two stories to each other as well as to a larger corpus, a number of differences between them are immediately apparent. Dona Dominga's version of her grandmother's adventure, for instance, features a decidedly black boy instead of two children of indeterminate color. The protagonist finds herself in an underwater city (as opposed to a hollow tree trunk) where she spends not a single night but rather two whole days. Then, instead of simply emerging from the tree trunk, she finds herself suddenly on earth again after having being escorted to the door of the Encante by a tall white man. In contrast to Seu Moreno, who recalls how his mother lingers on after her return, "a bit touched in the head," Dona Dominga reports that the woman dies immediately after recounting her ordeal. Finally, although in both cases, the Encantados yield to the authority of a Christian holy figure, Seu Moreno attributes Dona Claudina's return to a *promessa* made on her behalf, while Dona Dominga credits her escape to the miraculous effects of a medal with Christ's likeness.

In general, Dona Dominga's version of her grandmother's ordeal is considerably closer to the norm than is Seu Moreno's. Dona Claudina's initial abduction by a single Encantado as opposed to an enchanted pair, for example, is fully consonant with the tradition as a whole.[11] So is her description of a strange and wonderful underwater city. While her uncle departs from tradition in his references to the Encante as a terrestrial location, Dona Dominga insists on its more normal subaquatic character. In contrast to Seu Moreno's portrayal of a cramped and in no way alluring prison, she identifies the Enchanted City as "a truly lovely place."

Then too, although both storytellers assert that Enchanted Beings in the form of dark-skinned children lead Dona Claudina astray, the tall white man who leaves her at the underwater city's door fits the conventional description of an Encantado. Dona Dominga's assertion that her grandmother disappears at exactly six o'clock in the afternoon also recalls other Encantado narratives, as does her extension of Seu Moreno's single rainy night into two suspense-filled days. Finally, Dona Claudina's death immediately after she recounts her adventures provides a more predictable, as well as a more dramatic, climax than does Seu Moreno's description of her gradual demise.

The more conventional nature of Dona Dominga's story has several possible explanations. Her greater distance from the event in question is, perhaps, the most obvious. Because Dona Dominga, who is almost thirty years younger than her uncle, did not personally witness the protagonist's return after her supposed abduction, she has less knowledge of and loyalty to the original details of the occurrence. ("I heard this story from many people there in Silêncio do Matar," she explains. "I myself cannot say I remember it, but I heard much about it as a child.") Her telescoping of the two children into one, her substitution of the underwater city for the tree trunk, and her introduction of the white-skinned man who leaves Dona Claudina at the door to the Encante suggest a concerted, if not necessarily conscious, streamlining and transformation of the story to better fit existing narrative expectations.

The changes in Dona Dominga's story also have much to do with a specific social context and a particular historical moment. While Seu Moreno relives personal and communal experience through his recounting of his mother's story before an audience of friends and neighbors, Dona Dominga is clearly engaged in a confrontation with persons who not only do not accept the Encantados' existence but who have no allegiance to or firsthand knowledge of the *quilombo*. Although the presence of an educated foreigner probably upped the stakes in the minds of the participants, the battle had been going on long before my arrival.[12]

Seu Moreno, in contrast, has little need to insist upon the truth of stories no one openly challenges. Although some of the residents of Silêncio do Matar believe more firmly in the Encantados than do others, most tend to accept at least the possibility of their existence. One indication of the force of this generalized belief is the change in Carlinhos, who had scoffed openly at some of the stories told around the bishop's kitchen table, but who suddenly was full of tales himself once we reached his family home. One evening, as we rowed across a river lit only by a wedge of moon, I asked him point-blank if he believed in the Encante. "I do," he replied, "because there, out in the river, there is an *aningal* [a grove of philodendronlike water plants] where a small child disappeared, body and soul." When I then asked why he had dismissed similar stories in Óbidos, he responded with awkward laughter. "Sometimes, people exaggerate," he said finally, with a shrug.

Those residents of Silêncio do Matar who would appear to have doubts about the Encantados tend not to express these directly. "Look," one older woman confided to me as we sat alone in her outdoor kitchen, deveining a heap of tobacco leaves, "I don't know whether these things exist—I myself have never seen them. But I know many people who say they have, and who am I to say they didn't?"[13]

This reluctance openly to question the Encantados' existence (and, by extension, the storyteller's probity), so prevalent in the close-knit community of Silêncio do Matar, is largely absent in Óbidos. There, people from different backgrounds often argue openly about the existence or the exact nature of various supernatural entities. Although these debates may reflect in part a tension between rural and urban upbringing, this division is far too simple. Due usually to the influence of one or more relatives, persons born in the city may tell just as many Encantado stories as their rural counterparts. Furthermore, migrants from the countryside may eagerly abjure their "superstitious" past.[14]

Even the two coworkers who so annoyed Dona Dominga by their rejection of the supernatural as "tall tales and nonsense" recounted a considerable number of stories. While taking care to label her own accounts of the Encantados good examples of "the foolish things some people believe" (a comment that infuriated Dona Dominga), one of the women readily admitted that she herself used to fear these spirits of the deep. "Yes, yes, before I became modern I too believed these things," she declared with a self-conscious chuckle.[15]

The fact that the conversation took place in the bishop's kitchen—as opposed to the front steps of an individual storyteller's home—is in itself significant. Although the bishop himself was not physically present at this or any other storytelling session to which I was party, it is easy to imagine how the immediate setting—and an unspoken desire not to offend their employer with tales many members of the ecclesiastical establishment denounce as superstition—might influence the storytellers' behavior.

The existence or nonexistence of the Encantados is, in the last analysis, not the real issue. Squabbles over the truth of individual stories point to far more profound disagreements about the Amazonian present. Whereas some persons strive to portray themselves as fully comfortable with the larger social changes that have affected their own lives, others are clearly less happy with their own present situation. Thus, for instance, while Dona Dominga says she has no desire to return to Silêncio do Matar ("It is so small, one has to work so hard, and there is nothing at all to do once the day is over"), she is hardly enamored of life in the city. "I am here," she says, "because here in Óbidos, my son can study. There is the clinic when he gets sick and, besides, he likes the bustle [*movimento*]. But I wouldn't say that life is good here. I don't even know that it is better. Because I miss the trees, the river, even the sound of the wind on the water. Of course, nobody here has seen the Encantados. Why would they want to live in such a place, so full of dirt and noise?"

In keeping with the more confrontational context in which she tells her grandmother's story, there are racial overtones to Dona Dominga's account that are either lacking or far less important in her uncle's account. Just as she insists on the blackness of the small boy who leads her grandmother astray ("He was a person just like you or me," she notes, "but very black indeed"), so she stresses the fair skin of the Encantado who escorts her grandmother back to earth. When a lighter-skinned listener dismisses her tale as "superstition," Dona Dominga bristles. "I may be black," she tells me later, "but I am not stupid and I know what I have seen. This woman, has she ever lived there, deep within the forest? Of course she hasn't! Because if she had, she would not talk the way she does."

The absence of color references in Seu Moreno's account is hardly surprising. As he is telling the story in Silêncio do Matar, where virtually everyone is dark-skinned, there would be little reason to make mention of the children's blackness. In Dona Dominga's case, however, young Firmino is not just dark, but his very dark complexion sets him apart from other human beings and underscores the nefarious character of his behavior. (The boy is "a person just like you or me, *but* very black indeed," she says.) At the same time, the presence of a dark-skinned figure in an extremely powerful role normally reserved for European-looking entities is by no means entirely negative.

The substitution of Christ for Saint Anthony is also significant, in that the latter holy figure—like Saints Benedict and Thomas—is particularly revered among African Brazilians in many different regions of the country (Cascudo, *Dicionário,* 61–63). Moreover, many of these groups portray all three saints as dark-skinned. By invoking the medal with Christ's image as her grandmother's passport back home, Dona Dominga renders a community-specific story more universal. Her insistence on the power of baptism ("the priest's oils and holy water") and on Christ's power over hostile forces also makes the tale less folkloric and somewhat more acceptable in terms of the institutionalized religion that the bishop represents.

The ultimate point of Seu Moreno's tale is not just the awesome power of the black Saint Anthony—who is triumphant even over the forces of nature embodied in the Encante—but also the concomitant triumph of his mother, who emerges from captivity. The ability of Seu Moreno's father to obtain the saint's aid is itself an affirmation of an individual's power to shape his own and his family's destiny. Instead of simply accepting the loss that proves irreparable in the great majority of Encantado stories, the anguished son insists on confronting forces far more powerful than he.

Dona Dominga, in contrast, is in many ways more interested in affirming the existence of the Encantados, who represent for her a whole way—once, her way—of life. Her version of the story has the abducted woman return to earth for the express purpose of sharing her experience with fellow *quilombeiros.* ("Because the Encante exists," she says with an emphatic nod in the direction of her dissident coworkers. "She came back to earth just to let us know these things are true.")

In short then, Dona Dominga's story is as much about her own situation as a member of a social order increasingly characterized by competing backgrounds and beliefs as it is about her grandmother or the Encantados. Yet if it is for this reason quite different from Seu Moreno's account, both tales reveal a number of fundamental divergences from other Encantado narratives. For instance, even though Dona Dominga evokes a sumptuous underwater city, while Seu Moreno locates the Encante in a cramped and decidedly unlovely tree trunk, she does not dwell upon the underwater city's wonders in the way that other, non-*quilombeiro* storytellers are wont to do. The Encante represents one detail of a story whose real interest lies in the victim's joyous release to not just her family but the community at large.

The identification of the two black boys as Encantados in both stories also represents a departure from narrative tradition, not simply because the boys are black—a fact we already have noted—but also because they are children. Although the Enchanted Beings can, theoretically, assume any form at will, they are most likely to appear as particularly good-looking members of the opposite sex. It is precisely sexual attraction that leads the Encantados to kidnap those individuals who have become the unsuspecting objects of their desire. Quite often, the abduction is actually more of a seduction in which the bedazzled victim goes willingly to the river bottom.

To the extent that Dona Claudina is tricked into captivity by a pair of children who exploit her confiding nature, her case is very different. These Encantados' unextraordinary appearance suggests that even the most seemingly innocent and familiar figures may hold out a threat to one's very existence. No seduction, Dona Claudina's abduction is, instead, an outright betrayal. In this sense, the story holds out a clear warning to the listener about the dangers lurking in everyday and close-at-hand situations.

Finally, and most important, although our two storytellers do not agree on the details of Dona Claudina's escape from the Encante, this escape provides the unquestioned climax of both tales. In addition, both individuals credit a Christian holy figure with the protagonist's release. This happy ending and the confrontation between a saint (or Christ) and the Encantados are decidedly unusual in terms of the tradition as a whole.

In most Encantado stories told today in the Brazilian Amazon, the family of the abductee appeals not to a saint but to a shamanic healer. The *pajé* is believed to have the power to communicate with the Enchanted Beings, either by incorporating them within his or her own body or, less frequently, by assuming the form of a river creature and journeying to their underwater city. Usually in the case of an abduction by an Encantado, the *pajé* succeeds in contacting the victim, who often responds with a detailed list of instructions for obtaining his or her release. Most often, a family member is told to go alone to the riverbank at midnight and to anoint the monstrous snake who will appear there with the milk of a black cow (or the contents of an egg or the juice of a lemon).[16] Sometimes, he or she must shoot the monster in the forehead in order to disenchant the abductee, who will then reappear.

Not surprisingly, the family member in question almost always fails to follow through on the instructions relayed by the shamanic healer, thereby redoubling the abductee's term of enchantment. Although the well-known story of the Cobra Norato constitutes an exception to the rule (Norato does succeed in becoming disenchanted), the great majority of rescue attempts, like the conclusion that appears below, are notably unsuccessful. Although non-shamans do return upon occasion from the Encante, they are usually unable or unwilling to talk about their experiences. Moreover, most of those who reappear to family members tend to do so not in the flesh but rather in highly formulaic dreams (Cascudo, *Geografia,* 254–59; Chernela, "History").

5. And so, three days after that child had vanished,
        he appeared in the curer's session.
    So then, he said he hadn't drowned,
        he had been carried off to the Encante,
            and he was in that very pretty city
                beneath the river.
    But he missed his mother a lot,
        he was going to appear to her,
            and so, she should wait for him
                down by the river around midnight.
    Because he was going to appear with the third wave
        in the form of an enormous serpent.

    But that serpent wasn't a really a serpent,
        it was he who was wanting to be disenchanted.
    Then it was for her to splash the milk of a black cow
        over his forehead
            and he would emerge from that ugly shell.
    But she didn't have the courage.
    Look, the day arrived
        and she didn't even go there,
            she was so afraid.[17]

Because most of the tellers of the Encantado stories locate the saints in opposition to the Enchanted Beings, the saints are very rarely called in to fill the place of the shamanic healers (see Slater, *Dolphin* and Maués, *Ilha*). Whereas the Christian holy figures are said to wield *poder* (power), the Encantados possess *mistério* (literally, mystery or mysterious force). Likewise, storytellers speak of the *lei* (law or moral logic) of the saints in opposition to the Encantados' *ritmo* (rhythm or corporeal, intuitive direction). Not unexpectedly, contrasts between the two are often part of more detailed folk cosmologies that, while couched within an ostensibly Christian framework, frequently present a series of more or less striking departures from official dogma.

Many storytellers—including Seu Moreno and a number of his friends and relatives—readily admit that they do not understand the Encantados. "Who controls them? Just so, no one can say," they may assert, or "The Encantado? No one knows. It's just something that exists." However, their conviction that the Enchanted Beings belong to another, alogical order of being does not stop Seu Moreno's father from calling on Saint Anthony to aid his mother.

Even while Seu Moreno is quick to agree that the Encante is "another sort of dwelling place, another sphere" (*outra moradia, outro ambiente*), he nonetheless insists that, in situations of extreme need, human beings can call upon the saints—as opposed to the *pajés* who exist within as well as outside the *quilombos*—to intercede with the Encantados. Although Dona Dominga does not mention Saint Anthony, Dona Claudina's holy medal and, by extension, her identity as a baptized Christian allow her to slip away from her would-be abductors. The tall white man leaves the old woman at the door of the Encante because the image of the Christian deity around her neck ensures her passage back to the world of human beings. "Those Encantados," explains Dona Dominga in a later conversation, "they turn people into fish like them. But the man or woman who belongs to Christ will never grow gills, and so, they know this and they always let that person go."

Significantly, although I recorded a relatively small number of tales involving confrontations between saints and Encantados—just over a dozen in more than a year of fieldwork—every one of them was told to me by an individual associated in some way with a former *quilombo*. While not all the persons who told me these stories had actually lived in one of these communities, they inevitably cited a relative, usually a parent, who had.

Furthermore, although by no means all rescue stories told by residents of ex-*quilombos* involve saints, every one of the rescue stories involving saints that I did record in my travels throughout widely different parts of Amazonia were told by persons of African-Brazilian (and, more often than not, direct slave) heritage. While the number of narratives involving rescue by saints is relatively small, *quilombeiros* as a group tend to place a greater than usual stress on themes of concealment and escape from danger. Tales of marvelous islands full of tortoises and Brazil nut trees that simply vanish before the eyes of greedy outsiders and of golden mountains that melt away into the forest before miners can descend on them are not unfamiliar to a larger population. However, they are particularly prevalent among the descendants of runaway slaves.

Why should an association with runaway-slave settlements encourage stories in which the saints square off against the Encantados? Although much research remains to be done on every aspect of Amazonian *quilombos,* as well as on the Encantado stories as a body, I can offer several initial hypotheses. Structural similarities between the Christian saints and the African *orixás* (deities) provide one possible motive for the formers' presence in these tales. So does the community's need for a triumph over the special form of captivity that the Encante ultimately represents. Dona Claudina's return to earth underscores the power of the individual and the community to overcome superhuman forces through an act of faith. Her insistence on bearing witness ("She came back to earth just to let us know these things are true") likewise emphasizes the individual's responsibility not just to the divine forces that aid her but also to the group.

Today, if not in the past, descendants of the runaway slaves are unlikely to refer to the African and African-Brazilian deities known as *orixás.* Although their devotions to the Christian saints—which resemble those found among various other African-Brazilian populations—often contain African elements, these individuals are definitely not practicing *xangô* or *candomblé.* All the same, the ease with which the *orixás* have been syncretized with Roman Catholic saints within present-day African-Brazilian religions underscores the structural similarities between the two. Thus, while it is a Christian holy figure, not an *orixá,* who rescues Dona Claudina from the Encante, Saint Anthony acts more like an *orixá* than a shamanic healer, who, ultimately, is as close or closer to the underwater universe than he is to the world of human beings. (At the end of a particularly powerful *pajé*'s life on earth, he does not go to hell or heaven but rather to the river bottom to dwell among the Encantados.)

In addition, the members of runaway-slave communities, whose members lived in constant fear of discovery, punishment, and either death or a return to bondage, would be likely to feel a particular need for stories of betrayal and imprisonment to end in a triumphant escape. Although Brazil abolished slavery over a hundred years ago, older feelings of fear and distrust of a larger world are in no way foreign to present-day residents of the *quilombos*. The increasing loss of communal lands and personal freedoms to the multinational mining companies that began installing themselves in the region several decades ago stirs bitter memories. The fear of betrayal by fellow *quilombeiros* who would weaken the community by doing business for personal profit with these enterprises is very real. So is the notion that wage labor represents a new sort of captivity in the sense of forced servitude to powerful others. ("Once you become their employee," says one man who worked for many years in the giant bauxite refinery now located in Porto Trombetas, "you become a slave to their decisions. How are you going to refuse to work under inhuman conditions if you have sold your land and have no other way to feed your kids? When I was a farmer, I was very poor, of course. But the day I felt like fishing, I left everything to fish. When I went to work for the bauxite company, I made more money but my life was not my own.")[18]

Even though the threat of actual bondage has not existed for more than a century, Seu Moreno's version of Dona Claudina's abduction stresses the community's need to protect and restore its own. In contrast to those Encantado stories in which a family member is ultimately responsible for the permanent disappearance of the abductee, both his and Dona Dominga's accounts underscore the power of individuals to help one another and the active involvement of the entire community in its members' destinies. Despite the fact that it is Saint Anthony who finally scoops a bemused Dona Claudina out of the Encante, it is Seu Moreno's father—*and not a shamanic healer to whom he eventually has recourse*—who takes the initiative in obtaining her release. "But if my father had not made that *promessa* with the saint, she never would have returned, they would have carried her off right then and there," he pointedly concludes. The story's happy ending is a reflection on the power of a Christian—more specifically, a black Christian—saint. But again, as in Dona Dominga's account, it is also a victory for the individuals who join forces to find the lost woman.

In conclusion, the Encantado narratives tell not only of beings who move at will between the human and animal domains but also of social processes that assume different, ever-fluid shapes in different settings. The fact that communities founded by runaway slaves present special characteristics suggests the degree to which particular individuals and specific groups of people continue to transform and to redeploy to their own ends many aspects of a larger regional culture.

APPENDIX

Portuguese Originals of Translated Tales

1. Aí, ficou meio brabo, perguntava
        porque estava cheia de alho e pimenta malagueta,
                que estava fedendo muito.
    Aí ela falou para ele
        que tinha um boto que costumava
            aparecer na festa naquelas partes.
    Então ele disse,
        "Você está pensando que sou boto?"
    "Não falei isso!" ela disse
        mas não largou aquele alho.

    Assim que quando deu meia-noite,
        ele sumiu,
            foi embora.
    Procuraram em todo canto
        mas não acharam nada.
    E nunca mais apareceu por aquelas bandas.
        Mas ela ainda conta,
            conta, sim.

2. Eu acredito mesmo porque uma vez
        cheguei lá numa comunidade
            e fui dormir.
    Mas, olha só, não deu mesmo—
        peguei no sono
            só para acordar.
    Uma música alegre
        vinha do fundo,
            música de festa, né?

    Aí, quando foi de manh,
        fui perguntar para o povo
            que festa era aquela.
    Todo mundo olhou para mim
        —não tinha festa, não,
            ninguém não ouviu nada,
                só eu que escutei.

Mas vou lhes dizer,
era festa grande,
durou até a madrugada
—quem sabe se não foi alguém lá do Encante
fazendo anos, né?!

3. Os Encantados existem, mana,
eles já levaram
não sei quantas pessoas.
Agora, gente grande
tem mais defesa do que criança.
Porque pega aqueles santos óleos do padre
e aquela água benta.

Porque olha,
a minha avó também foi encantada, foi,
mas voltou do Encante.
Por isso que digo
que acredito no Encante,
porque ela voltou para contar.

Olha, curava os meninos dela
com um remédio que chamam paracuri,
e ela tinha mania de todo dia ir lá numa cabeceira
onde tinha muito por debaixo de uma mangueira.
Aí, quando foi nesse belo dia ela chegou lá
—eram as seis da tarde—
e lá, por debaixo da mangueira,
ela enxergou um pretinho,
uma pessoa como nós, mas pretinho mesmo.

E ele disse assim,
"Tia Clô, o que é que a senhora quer aqui?"
Ela disse, "Estou procurando paracuri."
"Pois, a senhora vá comigo que sei onde tem demais."
"Então vamos," ela disse.

Pelo menos, assim contou para nós
quando voltou.
Porque ela não soube mais dela
naquele momento.

Quando ela se recordou, estava numa cidade,
coisa tão linda ali
mas ela não sabe como ela foi para la.
E olha, quando deu o anúncio
que ela nao tinha chegado em casa,
todo mundo foi atrás,
procuraram a noite inteira
mas não encontraram ela.

Aí, passaram o dia inteiro do outro dia
e mais outro
procurando em tudo que era canto.
Por fim, o pessoal estava conformado
que ela não aparecia mais.
Mas justo quando perderam a esperança
no fim dos dois dias,
ela chegou.
Aí, todo mundo chorou, chorou
e ela disse, "Eu vim,
só para contar para vocês
o que passou comigo."

"Mamãe, onde é que a senhora estava?" perguntou o filho dela.
"Eu não sei, só sei que estava numa cidade,
e depois, um homem alto, branco
me trouxe ate uma porta.
E quando me acordei
eu estava de novo encima da terra."

Olha, foi só isso que ela falou.
E logo depois morreu
—nesse mesmo dia.
Agora, ela usava no pescoço um cordão de fio, sabe?,
com Cristozinho, assim.
Aí, eles resolveram
trazer ela de volta
porque ela tinha aquele Cristo no pescoço,
eu acho, pelo menos.

Que existe o Encante,
não cabe dúvida.

Ela veio encima da terra
só para avisar
que essas coisas são verdade.

4. Foi o meu pai quem fez promessa com o Santo Antonio
para tirar minha avó do Encante.
Que ela andava procurando um remédio que tem,
por nome de paracuri,
lá na beira
quando viu dois garotinhos daquele lugar.

Só que esses que apareceram para ela naquele dia
não eram aqueles dois, não
—eram os Encantados que tinham se apresentado
em forma de garoto.
'Dona Claudina, o que é que a senhora está procurando?'
Ela disse, 'Estou procurando paracuri.'
'Sei onde tem uma pulsão,' um deles falou para ela,
e aí foram caminhando, caminhando,
cada vez mais para dentro das matas.
Então, deixaram ela presa
no toco dum pau grande
e lá ela passou a noite.

A gente procurava, procurava,
mas embora escutou os gritos,
não podia responder.
Ela passou a noite inteira lá,
noite de chuva grossa.
E quando por fim conseguiu sair de lá,
manhã cedinho, saiu enxuta
enxutinha.

Aí, ela mostrou para todo mundo o toco do pau grande
onde tinha passado a noite.
Ela não foi para o fundo do mar,
mas foi coisa do Encante.
Os rapazinhos eram do Encante,
do Encante do fundo do mar.

Bom, depois,
ficou meio oscilada ela,
não demorou para morrer.

Mas se meu pai não tivesse feito
aquela promessa com o santo,
nunca teria voltado.
Ah não,
teriam levado ela naquela hora,
pode confiar.

5. Pois é, três dias depois daquele menino ter sumido,
apareceu na banca do curador.
Aí falou que não tinha afogado,
que tinha sido levado para o Encante,
que estava naquela cidade bem bonita
por baixo da água.
Mas tinha muita saudade da mãe dela,
ia aparecer para ela,
assim que era para ela aguardar ele
na beira por banda de meia-noite.
Que ia aparecer na terceira onda grande
em forma duma enorme serpente.

Só que não era serpente,
era ele que estava querendo se encantar.
Então, era para ela jogar leite de vaca preta
bem na testa dele
e ele ia sair daquela capa feia.
Só que ela faltou coragem.
Olha, chegou o dia
e nem foi lá,
tanto do medo que tinha.

NOTES

1. I am grateful for the support of the University of California Berkeley Committee on Research, which helped fund my fieldwork in Óbidos, as well as to the American Philosophical Society, which allowed me to do new research on *quilombos* in the Trombetas area during the summer of 1994. I also thank those representatives of the Roman Catholic Church in Óbidos and Oriximiná who greatly facilitated my contact with *quilombo* residents.

2. Although the *quilombos* of northeastern Brazil are far better known (see Price, *Maroon,* 169–226, for an introduction), there were also a number of these communities in western Pará. An overview of blacks in Pará during the time of slavery is available in Vicente Salles, *Pará.* For an important study

of present-day communities on the Trombetas River near Oriximiná, see Azevedo and Castro, *Trombetas*.

3. For Venezualan counterparts, see Madriz Galindo, "Encantos," and Guss, "Encantados." The section on the *yacuruna* (water people) of the Peruvian Amazon in Jaime Regan, *Tierra,* 173–85, provides an equally useful comparison. See also Harrison's discussion of snake-lovers in her *Signs,* 144–71; Leacock and Leacock, *Spirits;* and Figueiredo and Vergolino e Silva, *Encantados.*

4. The category *pajé,* an Amerindian term, encompasses various sorts of healers, including the particularly powerful *sacacas,* who are believed to undergo this sort of bodily transformation. Both *pajés* and *sacacas* may be referred to by the more general Iberian folk term of *curador—curadeira* for women—(healer). They are also sometimes known as *cirugiões,* (surgeons).

5. Although there are no formal studies of Silêncio do Matar, residents of the several dozen ex-*quilombos* have begun to hold annual meetings in which common problems are discussed and local traditions documented. Several mimeographed reports have been compiled by pastoral workers accompanying the *Raízes Negras* movement.

6. These prophylactics are an excellent indication of the hybrid nature of the Encantado stories; garlic has long been used to ward off vampires and other nefarious beings in European folklore, whereas chili peppers are distinctly American. Tobacco—commonly used in both native Amazonian and African-Brazilian cult activities—is also used to keep the Encantados at a distance.

7. The reader will note that this section of the story falls into two four-line stanzas. Often, though not always, stories told by women fall into divisions of two and four lines, while men's accounts are more apt to form stanzas of three and five lines. I thank Dell Hymes for first calling this patterning to my attention.

8. I thank Padre Manuel do Carmo da Silva Campos for his suggestion that I look into the *Raízes Negras* movement and Dom Martinho, bishop of Óbidos, for his hospitality during the summer of 1989.

9. *Mana* is a colloquial form of "sister" (*irmã*). The person to whom it is addressed is usually not a relative. In this case, Dona Dominga is speaking directly to her challenger.

10. Formerly, the visits of priests to isolated rural communities were far less common than they are today, and many people had little or nothing to do with organized religion. As a result, many people received baptism relatively late or, sometimes, not at all.

11. Because individual Dolphins are believed to fall in love with specific men, women, and children, it makes sense that the abduction should be staged exclusively by the impassioned Encantado.

12. For a quite different context in which varying stories play a com-

parable role in an ongoing debate with much wider social ramifications, see Slater, "Backlands."

13. Woman, age seventy-one, Silêncio do Matar. Widowed; raises tobacco "and other little things"; no formal education. 12 August 1989.

14. A similar phenomenon is documented for Greece by Charles Stewart in *Demons*. Stewart makes the point that a newfound allegiance to scientific logic is often less a motivation for abjuring "superstitious" traditions than a desire to emulate the upper classes.

15. Woman, age forty-four, born interior of Oriximiná (lives Óbidos fourteen years). Separated from husband; seamstress and cleaning woman; "a little" schooling. 9 August 1989.

16. These "recipes" have obvious parallels in European folklore. The blackness of the cow links it to the Devil. The lemon symbolizes cleansing; the egg, rebirth. Lemons and cows arrived with the Portuguese settlers.

17. Woman, age fifty-three; interior of Parintins (Terra Preta). Married; farming; no formal education.

18. Man, age fifty-two, Boa Vista. Married; rents boat for which he serves as pilot; no formal education. 18 July 1994.

REFERENCES

Azevedo, Rosa, and Edna Castro. *Negros do Trombetas: Guardiães de Matas e Rios*. Belém do Pará: Editora da Universidade, 1993.

Cascudo, Luís da Câmara. *Dicionário do Folclore Brasileiro*. 5th ed. Clássicos da Cultura Brasileira 4. Belo Horizonte: Itatiaia, 1984.

———. *Geografia dos Mitos Brasileiros*. 2d ed. Rio de Janeiro: José Olympio/INL, 1976.

Chernela, Janet M. "Righting History in the Northwest Amazon: Myth, Structure, and History in an Arapaço Narrative." In *Rethinking History and Myth: Indigenous South American Perspectives on the Past*, ed. Jonathan D. Hill, 35–49. Urbana: University of Illinois Press, 1988.

Figueiredo, Napoleão, and A. Vergolino e Silva. *Festas de Santo e Encantados*. Belém: Academia Paraense de Letras, 1972.

Galvão, Eduardo. *Santos e Visagens: Um Estudo da Vida Religiosa de Itá, Amazonas*. Brasiliana 284. São Paulo: Editora Nacional, 1955.

Guss, David M. "The Encantados: Venezuela's Invisible Kingdom." *Journal of Latin American Lore* 8, no. 2 (1982): 223–72.

Harrison, Regina. *Signs, Songs, and Memory in the Andes: Translating Quechua Language and Culture*. Austin: University of Texas Press, 1989.

Leacock, Seth, and Ruth Leacock. *Spirits of the Deep: A Study of an Afro-Brazilian Cult*. Garden City, N.Y.: Doubleday, 1972.

Madriz Galindo, Fernando. "Los Encantos, Elementos del Agua." *Boletín del Instituto de Folklore* 2, no. 2 (1955): 61–65.

Maúes, Raymundo Heraldo. *A Ilha Encantada: Medicina e Xamanismo numa Comunidade de Pescadores.* Coleção Igarapé. Belém: Universidade Federal do Pará, 1990.

Price, Richard, ed. *Maroon Societies: Rebel Slave Communities in the Americas.* 2d ed. Baltimore: The Johns Hopkins University Press, 1987.

Salles, Vicente. *O Negro no Pará sob o Regime da Escravidão.* Rio de Janeiro: Fundação Getúlio Vargas, 1971.

Slater, Candace. *Dance of the Dolphin: Transformation and Disenchantment in the Amazonian Imagination.* Chicago: University of Chicago Press, 1994.

———. "A Backlands Saint in the Big City: Urban Transformations of the Padre Cícero Tales." *Comparative Studies in Society and History* 33, no. 3 (1991): 588–610.

Stewart, Charles. *Demons and the Devil: Moral Imagination in Modern Greek Culture.* Princeton, N.J.: Princeton University Press, 1991.

Brinsley Samaroo

Animal Images in Caribbean Hindu Mythology

During the period from 1838 to 1917, some 551,000 East Indians were brought to the Caribbean colonies of British Guiana (238,909), Trinidad (143,939), Guadeloupe (42,326), Jamaica (36,420), Dutch Guiana (34,000), Martinique (25,509), French Guiana (19,296), St. Lucia (4,350), Grenada (3,200), and St. Vincent (2,472). This number was part of a larger Indian diaspora of about 1.4 million indentured Indians to Natal in South Africa, Kenya and Uganda in East Africa, Fiji, Malaysia, and the Seychelles (Vertovec, *Trinidad,* 4). Those who were indentured in Europe's Caribbean colonies came as part of the solution to the labor problem created by the abolition of African slavery beginning in 1838. Survivals of the Indian heritage are rare in many of the colonies to which the indentured immigrants came. Under the predominating Western Christian host culture, most of the East Indians became Christians and adopted the Western way of life advocated by the various agencies of the ruling powers. The exception to this general rule occurred in those colonies to which the largest numbers of immigrants came or in those that maintained continuous contact with the ancestral place. In the Caribbean, three settlements stand out in this regard: Guyana, Trinidad and

Tobago, and Suriname. It is in these places only that there remains any substantial vestige of Indian culture.

The major attribute required of these laborers by the plantocracy that had successfully agitated for this influx was the ability to do sustained agricultural work. Hence the emphasis in the selection process was on those in the fullness of their prime, between the ages of eighteen and thirty-five, who belonged to agricultural castes and had hard hands with corny palms as evidence of prior planting activity on the Indo-Gangetic Plains or in peninsular Madras.

But these immigrants brought to the Caribbean more than their calloused palms. They transported to the region cultural fragments from one of the world's ancient civilizations incorporating a world view that was markedly different from the predominating Western norm previously transported from Europe to the Caribbean. This cultural difference was, from the days of indentureship, a constant source of difficulty to the indentured immigrants and their descendants since their Asiatic lifestyle appeared strange, heathen, and generally alien to the host society. Even today, that fascination, fear, and apprehension regarding East Indian cultural practices remains in the region. At the same time, the settlement of this immigrant population, which resulted in the satisfaction of the plantocracy and the permanent settlement of about seventy-five percent of those who came, was due in no small measure to the stabilizing force that was provided through the cultural package brought by the Indians to the region. For it was that world view which provided the spiritual backbone that was so necessary for the successful application of their industry to the region. This was a cosmic view informed by such factors as a religious attachment to the land (Mother Earth, or Dharti Mata), the sacredness of the close-knit nuclear family that became the major basis of East Indian economic organization in the region, and a deep sense of duty to whatever task was assigned.

This paper attempts to select one thread of the complex skein of religious customs brought from India and transplanted in the Caribbean: the use of mythical animal images and the use of real animals as symbols in Hindu worship in the new environment. The use of animal images in worship on the Indian subcontinent follows the general pattern developed in ancient civilizations wherein "people who live by similar methods and techniques often produce similar cults just as they produce similar artifacts of stone" (Kosambi, *Culture,* 9). This trend has been observed in European Ice Age drawings and in the pre-

Columbian civilizations of the New World (Saunders, *Jaguar,* passim). One Indologist claims a clear Mesopotamian influence on Indian animal symbolism, tracing this to a trade connection between the two areas from around 800 B.C. This influence is particularly strong in the Indian use of serpent gods (Zimmer, *Art,* 71). The French scholar-priest Abbé J. A. Dubois, fleeing from the excesses of the Revolution in 1792, went to Madras presidency, where he remained until 1823. In Madras, he observed Indian customs closely. He noted a remarkable similarity between Indian and Greek gods and pointed out that, like the Greek gods, each Indian deity had a particular weapon and a particular sacred animal attached to him or her (Dubois, *Manners,* 633).

In most prehistoric civilizations, before people were able to understand the operation of natural phenomena, they deified those things that they were unable to explain logically. To the ancient Incas of Peru, whatever was unusual was declared a Huaca (abode of spirits) and therefore an object of obeisance. In India, cattle became an object of special veneration. The same veneration has been transferred to cattle in all areas of the Indian diaspora. One Hindu magazine, based in Trinidad but with a Caribbean-wide readership, explains the importance of the cow to the Caribbean Hindu: "What is called the sacred cow also includes the bullock. The cow plays a central role in the life of the rural-agrarian Hindu. It provides him with milk; fuel in the form of cow-dung; manure; dung used for building huts; beasts of burden; means of transport. The cow is useful in many ways. In addition to this, the cow inculcates in the Hindu personality a feeling of gratitude and affectionate respect for the animal kingdom" (I. Rampersad, "Cow," 43). In the same way that animals became important in Indian civilization, so too did plants become an integral part of Hindu worship. Their use as food for people and for animals; as preservatives, medicine, shelter, and items of trade; and as agents of environmental protection gave them a sustained importance over the centuries.

In India, divine sanction for the incorporation of these animal and plant deities as regular symbolic parts of worship was given in Brahminic texts as early as around 200 B.C. In chapter 9:26 of the Bhagavad Gita (Song of God), worshipers are enjoined: "If any earnest soul make offering to me with devotion, of leaf or flower or fruit or water, that offering of devotion I enjoy" (Sharma, *Gita,* 128). In chapter 7: 21, the range of deities is widened beyond plants and water to any divine form that a devotee may choose to worship: "Whatsoever (divine) form any devotee / With faith seeks to worship, / For every such (devotee) faith unswerving / I ordain same to be." Over time, a tradition developed whereby all that was produced by the earth became sacred as symbols of the divine. Many of these creations were from the animal world:

> Even from a distance, without ever entering the sacred court-yards, it is often possible to tell what deity will be found in the innermost shrine of a Hindu temple. At the corners of the outer walls surrounding the structural complex will likely be placed the figure of an animal. If it is a resting bull, the deity of the place is Shiva; if it is a bandycoot, or rat, the temple belongs to Ganesha; if it is a lion or tiger, it is dedicated to the Goddess, usually Durga: if it is a kneeling man with wings and a hawk-like face, the sanctum sanctorum houses Vishnu; and if it is a peacock, the god worshipped there is most likely Murugan. (Smith, *Mythology,* 67)

The functions of these animal *vahanas* (vehicles) are threefold. Firstly, the *vahana* carries the deity from place to place. It is also a companion or mascot of the deity, and finally, "at a symbolic level the vahana is said to manifest on an animal plane the attributes of the divine individuals themselves" (*Mythology,* 67).

Assured by divine sanction, Hinduism proceeded to create hundreds of deities who themselves became incarnate and assumed ever-changing rebirths (avatars) over the ages. The Indians who came to the Caribbean did not bring the whole pantheon of deities with them. What they brought was derived mainly from the Indo-Gangetic plain, whence most of them originated, and, to a lesser extent, from the Madras peninsula. Those who came were mainly peasants. "This peasantry," noted the Trinidadian author Vidia Naipaul, "hadn't been touched by the great Indian reform movements of the nineteenth century" (Naipaul, *Gurudeva,* 13). Thus the tradition that was brought to the region was neither the Vedic Brahminic tradition nor the ascetic mode of the advanced Bhakta (devotee) that had developed in the holy cities and shrines.

What was brought by the indentured immigrant was the folk-devotional tradition in a multitude of popular forms. This was a highly ritualized type of worship where form took precedence over content and in which day-to-day realities came before philosophical speculation. In this context, plants and animals, the configuration of the physical landscape, solar and lunar movements, and gender relations were the major areas of emphasis. To explain their operation, these realities became intertwined with divinity. They could be malevolent divinities or benevolent ones. Malevolent gods had to be constantly appeased, while benevolent ones were praised and their desirable attributes (strength, beauty, curative facility) prayed for.

Caribbean Indians of the indentured diaspora brought these beliefs and traditions in their heads as they crossed the *kala pani* (dark waters). In time, they also brought over a few of the scriptural texts—the major one being the *Ramayana,* which played a decisive role in shaping the character of the East Indians in the Caribbean: "We in Trinidad and the Caribbean should be proud of being part of this noble tradition of Ramayana, one which sustained our people for over 140 years in an unbroken tradition and without much contact with India in the early days" (I. Rampersad, "Ramayana," 10–11). The *Mahabharata,* a lengthy epic composed in honor of Vishnu and a virtual encyclopedia of Indian thought, was also transported as one of the sacred texts. The Bhagavad Gita, already quoted, forms part of this epic. The first exponents of the transported lore were a minority of Brahmins who had come as indentured workers. Later, as the caste system was reshaped in the new environment, other non-Brahmins emerged as self-appointed priests to carry on the tradition.

The practices brought from India to the Caribbean were not followed in exact replication of the modes used in the ancestral place. What happened from the late nineteenth century on was an exercise in homogenization of diverse fragments brought from two large and separate parts of India as well as of the traditions brought from hundreds of small communities within these two large regions. Why was this homogenization necessary? The immigrants understood, shortly after their arrival, that some kind of wholeness had to be created in the New World bastion against the strange and often hostile non-Indian world. In the colony of British Guiana, for example, there was the "reconstruction and redefinition of traditional social models . . . In the sphere of religion, the perceptual and conceptual universe of the ancestral land was concretised with the greatest authenticity and completeness" (Singh, *Guyana,* 16–17).

This attempt to standardize custom and practice, thereby inventing a new tradition out of the complex bits and pieces brought from India, occurred at two levels among the Indians of the Caribbean. We must seek to understand briefly the two tiers at which this process took place. In the Caribbean, caste (*varna*) was not destroyed despite the presence of strong factors that made the system inoperable on the Indian model. What occurred in the Caribbean was the simplification of caste into two easily understandable divisions. The majority of North Indians bonded themselves into a Caribbean Brahmin group, excluding the mainly Dravidian and lower-class and caste Indians who formed the Chamar caste. These people are often called Madrassees. It may be pertinent to note that in the orthodox classification of the caste system, namely Brahmins, Kshatriyas, Vaisyas, and Shudras, the Chamar category is not included. Chamar is in fact a subcaste (*jati*) of the Shudra caste. It appears that the Caribbean Hindus found the subcontinent's ordering of people into caste and subcaste too cumbersome, particularly when one could elevate oneself from a lower to a higher caste in the New World, where everybody was starting afresh. Among the higher, neo-Brahmin Caribbean group, the homogenization has been described in the following manner: "Homogenization first occurred substantially on the estates and in early Indian settlements on the island, where there evolved forms of egalitarian social interaction following the attenuation of the caste system, a Hindu lingua franca, a Vaishnavite bhakti religious orientation providing congregational worship, ritual services of Brahmin pundits to persons of all castes, standardized rites and ceremonies, and other social norms based on 'generalized' North Indian background" (*Trinidad,* 342). At the Chamar level, there has been an effort to simplify practices brought from the South (and from the North to a lesser degree) and to merge these into a bond at another level of society.

A major aspect of this homogenization has been the incorporation of the South Indian Tamil tradition, normally held in low esteem by the Brahminic or Christian tradition because of the animal sacrifices associated with this group. Those very upper-caste Hindus who had come from a tradition of animal sacrifice in India now dissociated themselves from that tradition. Possibly the predominant Western Christian tradition, which abhorred such practices, steered them away from the continuance of animal sacrifice in the New World. Here they offered leaf, flower, fruit, and water instead of animals.

In the Madrassee or Tamil tradition, a number of South Indian deities as well as pan-Indian female deities have become merged under the general rubric of the most powerful goddess, Kali Mai. Abbé Dubois, during his early nineteenth-century sojourn in southern India, noticed the sacrificing of animals to Kali, whom he calls the goddess of destruction. He cites the Kali Purana as the source of information regarding the kinds and qualities of those animals that are suitable for sacrifice (*Manners,* 388, 647). Another goddess who has been added to this lower-order standardization is Parmeshwarie (goddess of the universe), who is described in the Caribbean as a sister of Kali. The commonly believed legend is that Parmeshwarie was a Chamar maiden from North India who was so devoted to Shiva's consort, Parvati, that she was deified (*Trinidad,* 320). In the Caribbean, pigs are generally offered as a sacrifice to Parmeshwarie. Animals are most often used as sacrificial symbols in Kali Mai worship ceremonies, and it is in Guyana that the Kali Mai tradition has been strongest (*Guyana,* 17). There it has witnessed a particular resurgence since the late 1960s, mainly among Guyanese of Dravidian ancestry as well as other Hindus who are not a part of the orthodox pale (Bassier, "Kali," 1). From Guyana, the revival spread to Trinidad during the 1970s with the arrival of a leading Guyanese worship leader (*pujari*), whose goal was to boost a flagging Kali Mai movement. Today, the movement attracts thousands of followers who gather at various centers to seek blessings from "the Mother" (Guinee, "Kali," 8). In the French West Indian island of Guadeloupe, the movement has also taken root, with animal sacrifices as in Trinidad and Guyana (Hurbon, "Movements," 150).

The presence of animals is continuously noticeable in all these Kali Mai worship services. There is, first of all, actual animal sacrifice: a sheep, a goat, a young female pig, and a young hen or pullet. These are sacrificed at appointed times that the *pujari* deems to be auspicious, and the consecrated carcass is often carried away to be eaten by the person who offered it up initially in order to receive some boon from the goddess. In addition to actual animal sacrifice, the deities to whom obeisance is given are very close to animals. Kali herself sits on her lion *vahana,* and the god Shiva sits on his *vahana*—the bull Nandi. His girdle consists of the snake Vasuki, and out of his finger springs the symbol of sprightly life and eternal energy—the deer. As attractive as these animal images and symbols may be for the worshipers of Kali Mai, they spell terror for many other Hindus. Despite reservations on the part of higher-caste Hindus, Kali Mai worship—complete with its blood sacrifice and the high regard for animal images that accompany their deities—is becoming more popular both in Trinidad and in Guyana. In a period of greater economic hardships occasioned in part by severe structural-adjustment programs, more of the poor—Indian and non-Indian—are seeking solace in the Mother.

The *Vahanas,* or Animal Vehicles, of the Deities

As stated above, Indians in the Caribbean did not transfer all the animal deities of their homeland to the new environment. Those that were transferred were either those that could be found in the New World (such as the cow or bullock, monkey, snake, and swan) or those that possessed extraordinary attributes (the elephant and lion). In this selective transfer, there were animals that were sacred in India and present in the Caribbean that were not given high recognition in the New World. For example, neither the dog *vahana* of Bhairava, a godling from northern India and the doorkeeper of Saiva temples, nor the owl (Lakshmi's *vahana*) nor the rat (Ganesh's *vahana*) were highly regarded in the diaspora. The most popular animal image used in the Caribbean is the cow. Some of the reasons given for this importance have already been cited from the magazine *Jagriti.* One can add that the bullock (Nandi) is the symbol of fertility and is particularly suited to be the vehicle of Shiva. The cow (Nandini), equally used in Hindu worship, connotes agricultural production in abundance; her milk will rejuvenate mankind for thousands of years. Next in importance among the animal images used in Caribbean worship is the snake (Naga):

> Serpent cults have existed in most countries, originating when early man was most susceptible to the influence of the mysterious and the uncanny. Thus the serpent, because of its curious gliding movement, its hypnotic eyes, its ability to disappear suddenly, the fatal consequences of its bite, and the casting of its skin made it the subject of many myths and the object of both fear and veneration. This is particularly true of India, which possesses almost every known species of snake and which has preserved either in its archaeological remains or in its literature an unbroken continuity of evidence of the existence of the snake cult from the third milennium B.C. (Stutley, *Hinduism,* 198)

In Caribbean temples, the Nagas are ever-present. They are regarded as the guardians of the mineral wealth of the earth. The serpent Ananta (endless or infinite), whose other name is Sesa, is the protector of the sleeping Vishnu. Lord Shiva wears a garland of snakes as his symbolic ornament. In Trinidad, a new interpretation is given to this phenomenon: "Deplorable qualities like anger and false desires are as destructive to the human as the bite of a poisonous snake. Lord Shiva, who is above 'snake like' qualities—qualities which can 'coil' around the individual and keep him enmeshed in the world of Samsara—he who has complete control over them, actually wears them as ornaments" (D. Maharaj, "Shiva," 46). Another commentator points out that the snake of Lord Shiva represents the Kundalini Shakti (serpentine energy) that is present in each individual and that may be awakened by meditation (Umrau, "Shivatri," 7).

Then there are the theriomorphic figures that are part animal and part human. These icons seek to combine the most admirable qualities of selected animals with those of humans. Undoubtedly, the most important of these in the Caribbean is Hanuman, half human, half monkey. The monkey as a deity was a pre-Aryan inheritance in Hindustan. "The monkey cult, whether of totemic origin or not, had come to stay and Hanumat is worshipped by a vast population even in present-day India" (Bhattacharji, *Theogony,* 77). Hanuman's importance to Caribbean Hindus derives from the decisive role he played in the *Ramayana* story, where he assisted Rama in retrieving Sita, his wife, who had been abducted by Ravana, the king of Sri Lanka. For his many feats during the course of that long contest, Hanuman has secured the eternal veneration of Hindus everywhere and has emerged over the centuries as the protector of homes, the patron of acrobats and wrestlers, and a miracle healer.

As the *Ramayana* was transferred to the New World, Hanuman emerged as second in importance only to Rama. This is in fulfillment of God's promise that "as long as the Ramayana is sung in the world, his praise will be a part of it and he will endure in body" (Rambachan, *Hanuman,* 77). Among his Caribbean devotees, Hanuman is an exemplar of determination, resourcefulness, and energy, as well as a good minister of government—persuasive, diligent, and courageous (*Hanuman,* 48, 52). For this reason, he is "a tremendous source of strength for those who are often disheartened when they struggle for righteousness" (*Hanuman,* 73). The Hanuman Chalisa, which is an invocation requesting his blessings and protection, is a constant companion to most Hindus, who recite its mantras regularly. In the New World, Hanuman's praises are sung in the temples: "O Pawan Putra Hanuman, blessed art thou who have conquered all enemies and vices. Do bless me with divine virtues and guide me, so that I may be able to stand in defence of righteousness and in the promotion of Dharma" (Tewari, *Handbook,* 5). In the Caribbean, as Hindus seek to re-create their own tradition, Hanuman has been given human form, apparently to bring him closer to his devotees and to explain his possession of human qualities: "Summoned by Sugriva multitudes of Kapis arrived. The word 'Kapi' means a monkey as well as a tribe in the Kishkindas. Vali, Sugriva, Hanuman and the entire army were of the Kapi tribe. It is therefore believed that they were not really monkeys but the Kapi tribals" (Gangabissoon, *Ramayana,* 130).

Two others among the animal deities find prominence among Caribbean Hindus: Ganesh, the elephant-headed deity, and Singha, the lion. Despite the fact that the elephant is not native to the Caribbean, its historic usage as an animal in India and its possession of enormous strength have assured it a permanent place in Hindu mythology. It is the mount of Indra, the king of gods, the counterpart of Zeus: "Of all gifts, the gift of an elephant has the highest sanctity and indemnifies the donor against the danger of Hell. Eight celestial elephants (*diggaja*) guard the eight points of the Hindu firmament, and sculptured elephants adorn the walls of Hindu temples. The Goddess Lakshmi, the presiding deity of wealth, is iconographically represented with two elephants, one on each side of her. And who does not know of Ganesa, the elephant-headed god of wisdom and success?" (Choudhury, *Tradition,* 301).

Wherever Indians have gone, they have taken Ganesh with them. He is worshiped for many reasons. The 1992 celebrations in Trinidad recounted these: "Ganesh the god of good omen is worshipped by all Hindus. He is also worshipped as the god of wisdom, learning, success and power. His name is repeated at the beginning of everything as Vignesha or the remover of obstacles. Ganesh is also propitiated at the start of every activity whether marriage, house construction or writing a book" ("Ganesh," 14). In the Caribbean, there is a twelve-day celebration of the birth of Ganesh (Ganesh Chaturthi) that takes place in September. It ends with the immersion of the image of the elephant god in a river or in the sea. Ganesh is also praised as one of the originators of language: "I reverence Vani (the goddess of speech) and Vinyaka (Lord Ganesh) the originators of sounds represented by the alphabet, of the multitude of objects denoted by these sounds of poetic sentiments as well as of metres, and the begetters of all blessings" (*Anniversary,* 8; also *Ramayana,* 25; and *Handbook,* 3).

Like the elephant, the lion is not native to the Caribbean. Yet as a symbol of majesty and regal splendor, it is respected worldwide. In the Caribbean, as in India, Vishnu's throne is the Singhasan (lion's seat)—a symbol of his sovereignty. In the Caribbean too, the Singhasan has become the focal point in or out of the temple, where the pundit sits to preside over the proceedings of worship. It is present in Suriname and Trinidad as often as in Guyana (*Guyana,* 4).

The Vishnu Tradition

Of the *tri-murti* (three deities)—Brahma, Shiva, and Vishnu—dominating the Caribbean Hindu tradition, the Vishnu avatar is the most popular. In the popular mythology, Vishnu will descend to the earth whenever there occurs a serious breach of morality or an incident of the predominance of evil over good. This assurance comes from both the *Ramayana* and the Bhagavad Gita. Claiming that "the authority for our belief is enshrined in our scriptures," one group cites the relevant verses: "Whenever righteousness is on the decline and unrighteousness is in the ascendant I assume human form. For the protection of the virtuous, for the destruction of evil-doers and for reestablishing Dharma, I assume form from Age to Age" (*Anniversary,* 16; also *Gita,* 4:7–8).

Vishnu's *vahana* is the eagle Garuda. Garuda symbolizes the deity's possession of the eagle's ability to destroy enemies (the snake in this instance) or those threatened by disease. The Garuda mantra is offered by those going on journeys to hazardous places: "Om Tarksya (Garuda) cast down my enemies, trample the diseases and venom that might invade me." In addition to his use of an animal as his vehicle, Vishnu becomes reincarnated in at least five animal or part-animal avatars[1]:

1. Mina or Matsya appears as a fish. In this story, very similar to that of the Great Flood in the Bible, the fish warns of an impending flood and later appears to tow the boat containing the righteous to a place of safety.

2. The Kurma (tortoise) avatar represents Vishnu's appearance in the form of a tortoise. This avatar came during Satyug (The Age of Truth), when there was a serious conflict between the Devtas (gods) and the Danavas (evil men). The tortoise, with the assistance of a mountain (Mandrachal) and a snake (Vaisuki), achieved victory for the Devtas. The lower shell of the tortoise represents the earth; the curved upper shell, the sky; and the body, the atmosphere: the world in one body. The ascribed qualities of this animal became desirable attributes for devotees: restraint, calmness, and self-assurance. These enhance the mythological value of this animal in Hindu worship.

3. By about the fourth century A.D., the Varaha (boar) avatar of Vishnu was incorporated into the mythology. In this form, Vishnu res-

cued the earth from its control by the demon Hiranyaksa. The boar is also associated with fertility, hence its acceptance as a popular animal image.

4. The Narasimha (half-lion, half-man) incarnation of Vishnu symbolizes Hinduism's attempt to unite into one being the two greatest creatures on earth. Man represents the highest development of all creatures, the lion, the most powerful and fearless. At a more mundane level, Vishnu assumed this avatar to defeat the evil king Hiranyakasipu, who threatened to kill his son Prahlada, a Vishnu devotee. Brahma had granted a favor to this king whereby he could not be killed by man or beast, by day or by night. Vishnu therefore assumed this man-beast form and struck down Hiranyakasipu at twilight.

5. In the Kalkin avatar, which has not yet appeared, Vishnu will emerge on a white horse bearing a blazing sword to once again restore good in a world beset by evil. This avatar seems to have been conceived after the eighth century A.D., when successive defeats of Hindu empires by the Muslims inspired this wish. It is a hope similar to that of the Messiah promised to the Jews in the Old Testament.

Almost as popular as Vishnu in his various reincarnations is Shiva. In the Caribbean, Shiva has become the object of considerable veneration among his personal devotees (Saivites) as well as among the rest of the Hindu community of the higher and the lower castes, Caribbean-style. Here, Shiva becomes the "supreme personal god when he is identified with his Shakti or power. He is then omnipotent, omniscient, active God and the embodiment of such values as Truth (Satyam), Auspiciousness (Shivam) and Beauty (Sundaram)" ("Shivatri," 4). Many Hindus believe that he is the easiest god to please and that he unhesitatingly answers the prayers of his devotees. Shiva's consort is the goddess Durga, and together they convey the completeness that must be the ideal family life. Both Shiva and Durga are accompanied by a retinue of animals. Shiva's mount is Nandi, the bull; his girdle consists of Vasuki, the serpent. The *vahana* of Durga is either the tiger or the lion. After prayers have been offered to these deities, flags are hoisted either in the temple or at homes where these prayers are given. For Shiva, the flag is blue, for Durga, it is yellow; for the monkey god Hanuman, it is red, and for the elephant god Ganesh, it is orange. In India, the flags are raised in the temple compound; in the Caribbean, they are hoisted in the temple, at homes, or at the wedding tent. In a society where there are other religions in the same village each claiming adherents, Caribbean Hinduism finds it necessary to proclaim its presence even outside the temple. The public display of particular flags also serves as a protection against evil forces outside.

Animal Images as Part of the Popular Folk Culture

Many of the folk beliefs of the rural communities whence the immigrants came were transferred to the Caribbean. One researcher found that in the Gorakhpur area of the United Provinces of the nineteenth century, folk songs with animal images formed a salient part of the cultural landscape. Songs about cattle were abundant: "O husband! do not bring the ox with seven or five teeth, / the ox whose tail contains a knob / And the ox of black colour" (Srivastava, *Folk Culture,* 239). Similarly, animals in the ancestral place were regarded as indicators of impending events: "If the crow crows in the night / And the jackal howls during the day / Then famine will occur definitely" (*Folk Culture,* 239).

In Caribbean settlements, there was a similar widespread transfer of songs and beliefs. When a hen crows like a cock, it is a sign of hard times; a crying dog and the shriek of the night hawk are sure signs of death in the neighborhood; when birds, bees, butterflies, and wasps are seen flying from an area, it is a sure sign of impending natural disaster.

In the life-cycle rituals of Caribbean Hindus, animal images recur unceasingly. The author remembers vividly the observance of elaborate rituals in his village whenever a boy-child was born. The sixth day (*chatthi*) ceremony followed by the twelfth day (*barahi*) ceremony are particularly prominent. Recalling the birth of Krishna (an avatar of Vishnu), these *chatthi* and *barahi* ceremonies seek to re-create in the Caribbean the same joy that occurred when Krishna was born:

> Spread the news that Krishna is born
> Go and tell my father-in-law: he may give the city of Patna in his joy
> Go and tell my brother-in-law: he may distribute cows in his happiness.
>
> (Ramnath, *Laws,* 258)

The event is so important that the king would give a city as an expression of his happiness; the prince would give gifts of cows to express his joy. At a typical wedding, the giving of gifts symbolizes the appreciation of the bride or groom by the invitees. Although the gifts promised in this wedding song can hardly be afforded by the giver, their value is symbolic:

What will I give Ram at the door ceremony
For the door ceremony, I will give horses,
I will give elephants
What will I give him when he is going away
I will give him cows, I will give him Sita.[2]

Even before the actual ceremony, there is the building of the wedding tent (*maro*). In this song, the singers are representing the bride during the building of the *maro* and are comparing the couple to a pair of swans (Hansa). The male swan represents the principle of fertility, and the swan in graceful, lofty flight represents the migration of the human spirit from one avatar to another, always soaring higher and higher in pursuit of the Brahman:

In the water tank the female swan is sporting in one half of the tank
In the other half the male swan is also sporting
Half of my habitat is my parents' home
The other half is at my in-laws' place
Still the maro is not beautiful.

(N. Maharaj, "Folk Songs," 15)

For the marriage ceremony itself, the bride's feet are often painted with pictures of Suka, the parrot *vahana* of Kamadeva, the god of love, whose flowery arrow has found its mark.

Interpretation of Animal Deities

In the Caribbean, there is increasing controversy regarding the true function of these animal deities. Their use has been criticized both in India and in the New World by Christians who have not cared enough to understand the purpose of these *murtis*. Abbé Dubois pours scorn on the Indian use of these images: "Of all the different kinds of idolatry, the worship of animals is certainly one of the lowest forms, and one which most unmistakably reveals the weakness of human nature; what a sad spectacle it is when man, created in God's own image, with a countenance so formed that he might always be looking heavenwards, so forgets his sublime origin as to dare to bow his knee to animals!" (*Manners,* 636.) In the Caribbean, there was, from the very beginning, fear among the missionaries concerning these Hindu immigrants and their strange manner of worship. In October 1846, the Anglican bishop of British Guiana warned that "our clergy have much to contend with now that immigration has fairly set in to our shores" (Mangru, "Guiana," 69). Three decades later, that colony's *Royal Gazette* requested assistance for its coolie missions because of "Heathenism—which is a constant menace and will have a gradual effect on the morals of the colony" ("Guiana," 69).

The Canadian Presbyterian missionary John Morton, who started a mission for the indentured Indians in 1868, found the Hindu gods loathsome and their temples not worthy of any respect (Morton, *Trinidad,* 232–34). In the Caribbean, criticism based on the Christian unwillingness to understand Hindu beliefs has continued up to the present time. Over the last few years, the Hindus have been responding vigorously. Their major argument is that Hindus do not worship the image itself, but rather use it as a vehicle for conveying their praise or requests to God in his or her various manifestations. The image is not God but a representation of the divine. The many hands of the deity indicate the extent of the power of God to achieve boons for the devotee. Likewise, the animal that accompanies each deity represents particular qualities of that deity which the devotee would wish to acquire. In addition, the *murti* is made in a special manner with particular ingredients and is therefore a source of divine energy ("Love," 33). A publication by the Vedanta Sanatan Dharma tackles this controversy in a lengthy rebuttal of the Christian arguments. The main critic who is answered is the American evangelist Herbert Armstrong, whose sermons were regularly relayed to the Caribbean:

> The simple truth is that Hindus worship the metaphysical concept behind the idol or image. They do not worship the thing in itself as was done in the Old Testament or in primitive societies. In fact Hindus worship all aspects of Nature, being manifestations of God himself . . . Images tell us that they represent deep metaphysical concepts behind their forms. No one can expect to understand the Hindu faith if he fails to study Hindu symbolism. Images are symbols and aspects of the Godhead. No one worships an image. He worships its meaning. ("Misconception," 8–9)

Even now, the debate rages on and Hindus find it necessary to continuously explain to the larger non-Hindu community that there is a fundamental difference between idol worship and the use of icons as visual messages of the god who is being praised: "While we are asked to pray 'in spirit and in truth' this does not negate the fact that the mind needs images upon which to base its thoughts. So while we pray in spirit and in truth the fact remains that unless we are dead, the turbulent and restless mind keeps jumping from one place to another. To keep the mind steadfast any agnostic will agree that it is easier for us to view the object of our meditations to help us" (R. Rampersad, "Worship," 9).

In this essay, an attempt has been made to look at one aspect of the effort by the indentured immigrants to re-create India in the Caribbean. This reconstruction of the ancestral home indicates a deep-seated desire among Indians of the diaspora to rebuild a way of life that had sustained them for centuries on the Indian subcontinent and had given them anchorage in space and time. In the New World, the need for such rooting was even stronger. For they were in a strange environment in an unfree condition, and every attempt was being made to wean them away from their Oriental "heathenism" and their complex interpretation of the cosmos. Colonial society aimed at uniformity; Indians were creating diversity. In such circumstances, the Caribbean Indian had to create a tradition that could give personal satisfaction by its adherence to the original Indian tradition. At the same time, that tradition was expected to bind the larger (Indian) community and serve as a bulwark against the hazards presented by the non-Indian world. In the continuing search for solutions to these problems of adjustment, the task was made doubly difficult by the fact that the traditions brought from India were not brought in whole but in parts. There was also considerable heterogeneity in that fragmented tradition. Therefore, ancestral practices seeking to inculcate certain Indian values and norms of behavior had to be re-created. Through the repetition of these norms and values, the creation of a Caribbean tradition was actively set in motion. This practice, observed worldwide, has been called "the invention of tradition" ("Introduction," passim).

In the new Caribbean environment, this invention involved a selection of those norms and models that, over time, the Caribbean Indians judged to be relevant to their survival and prosperity. In this regard, caste was not abandoned but was refashioned to suit the conditions of the new home. People who would not have treated each other on terms of equality in India were now bonded as fellow travelers on the same boat. They called each other Jahagibhai (boat brother) or Jahagi Nata (boat relation). In the same manner, those vegetables and plants that could be found were incorporated in Caribbean pujas, and the names and places on this side of the water reminded listeners of the people, towns, and rivers of India. This was also the case with the animal images that now became an integral part of Caribbean mythology. We have seen that there was a selection of those that represented desirable attributes, those that could be found living in the region, and those that would find a generalized acceptance in the larger non-Indian society. With the increasing education of Caribbean Indians, there continues to be not a diminution of interest in these symbols but a rise in their usage. Modern technology has also enhanced the appeal of these images and has added to their beauty. In fact, this Caribbean-Indian tradition is being used more and more as a model for Indo-Caribbean people now resident in North America.

NOTES

The author wishes to thank the following colleagues for their useful criticisms of an earlier draft of this chapter: Professor Promode Mishra of the University of the West Indies, Professors Dan Smith and Robert Crane of Syracuse University, and Professor Anantanand Rambachan of St. Olaf's University.

1. This classification is partly drawn from M. Stutley, *Hinduism, the Eternal Law* (Wellingborough, Northamptonshire: Aquarian Press, 1985), 871.

2. N. Maharaj, "Some Aspects of Hindu Folk Songs in Trinidad," Caribbean Studies Thesis (Saint Augustine, Trinidad: University of the West Indies, 1974), 15. For similar songs in Suriname, see U. Arya, *Ritual Songs and Folk Songs in Surinam* (Leiden: E. J. Brill, 1968).

REFERENCES

Arya, U. *Ritual Songs and Folk Songs in Surinam.* Leiden: E. J. Brill, 1968.

Bassier, D. "Kali Worship in Guyana: The Quest for a New Identity." Unpublished paper presented at conference on East Indians in the Caribbean (Trinidad, 1979).

Bhattacharji, S. *The Indian Theogony.* London: Cambridge University Press, 1970.

Choudhury, D. K. L. "The Indian Elephant in a Changing World." *Contemporary Indian Tradition,* ed. C. M. Borden, 301–21. Washington, D.C.: Smithsonian Institution, 1989.

Dubois, J. J., Abbé. *Hindu Manners, Customs and Ceremonies.* Oxford: Clarendon Press, 1906.

Gangabissoon, S. *An Outline of the Ramayana.* N.p.: The Author, 1988.

"Grave Misconception of Hinduism in the West." *The Hindu Horizon* [Trinidad], 8 (1987): 8–9.

Guinee, W. "Ritual and Devotion in a Trinidadian Kali Temple." Master's Thesis, Indiana University, 1990.

"Hindus Mark Birth of Lord Ganesh." *Trinidad Express,* 6 September 1992, 14.

Hobsbawm, E. "Introduction: Inventing Traditions." In *The Invention of Tradition,* ed. E. Hobsbawm and T. Ranger. Cambridge: Cambridge University Press, 1983.

Hurbon, Laënnec. "New Religious Movements in the Caribbean." In *New Religious Movements and Rapid Social Change,* ed. J. A. Beckford, 146–76. Paris: UNESCO/Sage Publications, 1986.

Kosambi, D. D. *Myth and Reality: Studies in the Formation of Indian Culture.* Bombay: Popular Prakashan, 1983.

Maharaj, D. "Symbolism and Lord Shiva." *Jagriti '86* [Trinidad], 2 (1986): 46–50.

Maharaj, N. "Some Aspects of Hindu Folk Songs in Trinidad." Caribbean Studies Thesis, Saint Augustine, Trinidad: University of the West Indies, 1974, 15.

Mangru, S. "The Role of the Anglican Church in Christianizing the East Indians in British Guiana 1838–1898." Master's History Thesis. Georgetown, Guyana: University of Guyana, 1977.

"Many Ways to Show Love." *Jagriti 87* [Trinidad], no. 2 (1987): 33.

Morton, S. *John Morton of Trinidad.* Toronto: Westminster, 1916.

Naipaul, V. S. "Foreword." In *The Adventures of Gurudeva and Other Stories,* by S. Naipaul. London: A. Deutsch, 1976.

Paschim Kashi Silver Anniversary Brochure. Port-of-Spain, Trinidad: Mandir Marg, 1987.

Rambachan, A. *Hanuman: The Devotee of God.* Minnesota: Vijnana Publications, 1991.

Ramnath, H. *The Unwritten Laws of Hinduism.* Marabella, Trinidad: The Author, 1987.

Rampersad, I. "The Role of the Ramayana in the Lives of the Early Indentured Labourers in the Caribbean." *Jagriti '86* [Trinidad], 3 (1986): 10–11.

———. "The Symbol of the Cow." *Jagriti '86* [Trinidad], 4 (1986): 42–46.

Rampersad, R. "Hindu Worship Is Not Idolatry." *Trinidad Express,* 22 October 1992, 9.

Saunders, N. J. *People of the Jaguar: The Living Spirit of Ancient America.* London: Souvenir Press, 1987.

Sharma, A. *The Hindu Gita.* La Salle, Illinois: Open Court, 1986.

Singh, K. B. *Temples and Mosques: An Illustrated Study of East Indian Places of Worship in Guyana.* Georgetown, Guyana: Release Press, 1980.

Smith, H. D. *Looking at Hindu Mytholoqy.* New Delhi: Educational Resources Centre, 1988.

Srivastava, S. L. *Folk Culture and Oral Tradition.* New Delhi: Abhi Nav Publications, 1974.

Stutley, M. *Hinduism, the Eternal Law.* Wellingborough, Northamptonshire: Aquarian Press, 1985.

Stutley, M., and J. Stutley. *A Dictionary of Hinduism.* London: Routledge and Kegan Paul, 1977.

Tewari, R. *The Hindu Handbook of 1991 of the Edinburgh Hindu Temple.* Chaguanas, Trinidad: Edinburgh Hindu Temple, 1991.

Umrau, K. S. "Shivatri Celebrations in Trinidad." Caribbean Studies Thesis, University of the West Indies, Trinidad, 1992.

Vertovec, Steven. *Hindu Trinidad: Religion, Ethnicity and Socio-Economic Change.* London: Macmillan Caribbean, 1992.

Zimmer, H. *Myths and Symbols in Indian Art and Civilization.* Princeton: Princeton University Press, 1974.

Jeremy Poynting

From Ancestral to Creole: Humans and Animals in a West Indian Scale of Values

I begin by quoting a few short passages: "The stranger remembered how he'd once seen a large alligator killed by one of the villagers. The stunned reptile had been dragged out of the creek and left to the youths who pulled and poked at it in the middle of the road . . . A few moments later they'd lit a fire and set it against the beast" (C. Dabydeen, *Swirl,* 38); "Out of sheer boredom, he recalled, they would corner frightened bats, knock them to the ground with the short sticks they carried and then, in the truest spirit of democracy, elect one of them to unplug his bottle-lamp, bathe the helpless creature with kerosene, and set fire to it" (Kellman, *Coral,* 22); "The free Negro, like the French peasant during the first half of this century, has held it to be one of the indeafisible rights of the free man to carry a rusty gun, and to shoot every winged thing" (Kingsley, *Christmas,* 107); "But cane is we stubborn Cross, it don't give one scunt for Romance. / The secret is not to born or get dead quick, / Stone, nail, drown the puppies, the babies, / Cannibalize she nipple, mother-cord, devour she disease" (D. Dabydeen, "Christmas," 23).

What struck me about the novels from which the first two quotations came was not so much the scenes of cruel and apparently motiveless destruction of animal life, which are not uncommon in Caribbean fiction and poetry—the slingshotting of a bird, the pelting of a stone at a stray dog—but that in Cyril Dabydeen's *Dark Swirl* and in Anthony Kellman's *The Coral Rooms,* the episodes are not merely naturalistic portrayals of a casual heartlessness but are treated as symptoms of a much deeper crisis of humanity in the Caribbean. Although both works are self-contained and would appeal to readers without knowledge of their social and cultural contexts, it seems to me that reading them historically and pursuing their cultural subtexts begins to open up deeper layers of meaning that in turn shed light on Harold Sonny Ladoo's *No Pain Like This Body,* Cyril Dabydeen's *The Wizard Swami* and *Dark Swirl,* and Kellman's *The Coral Rooms.* I shall make briefer references to the work of V. S. Naipaul and Shiva Naipaul as well.

A few provisos before setting off.

First of all, I frequently refer to the region in general, whereas the reality is of considerable diversity in the arenas of animal-human contact. The extent to which the sugar plantation supplanted the natural world and, in contemporary times, the extent to which broad urbanization has transformed it has made Barbados, for example, very different from Guyana, particularly in relation to the latter's interior, where both savannah and tropical forest survive and support an animal life that is far richer than elsewhere in the Caribbean. It also seems to me significant that Guyana is the only country in the Anglophone Caribbean where a substantial Amerindian presence survives, although there is a smaller settlement in Dominica. This presence has, I believe, influenced the way Guyanese writers have focused on the animal-human interface, which they have done to a far greater extent than have writers elsewhere in the region.

Secondly, if I focus on the Indo-Caribbean strand of the story more extensively than on others, this is because it is not only the least known and deserving of greater attention but also because it is a rich vein. More Indian ancestral attitudes toward the natural world have survived the plantation experience to enter the bloodstream of the creolizing process, and those survivals offer rich metaphorical and ethical insights into animal-human connections.

The three key terms of the paradigm I am using, the ancestral, the plantation, and the creole, perhaps need brief explanation. The first I use simply to refer to the pre-Columbian Carib-Arawak world or to Africa, India, and Europe before the construction of the Caribbean plantation culture. The plantation I use as a shorthand for the whole post-Columbian system of European dominance over man and nature, the first major capitalist agribusinesses that gave rise to the labor systems of slavery and indenture and to the dominance of an attenuated form of European culture. By the creole, I mean that continually evolving, changing pattern of interculturation among all the fragments. The terms are not mutually exclusive. Elements of the ancestral survived, although transformed by the plantation; the creole clearly partakes of both.

The Amerindian Legacy

Of the Amerindian world view there is space to say only a little. (Earlier articles by Gary H. Gossen, Jay Miller and Vi Hilbert, and Joanna Overing are all apposite here, however.) The intrinsic actuality of the shared place of humans and animals in the world has entered the creole amalgam primarily through the inspiration later writers have drawn from historical references to it; and these references are frequently stereotyped in form. I can do no better than to quote the late Joel Benjamin's introduction to a valuable little Guyanese booklet, *Focus on Amerindians,* where he sums up the Amerindian ancestral legacy as including a "coherent and complex set of world views in which animal and human life blend in natural ecology with the physical environment" (Benjamin, *Focus,* x).

In other essays in the same collection and in the work of the nineteenth-century ethnologist Everard F. im Thurn, we are shown that the connections that the Amerindians made between themselves and animals existed at manifold levels. Whereas it is evident that the actual treatment of domestic animals was at times severely pragmatic, the methods of killing wildlife not necessarily humane, and the animal world not seen as wholly beneficent, what does stand out is the centrality of the belief in connection, the absence of species arrogance, and a fundamental sense of responsibility for the consequences of human action in a world shared with animals and plants. As elsewhere in the Americas, Amerindian peoples in Guyana traced their primordial beginnings to animals (tigers, snakes, the water *camoodi*) or from animal-human procreation. The Carib nation, for instance, was born from the fragments of a snake. And Makonaima, who created both humans and other animals, unlike the Judeo-Christian God who gives humankind dominion over the animal world, advised both to live in unity. Thurn noted that the Amerindian saw no such "sharp line of distinction, such as we see, between man and other animals, between one kind of animal and another, or between animals—man included—and inanimate objects" (*Indians,* 350.) Animals have spirits that "differ not at all in kind from those of men" (Thurn, *Indians,* 350). As a consequence, spirits can pass either way. At a domestic level, certain prohibitions on animals as food relate to the concern that at particular times, such as when a woman is pregnant, less desirable animal characteristics may be transferred to the unborn child because its spirit is too weak and undeveloped to resist the spirit of the slain animal. Parrots, for instance, were off the menu for fear of the child becoming too talkative (Jordan in Edwards, *Amerindian,* 66, 68).

In the Caribbean in general, the Amerindian world was destroyed more utterly by the impact of European colonial plunder and the plantation than virtually anywhere else in the New World. Only in the Guianas was it really possible for Amerindians to flee far enough away to ensure both physical and cultural survival. In Guyana, indeed, the Amerindian population has actually increased over recent decades, and belatedly, some real efforts have been made to replace the belittling stereotype of the Buck, held by all other sections of the population, for a real appreciation of Amerindian culture. But this culture is changing both under the impact of aggressive missionary activity and from the desire of some Amerindians for integration into the wider society.

I am principally concerned here, however, with what writers from other groups have made of the Amerindian legacy. In the past, there was certainly a tendency to see the Amerindian through familiar Eurocentric stereotypes as at best the noble savage or the child of nature, but often as the Buck who lay somewhere in the midpoint of the animal-human scale. A more enriching imaginative perception has been to see the Amerindian, or at least the legacy, as a potential bridge toward the repair of the human alienation from the natural knowledge of the richness of Amerindian mythological narratives and toward an awareness that some of the familiar creatures of folk legend, which are part of the imagination of all Guyanese groups—*massacouraman,* water *mumma,* and the bush *dai-dai*—all have Amerindian roots, frequently intermixed with the legendary animal-human creations of other groups. The work of a Guyanese artist, the late Aubrey Williams, and of the Guyanese writers Wilson Harris and Jan Carew, has led the way in making use of the Amerindian legacy. Harris's work in particular provides stimulus to the more recent writings of Cyril Dabydeen and Kellman.

Europe and the Plantation

It is tempting to cast the European—the creator of the plantation, the enslaver, the commodifier of his fellow human beings and of animal nature—in a uniform shade of infamy. If our business here were to weigh the European record in the historical scale of justice, that verdict might well be just; but I think that if one traces the flow of influence from the European legacy into Caribbean imaginative writing, the view has to be less monolithic. In the first place, the European construction of animal-human relations has itself never been uniform. In the nineteenth century, one can trace half a dozen different contradictory, overlapping strands, held in different degrees by particular interest groups and often held simultaneously by the same persons.

Folk Memories

Even in our own times, it is possible to trace older folk memories of a deeper sense of animal-human connection in European culture—present, perhaps, in coherent form up to the Middle Ages—in the animal-human folktales and fables absorbed from the so-called pagan worlds of Greece, Rome, India, and the Middle East and in the moralizing bestiaries with their mixture of real but fancifully described and wholly imaginary animals. Maybe the anthropomorphism of the children's story is the last refuge of this instinct. A continuing sense of this tradition may have been what attracted a white Jamaican, Walter Jeckyll, to be the first collector and transcriber of the wealth of African-derived Anancy stories at a time when they were generally despised. However, it was not really until the work of Louise Bennett and Andrew Salkey, in his *Anancy's Score,* that the tradition was fully recuperated as an adult one. There were other European contributions to Caribbean folklore: such figures of the popular European imagination as the *loup-garou* (werewolf, *lageru* in Trinidadian Creole) and the *diablesse* (devil woman), though again, as with Amerindian figures, there is almost certainly a coalescing with other, often African elements.

One may note briefly how the Jamaican novelist John Hearne alludes to the European prescientific vision of animal nature in *Land of the Living,* where Stefan Mahler, the refugee German-Jewish zoologist, sets out to jolt the scientific certainties of his "fact-constipated" students by giving a lecture on the medieval bestiaries, a comment too on his underlying unease with his own "European mania for rational definitions. Nothing can be safely understood until it is flayed, stuffed with analysis and niched in the museum of the mind" (Hearne, *Living*, 90.)

The Judeo-Christian Tradition

What seems to me intrinsic to the intellectual underpinnings of the European drive to colonial dominance and the ethic of the plantation, however, is the absorption into European Christianity of the Judaic sense of chosenness, both in the sense of being privileged in creation over all other natural beings, and thus having rightful dominion over them, and of chosenness over other lesser human groups, the blasphemy that led in its extremes to the abominations of slavery, of the Third Reich, and, as those odd footnotes to European history, of the animal pogroms that surfaced from time to time in fits of religious hysteria. The urge to dominion over all creation could soften at times to a spirit of paternalistic custodianship, but both derive from the same sense of human position, which was and is hierarchical and exclusive. Both are based on an absolute distinction between human and other orders of existence.

In the Caribbean, this tradition almost certainly had its main expression through the teachings of the missionary churches. One point of focus, the particular significance of the snake in African, East Indian, and Euro-Christian traditions, provides a neat example of the conflicting value systems of each of these cultures. In Christianity, of course, the snake is the prime exemplar of darkest evil, the creeping, legless thing that is the polar opposite of human uprightness (or at least the potential for it), a byword for deceit (a snake in the grass), and the Satanic serpent responsible for the Fall.

In the African religious traditions that came to the Caribbean, the Dahomean serpent god, Damballah, one of the surviving loas of Haitian vodún, is the giver of riches, one of whose signs is the rainbow, whose color is white. Within Hindu traditions, the snake has a similarly positive value—Shiva is the Lord of Snakes, Vasuki the divine snake revered as a symbol of fertility; and one of the highest forms of psychic energy, Kundalini, translates as "serpent power." I shall return to the literary exploration of this conflict toward the end of the essay.

The Industrial-Exploitative

The Caribbean saw the commodification not of animals but of man; and side by side with the expansion of the plantation system went a casual interference in nature for the benefit of profits from the sugar industry. In Jamaica, for instance, apart from the nonchalant destruction of habitat and the supplantation of wildlife by imported domestic animals, the plantation owners also imported several species, one of which, the mongoose, had catastrophic effects on several species of native animals, particularly lizards, snakes, and iguanas. Having inadvertently imported the rat, which destroyed a quarter of the cane crop, Europeans introduced the mongoose to eliminate this pest. The technique worked effectively for the sugar estates, reputedly saving £50,000 a year in the nineteenth century; but the rapidly spreading mongoose then in turn became a serious pest with a particular liking for the domestic fowls of the poor peasant proprietors.

In a climate of human brutalization and the ruthless drive for profits, it is scarcely surprising that, in the main, interest in Caribbean fauna and flora was the preserve of visitors. In general, it would seem that the limits of the sugar proprietors' and managers' interests was hunting and the table. Such documents of everyday life as *Lady Nugent's Journal* report the gluttonous consumption of wildlife and domestic animals at the planter's groaning table as yet another manifestation of the coarsening effects of plantation culture. She reports of one meal: "The first course was entirely of fish, excepting jerked hog. . . . There was also a black crab pepper-pot . . . six dozen of land crabs . . . turtle, mutton, beef, turkey, goose, ducks, chickens, capons, ham, crab patties . . ." (Nugent, *Journal,* 95).

The Scientific-Rational

The other strand of the European rationalist orientation toward animals, the scientific urge to collect, to classify, to arrange in hierarchies, came from outside the region, from European visitors to the Caribbean. To a large extent, this would still seem true today. In addition to more celebrated visitors such as Sir Hans Sloane (1660–1753), who visited Jamaica between 1687 and 1689; Charles Waterson, the eccentric Yorkshire squire who wandered in Demerara and South America between 1812 and 1824; Philip Gosse, who spent eighteen months in Jamaica in 1840 and 1841; and Charles Kingsley, there were numbers of amateur naturalists and collectors who left interesting and valuable accounts of Caribbean wildlife. Some of the species they described subsequently became extinct in the region. But even someone like Gosse, who wrote with a poet's eye of the birds he observed, expresses the doubleness of this tradition. There are Gosse's beautiful paintings and his proto-ecological sense that creatures needed to be seen in their natural environment, but one also learns that during his stay, Gosse shipped back to England no fewer than 1,500 bird skins and over 20,000 other biological specimens. It is significant, moreover, that the *Jamaica Journal,* which since its inception in 1965 has consistently attempted to encourage a local awareness of Jamaica's natural life-forms, has been forced to make extensive use of the work of such visitors in the absence of a genuinely native tradition.

The Romantic-Literary

The final strand of the European response to the animal world that found its way into the Caribbean was the romantic impulse, born in a spirit of opposition to the dominance of the industrial and the scientific. One can find in this impulse the desire, for instance, to celebrate animal wildlife for its freedom from the chains of social life or the wish to apprehend those correspondences between the human and the natural world that industrialization was burying. It is a profound tragedy that the first Europeans who came to the Caribbean were those imbued with the righteousness of the chosen regarding conquest over man and nature. The William Blake of "Auguries of Innocence" would have had no difficulty in understanding Amerindian, African, or Indian constructs of the relationships between human and animal life.

Initially, the English romantic tradition came into the Caribbean in almost wholly imitative forms. Later, one sees in the work of the authentically Caribbean poets A. J. Seymour and E. M. Roach a genuine localization of the use of animals as romantic symbols. In Roach's fine poem "Frigate Bird Passing," 1950, the "great hawk arrowing / The rare air" (Roach, *Poems,* 74) becomes the symbol for the soaring but imperiled poetic imagination. However, if one surveys a wide range of Caribbean poetry in English, the truth is that there are really very few poems (certainly in comparison with English verse) that focus on animal life, and in more recent work, in those poems that do, the inversion of the romantic image is made ever more explicit. For example, in Christine Craig's "Crow Poem": "My voice wants to say things / about blue skies, blond sand / yet a rasping, carrion croak / jets from my beak / sharp edged" (Craig, *Tigers,* 21).

Only in Wordsworth McAndrew's "To a Carrion Crow" does the bird rise out of the same maimed immurement in the squalor of carrion to the mythological splendor of a Promethean spirit who has dared to invade the heavens and been burned black for its impiety: "Nobody knows what you saw / when you passed through / but you burned in that sacred blue fire / and returned, black as coals, dumb . . ." (McAndrew, *Poems,* 8 [unpag.]). In each of these poems, one sees a working out, in Caribbean terms, of an inversion of an ostensibly English romantic tradition. Other repeated images in both fiction and poetry would include the outcast, the mangy pothound, or the pig rooting on the dunghill. Although it is not a particularly extensive element in recent Caribbean poetry, one sees in the work of Derek Walcott—particularly in the "Tropical Bestiary" sequence in *The Castaway*—a genuine Caribbean extension of the tradition of exploring animal creation as the source of metaphorical analogies for aspects of human experience. What I wish to discuss at this point is the extent to which elements of African and particularly Indian traditions of imagining animal-human connections have survived the destructive impact of the plantation experience and have become part of Caribbean writing.

The African Tradition

In "West Indian Culture Through Rasta Eyes," Dennis Forsythe gives an account of traditional West Indian belief systems, as reinterpreted by Rastafarianism, that has a great deal in common with Amerindian beliefs. Forsythe portrays Africans as representing their sense of relationship to animals in several interrelated ways: in animal stories where animals resemble people in their activities, but display the characteristics that are observed in animals; as gods (for example, Damballah, the serpent god who is portrayed as swallowing its own tail, an image of it being self-created); and as totemic symbols for the tribe, in which the perceived qualities of the animal are seen as defining the ideals of the tribe in their struggle for survival in the natural world. Animals with a powerful relationship to nature—the lion, tiger, elephant, and leopard—are most commonly found as totemic beasts, but of course, an animal with cunning and mental alertness such as the spider might also take on this symbolic role. [Anancy the Spiderman is seen, however, as functioning within the system of Babylon, the present corrupt society that the Rastaman has to overcome to gain spiritual enlightenment (Forsythe, *Rasta,* 214–36). Ed.]

Of all the peoples who came to the Caribbean, the Africans, in addition to the violation of their selves in slavery, may have suffered most grievously the sense of loss of the landscapes and animal-human ecologies that were part of their sense of being. In the poem "Mmenson," Edward Kamau Brathwaite writes a fanfare of loss: "Summon now the kings of the forest, / horn of the elephant, / mournful call of the elephant" (Brathwaite, *Masks,* 15). In "The Zoo," he makes that sense of loss more explicit. The way each creature manages to hold onto its particularity, nonetheless:

> cannot conceal the fact
> that where they play or flap
> is merely minor freedom for them:
> that all these birds and beasts:
>
> * * *
>
> are merely gathered here so we can gape &
> celebrate their public idiosyncracies—
> so we can pause, point, peel oranges,
> buy buns to throw,
> clutch at each other's sleeve
> and feel we recognize some old acquaintance
> sticking out his thong,
> our next-door neighbour the orang-
> outang.
>
> (Brathwaite, *Sappho,* 47–48)

The poem ends with the demand to "unlock / the ugly gadgets of the zoo," and the prayer that each of these creatures may find "release from this long xile's solitude still holding / them" (*Sappho,* 49, 50).

In the image of the zoo, Brathwaite finds an exact and troubling metaphor for the human experience of the plantation. In his own work, he searches out traces of the African survivals and seeks to express those sanctities. In "The Making of the Drum," he mixes the Hebraic image of the scapegoat carrying the people's sins with the African image of sacrifice where, although the goat must be killed to make the drum skin, it must also be blessed for its sacrifice (*Masks,* 7).

The East Indian Tradition

I think that, for a variety of reasons, far more of the ancestral traditions of Indian constructs of animal-human connections survived the plantation experience of the Caribbean and that this legacy, in creolized, Caribbeanized forms, has begun to enrich Caribbean imaginative writing. There are both intrinsic and external reasons why this should be so. In the first place, Indian imaginative constructs about the place of animal creation in the world are embedded at all sorts of levels in

Indian life: in ritual, iconography, dance, folktale, religious mythology, cosmology, written literature, and traditionally sanctioned patterns of ethical behavior. The subject is too vast to discuss in any depth, but what I feel is particularly important about the Indian tradition is that on the one hand it contains elements that remain in touch with the animism of the Caribbean's earliest inhabitants and that on the other it contains the sophisticated and ecologically explicit ethic of *ahimsa,* of non-injury to both humans and animals. Although like all ethical doctrines it has always been imperfectly performed, except perhaps by the Jains, nevertheless it remains a touchstone of Indian, especially Hindu, attitudes toward animal life in the Caribbean.

As with both Amerindian and African cosmologies, Hindu cosmology moves freely between human and animal creation. Of the incarnations of Vishnu, such as Mutsysa, the fish; Kurma, the tortoise; Varaha, the boar; Narasimha, the man-lion, roughly half are animal, half human. One text, the *Gita Govinda,* states that Vishnu became Buddha, one of the human avatars, out of compassion for animals, to end the cults of blood sacrifice. In Shiva, the Lord of Snakes, the serpents that encircle his neck and arms suggest a continuity with the horned ithyphallic god of the pre-Aryan Mohendro Daro, who is pictured surrounded by animals. Shiva is also known as Pasupati, Lord of Beasts. Two of the most loved of the lesser gods of popular Hinduism are, of course, Ganesh, the cheerful and benevolent elephant god, the remover of obstacles and the patron of grammarians. Hanuman, too, the divine assistant of Lord Rama, the monkey god, another guardian spirit, has a similar place in Hindu affections. The positive position of the snake (manifested in the serpent demigod Manasa and in Naga, a snake spirit; in Sesa, the thousand-headed snake on whom Vishnu sleeps; and in Vasuki, another divine snake revered as a symbol of fertility) has already been noted.

As with African and Amerindian world views, the whole of nature was in some sense divine. Thus, as part of the doctrine of the transmigration of souls, the passage from life to life could as easily pass through animals as humans. I was sitting with a group of Indian cane cutters on a veranda overlooking a canal in Guyana. An alligator surfaced. One of the young men pantomimed shooting it, to be reproved by an older man on the grounds that the animal might well be the resting place of a human soul. Although blood sacrifice has always been part of Hinduism (and a part that came to the Caribbean with the Madrassee immigrants in Kali–Mai puja), it was justified by the belief that the soul of the victim went straight to heaven. But there is also an equally long tradition of opposition to blood sacrifice and of approval of the moral practice of vegetarianism. The emperor Ashoka, for instance, forbade the killing of many species of animals. And although the Jain doctrine of the avoidance of killing any animal life, however microscopic, was followed by only a small religious minority, the doctrine of *ahimsa* provided an ethical code for relations between humans and animals that has continued to shape actual behavior. The reverence for the cow (*gow-mata*) is perhaps the most obvious manifestation of this code, and it is one that came to the Caribbean. The *Vishnu Purana* from the Gupta period of around A.D. 300 states that "[Vishnu] is most pleased with him who does good to others . . . who neither beats nor slays any animate or inanimate thing . . ." (Wilson, *Vishnu,* 234).

Inevitably, after a century and a half in the Caribbean, some of the wholeness of that tradition has been lost, its richness diminished—as Brinsley Samaroo argues in the essay that precedes this one—but much has survived of this world view in the consciousness of Indo-Caribbean people. Although the system of indentured labor that brought Indians to the Caribbean involved a harshness of regimented labor and quasi-servile relations (Indians described themselves as *bung* [bound] coolies), making indenture analogous to slavery, there was always one fundamental difference. Indenture was always a finite stage in the Indians' passage through the plantation (a maximum five-year term), and although generations were trapped in a cycle of backbreaking labor and rural poverty, there was—right from the point at which substantial Indian communities were present in Trinidad and Guyana—the opportunity for Indians to re-create their physical world, particularly their village communities, in ways and on a scale that Africans were never able to do. Kingsley, who is equally sympathetic, if paternalistic, to both Afro-Caribbean and Indo-Caribbean life, makes an observation in his *At Last: A Christmas in the West Indies* that touches on this difference of experience and its apparent consequences in the two groups' attitudes toward animal life. He notes the Indian fondness for "dumb animals" as an excellent sign that their "morale is not destroyed at the root . . . A Coolie cow or donkey is petted, led about tenderly, tempted with tit-bits. Pet animals, where they can be got, are the Coolies' delight, as they are the delight of the wild Indian [read: Amerindian]. I wish I could say the same of the Negro. His treatment of his children and of his beasts of burden is, but too often, as exactly opposed to that of the Coolie as are his manners" (Kingsley, *Christmas*, 124).

Nevertheless, the experience of being uprooted from India, the experience of the plantation and of settlement in culturally heterogeneous societies, could not leave the Hindu world view untouched. There are thus a number of stories and episodes in novels where the Indian-Hindu attitude toward animals is juxtaposed in comic or tragicomic ways with the heterogeneous Creole world that surrounds it. The way in which the New World environment subverts meanings is explored in V. S. Naipaul's *The Mimic Men,* a complex and rich work that touches in two ways on the theme of this essay. There is a point in the novel where the narrator's father abandons his conversion to Christianity and becomes Gurudeva, the leader of a millenarian political-religious protest movement. The news reaches the narrator that a famous racehorse has been found slain in a ritualistic way. He recognizes the pattern of the ancient Aryan horse sacrifice of Asvamedha—"a thing of beauty, speaking of the youth of the world, of untrodden forests and unsullied streams" (V. S. Naipaul, *Mimic,* 140)—but for Gurudeva's followers, the sacrifice has quite a different meaning: an act of colonial rebellion, a punishment of the former slave owners, the wealthy French Creole family who own the horse and have named it provocatively after the leader of an unsuccessful slave revolt. The narrator cannot decide what his father's motive has been: political revenge or "an attempt at the awesome sacrifice, the challenge of Nemesis, performed by a shipwrecked man on a desert island" (*Mimic,* 142). Whatever the motive, the narrator feels that the beauty of sacrifice has been sullied by its association with the old island struggle between master and slave. As in Roach's "Haitian Trilogy," however, there has been a transference; meaning has been altered (*Poems,* 90–93).

In the image of shipwreck in *The Mimic Men,* V. S. Naipaul explores a deep sense of alienation from the Caribbean landscape. His Indian narrator, K. K. Singh, begins to see himself as an intruder in a world that is already possessed by the conflicting visions of former slave owner and former slave. The French Creole Deschampneuf family see the slave-made landscapes of Isabella through an idealizing, softening, pastoral myth, whereas the island is a nightmarish vision, "a garden of hell," for his friend Browne. For Browne, there is no Edenic tropical paradise, but a landscape "as manufactured" by the patterns of slave sugar cultivation as any artificial European park (*Mimic,* 147).

Singh's vision of a world made by the plantation is secondhand, but in Ladoo's novel *No Pain Like This Body* and in Arnold Itwaru's *Shanti,* there is an even more direct sense of alienation from the world created by the plantation. In both works, this sense of estrangement is powerfully conveyed not least by an inversion of the Hindu sense of oneness with the animal world. And in both, animals as part of the alien environment are experienced as unremittingly hostile or unpleasant. In *No Pain Like This Body,* for the abandoned Hindu villagers of Tola Trace the natural world and animal life are both literally a source of their misery and also the source of the metaphors they use to describe their experience of human and cosmic malevolence. Snakes and scorpions are natural enemies. Pa, the sadistic persecutor of his wife and children, is like a snake "watching with poison in his eyes" and "smarter than a snake" when he starts pelting the snake holes in the rice bed to make his son Balraj come out of the water so that he can beat him (Ladoo, *Pain,* 16, 18). When lightning falls on Tola Trace, it falls like snakes. Scorpions, too, are both the literal and figurative sting in the tail of Ladoo's claustrophobic world of suffering. Thus, when one of the children, sick with fever, is put inside the rice box as the only dry place in the hut, he is stung by the scorpion and dies from the effects. Like the lightning, scorpions are described as "fire stingers" (*Pain,* 47). When the rains come, the family is overwhelmed by the stinging, biting insect life that comes out of the walls of their hut.

When the characters in *No Pain Like This Body* try to make sense of their lives, they make comparisons between themselves and animals that are low in the chain of being. In part, Ladoo portrays what he sees as the self-contempt of a low-caste community, when for instance the comparison is made between the *crapaud* fish (tadpoles) the children are toying with and the way the sky god toys with their lives. Pa eats "like a pig," and it is the villagers' reproach to their venal pundit that "he is a modderass chamar. . . . He fadder used to mind pigs in Jangli Tola" (*Pain,* 98). One of the children sings to his mother: "you ugly like a rat, rat, rat." When the child dies, the pundit gives Pa the comfort of the farmyard: "You just have to ride you wife and make anodder chile" (*Pain,* 72).

Ladoo's point is not merely about the miseries of the low-caste people but also about what he saw—and I think it relevant to mention that Ladoo came from a Christian Indian family—as the almost complete severance of Indians from any sense of living ancestral identity in the New World. There is one brief moment of grace during the child's funeral when the villagers are brought together by compassion to a sense of connection with the natural world: "There was life in the wind as it left the corners of the sky and swept the face of the earth . . . there was love in the night birds that made strange noises beyond the river; there was love in the people as their hearts reached up to the sky and their souls mixed with the void" (*Pain,* 95).

Such a moment emphasizes how great has been the loss, but it also points to the fact that the tendency toward closure in Ladoo's work is never quite complete. If the confused story that one of the children tells after a brother's death is full of the now-familiar images of snakes and scorpions, of birds that are not really birds but jumbies (zombis), pariah dogs that are not really dogs but evil spirits (or, at another point, *lagahu*), this metamorphosis points outward in several contradictory ways. There is here a refinement of the profound sense of alienation, of course, but Ladoo also shows the beginning of an acculturation process as these Indian children show how they are absorbing creole folklore (already in 1905, the period in which the novel is set). He further shows powerful residues of the ancestral vision of connection between the human and natural world. What we have then is not so much the emptiness of absence as the pain of the inversion of the kinds of pieties that I have suggested were part of the Hindu world view that was transported to the Caribbean. Ladoo thus attests to their continuing power.

In Itwaru's *Shanti,* the sugar-estate workers are similarly portrayed as people who "did not know India," who are wholly cut off from a real sense of ancestral continuity. Like Ladoo's, Itwaru's background is Christian Indian; and although Christianity in the novel is associated with a destructive colonial arrogance, one detects in the very bleak vision of cultural impoverishment the legacy of Itwaru's own separation from Hinduism. As well as being a deracinated people, Itwaru's characters are trapped within a plantation life where, in the view of Booker the overseer, the women, for instance, are "little more than self-conscious beasts" in "the practised certainty" of the rhythms of labor. "Animals, Booker surmised, vigorous, fuckable female animals at his disposal and pleasure" (Itwaru, *Shanti,* 18).

Human life on the plantation is portrayed as a constant round of brutal conflict, as individuals are forced to fight for survival: overseer against worker, drunken worker against worker, man against woman, flogging and whipping parents against child, man against animal (Tillak becomes a castrator of bulls, an activity he delights in as it eases his own impotent rage). Animal life, too, is involved in the same tense, snapping hostility: braying donkeys, barking dogs, crowing cocks constantly disturb. When, as they frequently do, people insult one another, it is in terms of animals: "Coolie-dawgs," jackasses. Animal life becomes part of an unremittingly hostile world, constantly preying on the girl Shanti's sense of vulnerability and exposure. When she took a bath: "she was relieved there were no crapauds this morning, none of those huge menacing toads which had never harmed her but which she was afraid of nonetheless, those ugly jumping creatures in the slime-black urine-stink muddy drain at the side of the cubicle" (*Shanti,* 41). Even outside the squalor of the plantation, there is only the "unknowing bush of snakes, thorns, poisonous flowers, poisonous fruit" (*Shanti,* 79).

Human activity is seen as part of this animal hostility. When Shanti witnesses the Christian Indian schoolmaster's self-righteous brutality, she sees the mask of an animal: "like an alligator, he would suddenly and furiously attack" (*Shanti,* 67). When the schoolmaster's wife accuses Shanti of letting her husband look at Shanti with lust, she becomes a carrion crow in Shanti's eyes: "The crow swelled its wings in Eve's sudden stagger backwards, her arms fanning the air for support. 'SHAAAN-TI!' she cawed in alarm . . . " (*Shanti,* 70–71).

Both Shanti and her boyfriend, Latchman, see Reid, the Indian-hating Afro-Guyanese policeman, in terms of his being a caiman, an image that mixes with Latchman's dreams of animal hostility: "In his dreams the massive door of the sky of night would swing thunderously shut, leaving him outside in the crepuscular eye of the primordial reptile, the gruesome caymans' vigilant hiss and growl as they crawled out of their riverbank places into the sleeping village of the world to devour him. . . . Like the cayman, Reid was huge and menacing. . . . His was a reptilian rage which pounced when one least expected" (*Shanti,* 72–73).

Where echoes of a positive Hindu animal imagery survive in the novel, they have been subverted by negative Christian symbols. The schoolmaster is shamed by his lust for Shanti, and the "penile snake of his erection" is not the frank Hindu image of fertility, but the Christian symbol of evil, as is the green slithering snake that appears in the tree when Shanti tells Latchman of her pregnancy (*Shanti,* 88). This same shift of image occurs more obliquely in Shiva Naipaul's *A Hot Coun-*

try, where Dina Mallingham's father has metamorphosed from Hindu *Mahalingam* (great penis) into buttoned-up, sexually repressed Christian Indian schoolmaster Mr. Mallingham. Throughout the novel, Dina's attempts to escape from the repressions of her childhood are constantly impeded by her learned fears that the natural is the source of a disordered and barbarous luxuriance in which people revert to becoming "unreflecting creatures of appetite" (S. Naipaul, *Hot,* 149).

Ladoo's, Itwaru's, and Shiva Naipaul's novels speak of powerful and unresolved wounds. At best, there is survival and resistance, but little to be salvaged from any of the cultural elements (particularly Hinduism), which exist only in damaged and oppressive forms. Although Cyril Dabydeen's work, too, has a deep sense of colonial oppression and its estranging effects, what I find particularly refreshing in his poetry and his novels *The Wizard Swami* and *Dark Swirl* is his willingness to enter into a more free-flowing and complex logic of possibility. Dabydeen begins from a position of comfortable if often ironic ease with the Hindu tradition, and rather than seeing its uprootedness from India and its contact with other cultures as the source of inevitable decay and pollution, he sees the possibility of an enriching process of interculturation. It is at this point that some brief reference to the influence of Wilson Harris is in order.

In recent years, Harris has spoken explicitly on ecological issues, but it is almost an incidental element in his earlier novels that I want to take up here, because it is this element that I believe has been most influential in the work of Cyril Dabydeen and Anthony Kellman. I refer not only to Harris's espousal of the nonnaturalistic tradition in the novel but also to the way in which he has used Amerindian myth and belief structure. In *The Palace of the Peacock,* as the voyage upstream begins to fall apart and members of the crew meet their sudden death, da Silva's old certainties begin to crumble and his consciousness becomes open to his subconscious. What enters his subconscious, it seems, is a folk memory that takes an Amerindian form. Da Silva is arguing with Cameron, the rational man, that he recognizes one of the flocks of parrots flying overhead:

> "Don't pick at me," da Silva said. "The impossible start happen I tell you. Water start dream, rock and stone start dream, tree trunk and tree root dreaming, bird and beast dreaming . . ."
>
> You is a menagerie and a jungle of a fool," Cameron's black tongue laughed and twisted.

> Everything Ah tell you dreaming long before the creation I know of begin. Everything turning different, changing into everything else Ah tell you." (Harris, *Peacock,* 110–11)

Cameron continues to mock da Silva, finally in exasperation flinging a stone and wounding a bird. Da Silva is beside himself with distress: "O Christ, shut up," said Cameron. "I didn't pelt you . . . You is bewitched . . . that's what . . ." Da Silva muttered wildly—"I tell you when you pelt she you pelt me. Is one flesh, me flesh, you flesh, one flesh. She come to save me, to save all of we. You murderer! What else is you but a vile murderer? . ." (*Peacock,* 115). In his rage, da Silva stabs and kills Cameron. The episode is not specifically ecological in its significance, but in the way Harris suggests a subconscious faculty that has access to primordial ways of imagining the world and in the way he frequently works extended animal metaphors as analogies for states of human consciousness into his earlier novels—Christo, who disguises himself as a tiger in *The Whole Armour,* or Mohammed, who is freqently identified with a bull in *The Far Journey of Oudin*—he provides a creative encouragement to the kind of direction we see in the novels of Dabydeen and Kellman.

Cyril Dabydeen's *The Wizard Swami* is a transitional work in the sense that it grows out of the kind of comic realism used by V. S. Naipaul in *The Mystic Masseur,* which is based on the premise that those Caribbean Hindus who pretend that they are still in India are suffering from a delusional form of madness. Devan, the wizard swami from the village backwoods, is just such a figure; but it is what Dabydeen does with Hindu animal symbolism in the novel that I wish to discuss. Through a series of comic mischances, Devan finds himself as the ignorant but enthusiastic trainer of a racehorse called Destiny. Apart from the ironic play on the motifs of karma and providence in the novel, the horse is also the nexus of all the contradictory forces of an ethnically plural and secular society that constantly undermine Devan's simple-minded Hindu revivalism. Thus, although Devan sees the horse as the flag bearer of Hindu hopes, a simultaneously new and very old symbol for a revivalist Hinduism, the Aryan horse ("fast . . . agile, pistons in the hooves") replacing the placid cow, for others Destiny is a Guyanese symbol because it is "bred from the lush grass of the mother soil in the country of many waters, sugarcane, rice, bauxite" (*Swami,* 135) and is in competition with a horse from Trinidad. The horse also becomes an unintended sacrifice (ironic Asvamedha) to Devan's and his patron's clumsy confusion between two orders of agency, the secular and the magical. (The patron lets Devan think that his faith is healing the animal's lameness, whereas in reality he is using the services of a very unscrupulous druggist.)

Thus far, the novel makes much the same points as V. S. Naipaul's *The Mimic Men,* although without Naipaul's dread that the tradition is at a dead end. But Dabydeen takes the image further, and in going back to its original Vedic poetic core, he frees it from culturally restrictive readings and restores to it its universal, cosmic force as the image of a free-wandering nature. Evoking the images of the *Rig Veda* and the *Brhadranyaha Upanishad* and Sylvia Plath's poem "Ariel," Dabydeen presents Destiny as a free, creative force whose meaning is open to all: "galloping into a mirage-like stasis and eating up the dirt at the same time, pulling the ground away from under its feet . . . Now, at any moment, this horse could take off from the ground, a flying pegasus. Hindus bawled out as the rhapsody of this image gripped their imagination, tormented them" (*Swami,* 135). It is significant that, during the race, Destiny throws his jockey: "Wild, wild, de haas gone wild," the crowd shouts, and Devan senses the revolt as something occurring in his own mind "as if the horse, in the frenzy of his mind, was running across the entire country" . . . (*Swami,* 140). Devan's certainties are shaken and the future he must look for is one without sectarian restriction.

If in *The Wizard Swami* Dabydeen brings Hindu animal symbolism into the mainstream of the Caribbean novel, in *Dark Swirl* he very explicitly confronts animal-human relations at manifold levels: actual, epistemological, and mythical. The narrative is organized around the arrival of a European naturalist in a rural Indo-Guyanese village in the remote Canje region of Guyana. He is a collector of specimens, bookish, concerned with mapping out abstract theories and testing them empirically; he is also a superior and arrogant man who is amused and sometimes horrified by the superstitions of the villagers. Yet he senses something "mystical" in their attitudes that interests him.

The novel is not, however, simply a poetic fable about the conflict between the positivistic values of an ordering, classifying science and a fluid, magico-religious culture with its intimations of natural correspondences, of the oneness of all things. That might well have been the ancestral world view of the villagers, but the years of separation from India, the trauma of the plantation, and the exposure to European colonialism has made their attitudes more confused, fragmented, and contradictory. On the one hand, although they live close to the natural world, they have neither any curiosity about it nor any philosophy of their place in it. They constantly mock the stranger for his interest in the specimens he collects. But they also have deeper responses that emerge in their dreams and nighttime fears. In the darkness, the villagers come face-to-face with their sense of estrangement from the landscape, this "hostile place": "They could hear in the wind echoes of an ancestral past of indigenous men and women fleeing into the bushes; of sugar plantation owners, white-white, who buried slaves alive under silk-cotton trees . . ." (C. Dabydeen, *Swirl,* 24). The fear of this hostile place is manifested in particular in the villagers' fears of what may lie in the creek at the center of the village, fears that they symbolize in the protean animal-human figure of the legendary *massacouraman* (with its roots in Amerindian myth) and in the revenge they exact on the harmless alligators they occasionally catch, substitutes for this object of their fears. The stranger has been puzzled and revolted by his witnessing the ritual burning of the reptile and the chant of the village youths: "Massacouraman . . . Massacouraman" (*Swirl,* 38). But alongside these fears are other, more comfortable images of connection that surface in dreams: "Nearly everyone, at one time or another, had imagined strange reptiles crawling out of the creek at nights and inhabiting the space under their beds, or even crawling into the beds and lying next to them" (*Swirl,* 8).

These contradictory feelings are brought to a head by the presence of the stranger and the relationship between him and Josh, a boy whose sensitivity marks him as different from the other village children. Josh is obsessed by the creek and has an especially acute imagining of the creature that all suspect lives in its depths. He refuses to swim in the creek because he fears that the creature will pull him down into the mire and mud. But Josh also senses that the creek is a source of life, and he feels angry that the collector might pick out all the animal life in it "until nothing was left in it save for the old cans, shoes and bottles that the villagers threw into it" (*Swirl,* 14). This kind of feeling is seen dismissively as part of Josh's eccentricity.

However, when the boy falls ill after "seeing" the creature, both the villagers and the stranger begin to take him more seriously, although both are ambivalent in their responses. The stranger is both dismissive and curious, but as he begins to feel that there might be something there, he has visions of capturing it and taking it back to a zoo in Europe or the United States and making his reputation. The villagers are split between feeling that it is the stranger's presence that is responsible for the leviathan's activity and hoping that he may become their savior by freeing them from its curse. But when the stranger lets it be heard that he wants to carry the creature away, he sets off an instinctive resistance. Josh's father, Ghulam, for instance, begins to believe that the stranger is threatening to take away something that is theirs, that the "commotion" in the creek is "inside his own bloodstream . . . hot, burning" (*Swirl,* 40). He feels that while the creek contains some terrifying natural force, it is also their source of life. Another villager laments: "De creek give life to we—de creek can't dead" (*Swirl,* 49). Still others feel the same, although the dominant group wants to fill up the creek so that both creature and stranger will go away.

The majority of villagers, as well as the stranger, want to control and dam up the energy the creature stands for. Yet both sense something beyond them. Josh's father in particular is forced into reflecting on the connections between his responses to the stranger and the possibility of the *massacouraman's* existence and his own tenuous sense of identity as a Hindu cut off from his roots. Like the other villagers, Josh's father is perplexed by what the stranger finds so interesting about the local wildlife, but he decides to wander out at night, as the stranger does, in the hope that through imitation he might find some clue. In the darkness, he feels uneasy, watched, but presses on: "willing himself to be at one with everything, as if his spirit could be with the insects, reptiles, animals and plants . . . It was then he felt himself to be most truly Hindu and yet something else. . . . Whatever they had been, he sensed they were becoming something else" (*Swirl,* 39). Before long, Ghulam is locked in the same obsessions as his son, brooding at home: "His mind festered with thoughts which seemed both alien to and rooted in his spirit" (*Swirl,* 69). Dabydeen very explicitly connects the question of identity with that of ecological belonging:

> There was no getting away from thinking about the massacouraman, how he embraced it and feared it and simultaneously denied it because he felt it wasn't truly part of himself or the villagers. Was it because they were a transplanted people? Yet he also sensed that they had begun to see themselves less and less in this light on the Guyana coastland, that somehow the landscape was changing with them, that the

> birds, insects and other animals were also going through a slow transformation. Was the whiteman trying to stop that? (*Swirl,* 69)

He is not, for the stranger goes through his own crisis of identity, shedding the rigidity of his scientific rationalism and opening his mind to the sense of correspondences he finds latent in the villagers' way of seeing. But long before the stranger's breakdown, far from setting out the stranger's and the villagers' world views in simple oppositional terms, Dabydeen suggests that it is the stranger's presence that actually leads the villagers to a deeper awareness of their world. Encouraged by the example of Harris, Dabydeen's work, although retaining a strong sense of its Indo-Caribbean roots, has moved into a rich territory where all the region's cultures have become its province.

Kellman's work perhaps does not have a similarly strong sense of Africanism, but it too searches the rubble of ancestral cultures for creative ways forward from colonial mimicry. In *The Coral Rooms,* we are introduced to Percival Vere, a career civil servant in the very man-made environment of the multistoried Federal Bank of Charouga. Rendered psychically vulnerable by fatigue from overwork, Percy's conscience has begun to trouble him. There is Burrowes, the alcoholic and deranged former competitor for Percy's position at the bank, whom Percy had successfully set up for blackmail and sexual disgrace. But operating at a deeper level of dreaming consciousness is Percy's memory of his boyhood exploration of the island's limestone caves and the way he and his friends had treated the cave's bats:

> Out of sheer boredom, he recalled, they would corner frightened bats, knock them to the ground with the short sticks they carried and then, *in the truest spirit of democracy,* elect one of them to unplug his bottle-lamp, bathe the helpless creature with kerosene, and set fire to it. . . . He had been faithful on the day his turn came *to carry out the ritual.* After replugging and relighting the lamp, he lowered the tongue of yellow flame and, with great deliberation, painted the bat's breast with it. The soot spiralled up into their blackening nostrils. The bat writhed like a demon on the fetid floor, scarfed with fire and shrieking in the most terrible way. The fire came leaping from its eyes and the acrid smoke from the burning flesh made the boys tug at their noses. They could hear the other bats flapping with what seemed like concern. (Kellman, *Coral,* 22–23 [emphasis mine])

The resemblance of this passage to Cyril Dabydeen's description of the massacre of alligators in *Dark Swirl* is significant (and I know that Kellman had not read *Dark Swirl* at the point of writing *The Coral Rooms*). There is the same emphasis on the ritualistic properties of the action, the same use of fire, and the half-repressed perception that the slaughtered creatures have some affective sensibility. In addition, *The Coral Rooms* consciously locates the action as part of a postcolonial failure of political choice. As in *Dark Swirl,* the action signifies a deeply rooted failure of human sensibility. In Kellman's novel, the failure is less explicitly signified as occurring in human relations to animals, but is meant more as a psychic blockage to the recognition of the animal-natural in humanity.

We are shown glimpses of this incipient spirit in Percy when he is gamboling playfully on a beach with Materia, his wife-to-be, soon after he has met her. Playing freely in the water, he is like a sea snake, but it is not long before his and Materia's marriage becomes a matter of self-protective routine. The spirit is there in quiescent form in Percy's mother who, after being widowed, had plunged even further into the care of her garden, who is first seen in the novel feeding guinea grass to the little black-bellied sheep, the pets she keeps, each called Lammie, although each is dispatched to a butcher when it ceases to be lamblike. Mrs. Vere, however, is sufficiently in touch with the spirit of connection—I think the reference to guinea grass is intended to connect her animal husbandry to something African and repressed—to be the only person to have some glimmer of understanding about why Percy has to throw up his job and go on his quest to rediscover the caves of his boyhood. The spirit is there in repressed form in Percy himself just before he sets out, during his last visit to his mother. He confronts Bassie, his mother's servant, with whom he has been having a casual, exploitative affair. This time, he sees her truly for herself, experiences a real urge for connection with her; she is frightened by what she senses in him—"his tigerish presence"—and on the point of his starting to "leave his own body to inhabit hers," she lets out a cry "which *butchered* the beginnings of the newest and purest relationship they could have imagined possible" (*Coral,* 61 [emphasis added]). Past misdeeds are not so easily overcome, and Percy's feeling that he is still at this stage a dead man prevents any further move to real understanding.

The historical dimensions of Percy's sickness become clearer as he embarks on his journey to rediscover the caves. At his first stop at an old plantation, "There was a whisper of wind that seemed to carry voices from centuries gone, voices suppressed and urgent" (*Coral,* 68), but he is rudely ejected from the property by the owner, a crusty, irascible white man. Just before this, Percy's jeep has gone off the road when, in a distracted reverie, he "beheld four white lions, mouths agape, leaping towards the jeep" (*Coral,* 67). When he recovers from his alarm, he sees that the lions are part of the statuary of the old plantation house, a double image of the continuing power of the old imperial consciousness in the making of Percy's life and, perhaps, in their whiteness and ultimate fixity as statues, an image of African loss.

Percy's quest begins in earnest when he meets Cane Arrow, an old African man who leads a maroon existence in the mouth of the cave. Cane Arrow is a "natural man" in touch with the vegetable and animal environment but also a man like Percy in flight from the world and from himself, though more sharply conscious than Percy of the damage inflicted on him by the continuing slavery of work on the plantations, a present and a past that Percy keeps well away from his consciousness. In a novel with a rich vein of comedy, Percy's first meeting with Cane Arrow begins when he sits down in a dimly lit gully on what he thinks is the root of a silk-cotton tree: "It heaved with a vengeful startled howl, capsizing him in an instant. . . . The root was staring at him now with piercing eyes set in a dark wrinkled face. . . . The old fellow stood there clinging to the soil, sculptured root in brown pants and faded cream shirt, elephantine skin scabrous, reef-like" (*Coral,* 71).

As a natural man, Cane Arrow becomes Percy's chief bottle-lamp and guide to the caves although, as in all quests in mythology, Percy's journey into the depths of the caves, into history, and into himself, must be made on his own. Despite the fact that he has equipped himself methodically with all the technology he might need for his adventure, when Percy makes his dive he does so purely within his own physical capacities. Deep inside the cave, Percy experiences a vision of an Edenic Amerindian settlement, a world in perfect harmony with itself and with nature, but as he watches, he sees that one of the women wears a gold crucifix and he reflects: "Even here in this Eden, cultural confusion, assimilations of greed, pollution of the dialect" (*Coral,* 83). When he looks again, "trying to recover the pastoral purity of his first vision[, a]ll he saw was a tableau from a museum, the stone axe suspended in mid-fall" (*Coral,* 83). History cannot be undone and when he looks and listens again, he hears or sees that it is the woman who is mocking the false pastoral vision, as she metamorphoses through the races in his gaze: "She was Amerindian, she was African, she was brown-skinned Materia, and as he listened more carefully to her, he heard not mockery but joyous laughter ringing out worlds of possibilities, coalescing visions and revisions of races and their juxtapositions. Creole magic" (*Coral,* 83).

There is no going back. There is, perhaps, in the Caribbean no recovery of the ancestral worlds of animal-human connectivity. But what Percy goes through is an absorption of the elements of that past into the potentialities of the present. He can discover "an intensified compassion for the Amerindian and the slave" (*Coral,* 88) and all that they have lost. In that act of compassion, of seeing more clearly, he forces himself "to see, to hold and be held by, an inescapable self, true as sunlight, pure as cave springs" (*Coral,* 88). The nature of this self is imaged almost wholly in animal terms. He is "moulting a restrictive skin," he is "growing new antennae of sensitivity" (*Coral,* 88). Like the Amerindian shaman, like the stranger in *Dark Swirl,* he expresses this sense of animal connection by vomiting without control. What Percy vomits is the "waste his soul's island had accumulated" (*Coral,* 89). His "sacrificial body" becomes the duct releasing: "all the fat black-bellied heads of corporations, political animals, newspaper publishers, lawyers, all scrambling for a piece of earth to plant a flag in the name of the king of the I" (*Coral,* 89).

I note the ironical use of animal references to those who have set out to continue the plantation drive for "man's" conquest over nature and the dangers of the arrogant humanocentric cult of the "king of the I." Percy must return to Materia and to contemporary life, but we guess that he will go with an awakened creole consciousness in which an ancestral sense of natural connections will have a freer, more compassionate play.

REFERENCES

Benjamin, Joel. Preface to *Focus on Amerindians,* ed. Walter F. Edwards. Amerindian Languages Project. Georgetown: University of Guyana, 1980.

Brathwaite, Edward [Kamau]. *Masks.* London: New York: Oxford, 1968.

———. *Sappho Sakyi's Meditations.* Mona, [Jamaica]: *Savacou* 16, 1989.

Craig, Christine. "Crow Poems." In *Quadrille for Tigers.* Sebastapol, Calif.: Mina Press, 1984.

Dabydeen, Cyril. *Dark Swirl.* Leeds: Peepal Tree Press, 1989.

———. *The Wizard Swami.* Leeds: Peepal Tree Press, 1989.

Dabydeen, David. "Christmas in the Caribbean." In *Coolie Odyssey.* London: Hansib, 1988.

Edwards, Walter F. *Focus on Amerindians.* Amerindian Languages Project. Georgetown: University of Guyana, 1980.

Forsythe, Dennis. "West Indian Culture Through Rasta Eyes." Chap. 8 in *Rastafari: For the Healing of the Nation.* Kingston, Jamaica: Zaika, 1983.

Harris, Wilson. *The Far Journey of Oudin.* London: Faber and Faber, 1961.

———. *The Palace of the Peacock.* London: Faber and Faber, 1977 [1960].

———. *The Whole Armour and The Secret Ladder.* London: Faber and Faber, 1973 [1962].

Hearne, John. *Land of the Living.* New York: Harper, 1962.

Itwaru, Arnold. *Shanti.* Leeds: Peepal Tree Press, 1988.

Jordan, Phyllis. "Amerindian Customs After Birth." In *Focus on Amerindians,* ed. Walter F. Edwards. Amerindian Languages Project. Georgetown: University of Guyana, 1980.

Kellman, Anthony. *The Coral Rooms.* Leeds: Peepal Tree Press, 1993.

Kingsley, Charles. *At Last: A Christmas in the West Indies.* London: Macmillan, 1885 [1871].

Ladoo, Harold Sonny. *No Pain Like This Body.* Toronto: Anansi, 1972.

McAndrew, W.[ordsworth] A. *Selected Poems.* N.p.: N.p., 1900? (A self-published chapbook, unpaginated, probably printed in then-British Guiana.)

Naipaul, Shiva. *A Hot Country.* London: Hamilton, 1983.

Naipaul, V. S. *The Mimic Men.* New York: Vintage, 1985 (1967).

Nugent, Lady Maria. *Lady Nugent's Journal.* London: Institute of Jamaica, 1939 [1839].

Roach, E.[ric] M. *The Flowering Rock: Collected Poems, 1938–1974.* Leeds: Peepal Tree Press, 1992.

Salkey, Andrew. *Anancy's Score.* London: Bogle L'Ouverture, 1973.

Seymour, A. J. *Selected Poems.* N.p.: B.[ritish] G.[uiana] Lithographic Co. Ltd., 1965.

Thurn, Everard F. im. *Among the Indians of Guiana.* London: Kegan Paul, 1883.

Walcott, Derek. *The Castaway and Other Poems.* New York: Farrar, Straus & Giroux, 1965.

Wilson, H. H., trans. and ed. *The Vishnu Purana.* Calcutta: Punthi Pistak, 1979 [1840].

Kandioura Dramé

The Trickster as Triptych

When, in the 1930s, Francophone writers of colonial Africa and the French West Indies turned their attention to the immense wealth held in their oral traditions, they focused on the folktale. Although a great deal of collecting had been done by European travelers and ethnographers, the interest of such writers as Ousmane Socé, Birago Diop, Léon G. Damas, Bernard Dadié, Léopold Sedar Senghor, and Abdoulaye Sadji was in part rekindled by Claude McKay's novel *Banjo,* a landmark book for writers who would later be identified as the negritude generation.

In this novel, McKay was able to show that the folktale can be effectively used in the novel to convey a sense of identity. It functions as the path that his uprooted, exiled characters can take to go home. For the wanderers, the rediscovery of the folktales of their countries functions as a "homecoming." It is particularly significant that this process of homecoming has to be initiated by Ray, the character who has traveled farther from his homeland than anyone else in the novel. It becomes the self-imposed duty of this bright Jamaican student to bring together, in France, blacks from many parts of the world and to encourage them to "go home" by daring to "remember" the scattered parts of their cultural baggage. Faced with the profound skepticism of these tough uprooted sailors and dockers, these wanderers of the seas who grow roots in no soil, Ray discovers the miraculous power of performance. For a storytelling session is a performance, a dramatic incarnation, an embodiment of the mysteries of folktales. His own performance is soon followed by others, and they quickly turn the gathering into a collective homecoming away from home.

Undoubtedly, many of these writers were aware of the work done by ethnographers in collecting tales. But McKay's example held a special attraction for them primarily because it elevated the tales to the level of literature, a creative activity worthy of serious, adult attention; whereas many colonial observers continued to view folktales with suspicion, following in the footsteps of Golberry, who wrote in 1802: "Like children, the most mature black men apply a whole day's attention to futile activities, to conversations which to us would be nothing more than chatter. They spend entire days making up tales and stories. For the most absurd tales, the most unbelievable stories are the supreme delight and the greatest entertainment of these men who reach their old age without growing out of childhood" (in Dadié, "Conte," 70).[1]

Another factor that encouraged negritude writers to adopt the folktales was the thesis developed by Ray that all black cultures had a common matrix, a common heritage, and a common predicament. And so it was that this most Afrocentrist of all negritude views had already been outlined by McKay in 1929, in the heyday of the Harlem Renaissance. The result of the attraction that McKay's model exercised on young negritude writers was the unleashing of extraordinary creations. Some of these writers, like Diop, became closely associated with the writing of tales. In his case particularly, it has been a felicitous choice, one that has "secured for him an enduring place in the corpus of modern African literature" (Irele, "Tradition," 69). The focus of negritude on the thesis developed by Ray in *Banjo* liberated a great deal of creative energy among the young writers in the work of the transposition of tales from African and Caribbean oral traditions, but little or no effort went into comparative studies of these cultures. In many cases, it was enough to point out thematic and formal similarities between tales from different parts of the African diaspora in order to bolster the paradigm provided by Ray.

Parallel to this development was the concept of African cultural retentions or survivals in the New World advanced by a school of thought among Africanists in the social sciences. The works of M.

Herskovits, R. Bastide, W. Bascom, and R. D. Abrahams, among others, demonstrated with renewed methodological vigor the strength and feasibility of African cultural-retention studies in the areas of religion, art, music, and lifestyle in general. The success of this school of thought was in turn amplified by Présence Africaine (the publishing house and its journal), which published many of its writings on the subject. However, the limitations of such views were soon exposed by E. Franklin Frazier, who was eager to unveil the inadequacies of retention studies based essentially on generalizations that could as easily be made of many different cultures and failed, therefore, to isolate rigorously any cultural specificity. Frazier remarked, for example, that his study of a black American family reunion could not, with any scientific seriousness, be truly similar to a Pennsylvania Dutch family reunion (an observation he held to be true) and an African family reunion (as Herskovits noted in a review of Frazier's book *The Negro Family in the United States*) (Abrahams, *Man-of-Words,* 40–44).[2] Furthermore, given both the deliberate effort made by the plantation economies of America to work consciously toward the dismemberment of potential slave communities and the great ethnic diversity among the slave populations, the retention scholars were forced to face the difficulty of tracing cultural links directly to specific African ethnic groups.

The frustration that manifested itself in a temporary halt affecting retention studies as a result of this criticism forced comparatists like Abrahams to think of an alternative method that would take into account legitimate scientific arguments on both sides of this increasingly festering debate. In a brilliant essay on plantation cultures, Abrahams developed the theory of studies not of African retentions per se but of African continuities instead (*Man-of-Words,* 40–54). Continuities, he maintained, were more fruitful to the researcher than any efforts at establishing with certainty a putative direct and specific link between black cultural expressions in "the institutional systems of . . . Africa" and "the New World plantation" (*Man-of-Words,* 54).

The new element that makes Abrahams' approach a formidable one is that it takes into account the mutability of cultural traits and shows the vulnerability of studying cultural features as static. Leaving aside such binary oppositions as New World versus Old World, African cultures versus plantation cultures of America, Abrahams anchored his research in the realm of "expressive continuities" as manifested in the "patterns of performance of simplified models of social organization in the Old World" that furnished "the basic groundwork" in the creation of "an Afro-American creole culture" (*Man-of-Words,* 45, 54).

The negritude writers I mentioned in my preliminary statements focused attention, in their renderings of African tales, on the three most durable, most resilient, and most adaptable characters that have come out of Africa. They are Bouki, aka Uncle Bouqui, aka Hyena; Leuk, aka Compère Lapin, aka Brer Rabbit; and, last but not least, Ananse, aka Brer Anancy, aka Spider. These three characters are found in Africa, in Louisiana, and in the Caribbean. They were individually identified a century ago as transcontinental characters, but they may be more properly described as a triptych. The goal of this essay is a presentation of these characters in African oral literature studies and an interrogation of the defining traits of Uncle Bouqui, Brer Rabbit, and Brer Anancy in the Americas. For the moment, however, such a transcontinental/transcultural attempt at comparison can only be a meditation on possibilities. Only a team of full-time researchers from all the cultures and disciplines involved could effectively accomplish the task of providing definitive scientific propositions on such a broad subject. Such a team might include folklorists, anthropologists, historians, and literary critics. Even so, its effort would be limited if it did not include creative writers in its work. It seems to me that if Derek Walcott's rich and complex plays, *Dream on Monkey Mountain* and *Ti-Jean and His Brothers,* can be enjoyed by all those who love a good story, they can only be fully understood by those who are also able to read the Saint Lucian and Martinican folktales in the two plays. Conversely, one can enjoy "La geste de Ti-Jean" (The Saga of Ti-Jean), but reading the play opens the door to a larger understanding of the saga (Laurent and Césaire, *Contes,* 213–45). In a sense, creative writers often do more than use these tales as a cultural intertext. They also interpret them for the world.

I would like to start by discussing the remarkable work accomplished by a noted team of researchers comprising anthropologists, folklorists, and at least one literary scholar of the narratological persuasion who undertook in the 1970s a broad taxonomic and heuristic study of African tales under the aegis of the French research center C.N.R.S (National Committee for Scientific Research) (Bremond et al., *Recherches,* passim). The original goal of the project was the creation of a simple, rational, and practical system whereby a complete index of African tales could be drawn. Carrying out such a project based on a limited set of Dogon folktales collected by Denise Paulme and Geneviève Calame-Griaule seemed at first ideal in view of the apparent or presumed homogeneity of the data. However, organizing the folktales in question into a thematic grid proper to the Dogon revealed itself to be arbitrary and myopic. The interferences of similar folktales from the region excluded all hope of exclusivity. It became necessary to develop the project into a comparative perspective that included similar data from other ethnic groups of West Africa. Redefined in this way, the project became a three-pronged task of establishing an index (no longer specified as Dogon), "an analysis of the relationship between culture and literature through a corpus of homogeneous [Dogon] tales" (Seydou, "Analyse," 6), and a multiethnic comparative study of themes. It also became necessary, in light of the new project, to include within the data texts in translation. The scholars brushed aside the obvious dangers involved in such a decision. The enlarged and redefined project drew on a great number of folktales translated from a variety of ethnic groups and languages. Many of the texts were only available in French translation, while others had to be retranslated from English into French. Heterogeneity was favored over homogeneity in the name of comparative imperatives.

Comparative ambitions in the domain of folktales can lead to embarrassing analytic dead ends. For one thing, the immense task involved in a systematizing analysis of a forest of intermingled texts, themes, and forms from distinct cultural areas can lead to intellectual paralysis. A universalizing, globalizing urge aided by the intellectual paralysis thus provoked may lead to little more than a compilation of thematic similarities across cultures with little or no insight into the individual cultures themselves. It is difficult to draw from such an index alone any genealogies of structures and motifs. At most, a paradigm based on a system of similarities provides a starting point for further research. The next step should be an analysis of the differences that exist between the tales that constitute an apparently homogeneous set before any cross-cultural comparisons are made. As Christiane Seydou put it: "As is the case in linguistics, the differences prove to be the pertinent factors and the similarities should encourage the search for these differences rather than the artificial and obviously dangerous construction of a common system of signification" (Seydou, "Introduction," 7).

But to provide a complete synthesis of cultural signs and to decode these signs, one needs a complete set of tales from each culture with precise references with regard to the linguistic and social context. The difficulty of the task is, once again, monumental. Should all attempts at such precise comparative studies be abandoned? Without going this far, it is clear that the individual scholar may be more effective by turning his or her attention toward the study of individual texts. After all, each tale being, in itself, an orderly form of syntax that is organized according to the internal logic of its own purpose and semantic imperatives, it can be viewed from a number of useful methodological perspectives. These can be structuralist or semiological, symbolic or discursive. The goal is to arrive at a heuristic method of unveiling epistemes. In other words, the formal analysis of tales combined with the study of the cultural context can reveal multiple semantic processes at any given time.

Despite the difficulties reviewed by Seydou and summarized above, the research of the C.N.R.S. team has successfully tackled a number of interesting problems in the analysis of African folktales. The collaboration of Calame-Griaule and V. Görög-Karady on the treatment of the theme of magical objects in West African tales compares these with European tales of similar theme as analyzed by G. Dumézil in *Mythe et épopée*. The result shows that if the tales in question bear striking resemblances at the structural level, their popularity in West Africa can only be explained by specific West African cultural exigencies. For example, whereas the European versions insist on the individual nature of the adventure, the African tales emphasize the consequences of actions taken by the characters with respect to collective interests. Social discipline appears to be favored over the quest for individual pleasure, these two moral positions being represented by a positive and a negative character (or a moral and an immoral act) in the tales. The representation of this moral conflict is understoood as a permanent feature of the human condition and explains its permanent inclusion in all initiatory tales. Finally, whereas Dumézil identified three hierarchical ideological functions that determine Indo-European social order—magical power and law, physical force, and productive fertility—the African tales redistribute all three functions in binary oppositions and, in so doing, reflect a fundamental thought system based on dualism, rather than trinity: male-female, good-bad, and so forth.

Paulme's typology of the African trickster reviews a sample of West African tales in which Hare, Tortoise, Spider, Jackal, and so on are featured (Paulme, "Typologie," 569–600). The tale motifs arrived at are then classified "according to the opposition and alternance of amelioration (A+, A-) and deterioration (D+, D-) in the position and/or status of the characters, as viewed from the trickster's perspective" ("Typologie," 600). Paulme's analysis distinguishes the African trickster from the Amerindian trickster. For whereas the latter "is generally a chief or ancestor whose adventures take place in the mythical past, the former is rather an astute weakling whose . . . tricks are set in everyday life and social context" ("Typologie," 600). If the flamboyant trickster appears indispensable to African tales, his tricks are not always successful; sometimes they backfire. The failure of the trickster is always linked to an action on his part that is considered excessive. When his goal, while affording him an advantageous position, does not seriously endanger social order, he is approved, even admired by the audience. When he becomes an agent of disorder and conflict or the embodiment of selfishness, he is punished and humiliated. These are, in fact, the rare situations where Hare is defeated, outsmarted by the disastrously stupid Hyena.

Paulme's essay sheds light on the important fact of the individuality, the distinctiveness, of the tricksters. In the final analysis, there is no such a thing as "the African trickster." The plurality of tricksters is too often neglected in studies on animal figures in African folktales. In reality, Hare has little in common with Spider, and whatever they may have in common does not make them interchangeable figures in the tales.

Contrary to his colleagues, Claude Bremond deliberately set his analysis at the level of form alone without regard to the contents of the tales. In establishing his "Principles for an Index of the Ruses," Bremond takes a random sample of African tales and applies to them a detailed reading of their narrative sequences in order to arrive at a representation (both as a digital numeric grouping and a literal grouping) of "the syntagmatic structure of the tale" (Bremond, "Principes," 601–18).

According to Bremond, if we exclude all thematic concerns from consideration, we are able to see in a tale such as "Hare Rides Elephant" the abstract functions that characterize a ruse: (1) according to its external finality; and (2) according to its internal mechanism. For example, Hare wants to carry out vengeance against Elephant and tricks him into playing along by teasing his vanity. "I will," says Hare, "serve as your hat," and Elephant does whatever Hare tells him. The ruse employed by Hare is numerically encoded by Bremond to designate the means and goals that are involved.

All ruses that present the same formal identity (vengeance by seduction) are classified in the above-mentioned category. Only the formal kinship of the ruses—same finality (goal), same kind of bait—authorizes their classification in the same category. Consider another tale from the same people as "Hare Rides Elephant." In this case, Gazelle was tricked by Leopard out of his share of meat. Now Gazelle wants revenge. He invites Leopard to a feast but directs him to sit on a mat that covers a trap. The closeness of the two tales may indicate the persistence of a problem among the people, and storytellers may be revealing the degree of society's concern through this formal recurrence. In this regard, an index of ruses, which is a strictly formal approach, may allow for numeric and statistical operations about frequency and recurrences in a way that would be harder for content analysis to achieve. In other words, it becomes possible to "poll" a people's folktales in order to gain insight into their preoccupations.

Bremond tends to see motif as subordinated to function. The lone motif cannot be used as a principle of analysis and classification. And whereas a motif index is indispensable to the scholar who wants a better understanding of a historical event, a ritual, or a myth, for the scholar who wants to understand the significance of a recurrence in the present context of a society, a tool such as the index of ruses is more helpful. In other words, although motif indexing is invaluable to the historian, the sociologist gains more by using an index of functions. In this way, Bremond's essay on the narratology of the folktale strengthens and "takes D. Paulme's typology . . . one degree deeper by attempting a formal analysis of the trickster's stratagems" ("Principes," 618).

As can be seen from the essays discussed above, the C.N.R.S. team was able, from various perspectives, to shed light on the ways in which folktales can function as cultural products. From the perspectives of both form and content, the folktales emerge as versatile artistic creations that are not only recyclable but highly transformational. Working from different approaches, the members of the team have produced a number of very finely crafted constructs on the modalities of reading African tales. But, although Seydou insists, in comments made in passing, on the very important fact of folktales as literary creations, no special treatment is devoted by the team to this distinguishing quality. The linguistic crafting involved in the telling of a story is wholly ignored in their important contributions to the study of folktales. The lack of concern for the artistic quality of the folktales is evident in the authors' neglect of the languages in which their data were produced.

M. E. Kropp Dakubu's recent treatment of an Ananse story foregrounds precisely the fundamental importance of language in the decoding of the folktale and fills a gap left in the work of other commentators. A major distinction emerges at this point between the highly technical typologies of themes (Paulme) and the highly abstract narratological principles for indexing ruses (Bremond), on the one hand, and the literary-linguistic analysis of a folktale provided by Dakubu. Whereas the first two studies produce generalizing, universalizing principles of cultural determination in a single society or comparatively across several societies, Dakubu's essay entitled "Why Spider is King of Stories: The Message in the Medium of a West African Tale" provides a deeper, more balanced analysis of the folktale as art, as oral literature (Dakubu, "Spider," 33–56). While the Paulme and Bremond methodologies require a set of tales in order to validate their sociological, narratological, and anthropological imperatives, Dakubu tends to focus on the search for the most meaningful, most intricate tale. Whereas the former methodologies can free the scholar from the requirements of erudition demanded by a serious analysis of contents across cultures (particularly in Bremond), the latter is based, essentially, on a firm grounding in the culture and language of the storyteller. Only then does it really become possible to study the poetic quality of the story.

Dakubu defines the subject of his essay as "the relationships that are found to exist between the internal, language-specific lexical structures of variant texts of the 'same,' in different languages" ("Spider," 33). The languages in question are all spoken in Ghana. They are Dagaare, Asante, and Waale. Although many versions of the tale exist, Dakubu wisely relies primarily on the version recorded on tape in Dagaare, the version in Waale, and Rattray's version, which offers the Asante text and its translation into English. Working from these texts, the scholar establishes "an outline of the story that includes the elements . . . that are common to all three 'full' or extended" versions ("Spider," 38). The following is a brief summary of the "basic" story.

God had three sons: Night, the eldest; Moon; and Sun, the youngest. He sent them away to set up their own houses. The time came when God wanted to make the youngest son king, and he devised a contest for his children. Whoever names the yam he has dug up will be given the leopard skin and become king. To make sure that God's will is done, Spider invents a stratagem. He diguises himself as a bird and sits on top of God's gate. He is able to hear God's spoken words, reports them to Sun, and coaches him successfully through the contest. The outline of the story is followed by what amounts to a very close and detailed textual and lexical analysis of the tales. Dakubu is able to show that the "apparently decorative aspect of the text is in fact crucially related to its meanings" ("Spider," 33) by providing an analysis of puns, wordplays, word-echoes, and associations found in the story in order to reconstruct a whole field of significations neatly layered beneath the surface of the stories. This is done particularly well with the two most compelling versions, the Dagaare and the Asante.

Through a close phonetic and etymological analysis of the names of God (*nmene*) and his three children—Sun (*nmenaa*), Moon (*nmaraa*), and Night (*yeunuu*)—Dakubu makes two important discoveries that may actually escape a casual Dagaara listener during the performance: (1) that all phonetic, etymological, and semantic systems of the tale's lexicon "depend on the name of God" ("Spider," 49); and (2) that the interrelatedness of these elements is not only highly significant, it is also what makes this particular tale a work of art. Thus the association between God and Sun, his youngest son, signifies the closeness between the two, whereas the name of Night has no links with either God or Sun, or even Moon. Night is relegated to the "darkness" outside the linguistic system. The names of the three sons also reveal a progression from light, to intermittent light, to absence of light (and are thus encoded contextually within the tale), so that they appear to reverse the names of the food items they name to answer their father's question. The food items range from the most domesticated (Night's answer), to the semidomesticated (Moon's answer), to the wild (Sun's answer). Night names a yam that is commonly cooked by the Dagaara; the dish is made with hot pepper and must be eaten while still hot from the pot. Moon names a yam that must be carefully prepared to avoid irritation of the throat. Sun names a yam that is wild, rarely eaten, but perfectly edible and harmless.

This wild yam happened to be the name that God was thinking of. It is precisely the name that Spider teaches Sun, who happens to be the one God was thinking of as the king of men. Spider is therefore the agent of God's will, whose attributes are elucidated through another associative system unveiled by Dakubu. Spider appears to be related both to God and to Sun.

> Spider and Sun, the ruler of the earth, are both directly under God, their closeness to him signified by closeness in name, but Spider appears outside the tensions between civilisation and chaos that the three sons and their dependent system represent. This gives Spider his freedom of action: he is answerable only to God, and not to any human code of behaviour. He may use means that would be condemned if he were a member of human society, but he is not. He ensures the fulfilment of God's will, which is human good, namely, the rule of civilisation and light rather than chaos and darkness, and so he is friend to God and man, despite his casual attitute to particular man-made social rules. ("Spider," 51)

Applying the same principles of analysis used for the Dagaare text to the Asante text reveals that the latter is more political and legalistic. Whereas the Dagaare tale "emphasises cleverness as an intellectual linguistic game, and uses it to express a theological idea of the power structure of the universe," the Asante version "emphasises cleverness in the validation and manipulation of power relations, projected on to celestial bodies, and is concerned that legal limitations on them be enforced" ("Spider," 54).

In light of this impressive analysis, it appears that in Ghana the same folktale told by two different storytellers assigns different functions to Spider. An agent of God in both stories, Spider embodies cosmological order in one story and social order in the other. Nevertheless, in both instances, its cleverness or deviousness is equally emphasized.

Dakubu concludes this admirably executed interpretation of the tales by suggesting that the Asante version reflects Akan culture, where political thinking features prominently, whereas the Dagaare version reflects Dagaara metaphysical concerns. Finally, the study makes an eloquent and welcome plea for these texts to be seen less as the representation of "a body of consistent philosophy" than as the products of the imagination and linguistic talent of very gifted storytellers. In particular, the Dagaare story, entitled "How Spider Became King of Folktales," which "was told by a schoolboy . . . who was in his early teens," achieves greatness by constructing a complex punning system of interrelated meanings. Indeed, if Ananse speaks a "religious language" that may suggest "passages to the sacred," according to Dakubu, "his tales do not expound a systematic theology" ("Spider," 55). In the final analysis, Spider's legacy may be artistic creativity as manifested in a web of texts.

If nothing else, the relations among these texts reveal the central importance of the text itself in tale telling. The importance of who tells it to whom in what context depends, finally, on the importance of what is said. In the perception of the participants, the words are central: The performance situation matters, but the tale itself consists of organized words. To push the message home, this tale is *about* words. As in so many tales, exclusive possession of the right word is the key to power and glory. The proper organization of words is so important to the proper distribution of power that the two are joined in one figure, Spider, by divine fiat. Civilization demands not only language but text.

Dakubu's meticulous analysis of the Ananse story told by a teenage boy reveals a genius at work, and his plea to see this performance as such is commendable. Too often, the storyteller is buried and forgotten under the elaborate constructions of the erudite commentators. While recognizing and giving praise and prominence to the poetic work of the talented young storyteller, Dakubu also warns against framing the story as a conscious religious narrative. Although the temptation to conflate artistic liberty and religious dogma may be difficult to resist where oral traditions are concerned, we know enough to realize that, in this case, such an act would be no more than another form of unwarranted appropriation. But Dakubu is careful not to deny the existence of a mythical dimension to Ananse. Paulme evokes this aspect of the animal figure in her study "Typologie." She remarks that while Hare remains a secular figure, Spider still retains some mythological traits. He is sometimes a Promethean figure. For instance, he reveals fire as well as agricultural products to humans. At the same time, he is credited with the introduction of diseases and death among humans. Unpredictable, he is sometimes the agent of scandal and disorder in society. In this regard, Paulme's observation that Spider is the embodiment of movement and creativity is quite perceptive.

Is it likely that Spider's identity has evolved over time to become a *fusion* of the sacred and the profane, an embodiment of this duality? Has this dualism survived during Spider's passage to America? For an answer to this question, we must turn to Peter A. Roberts' essay on "The Misinterpretations of *Brer Anancy.*" By giving a historical perspective on the appellation Brer Anancy, Roberts makes a major contribution to the study of animal figures in African-American folktales in this concise article. Going back to the earliest commentators in nineteenth-century New World Africanist scholarship, he shows how the word Ananse has evolved, through European misinterpretation, into *nancy,* which in turn has been described as a term invented by Jamaican blacks to designate Anancy. He notes that although "current usage in Jamaica and throughout the West Indies today has both terms *Nancy* and *Anancy,*" the former was most likely a misinterpretation on the part of the Europeans. It follows from this that the Africans knew quite well the proper term by which to designate this character. He adds: "*Ananse* is a West African word for 'spider,' and this is recognized by commentators from the earliest years, but what is also recognized is that not all the stories have Ananse as a character" (P. Roberts, "Misinterpretations," 98).

Roberts sees in the existence of the two appellations of Spider and in his shifting "identity" in the "Anancy stories" "simply another example of variation and syncretism which characterize many aspects of the development of Afro-American language and culture" ("Misinterpretations," 99). Although I do not question the existence or importance of syncretism as a cultural feature of African-American language and culture, cultural continuity seems a more appropriate description in this case. In fact, syncretism itself, at least in religious terms, may be just as African as African-American.

Having said this, the notion that Ananse is a composite character of spider and chameleon deserves to be meditated upon. Roberts arrives at this notion through L. D. Turner's 1949 work *Africanisms in Gullah Dialect,* which cites the word *nanse* in Gullah as meaning *spider* and gives the Twi and Ewe equivalent Ananse, followed by *nansi* as *chameleon* in Bambara. Roberts suggests that since "the basic idea associated with 'chameleon'—change in physical form—characterizes almost all the stories, whether or not they contain a spider character" ("Misinterpretations," 98), this is consistent with the shifting character of Spider in the West Indies. It is hard to establish an etymological correspondence between Bambara and Twi or Ewe. Yet the suggestion is compelling, especially in view of the role of Chameleon in Bambara mythology.

The late Amadou Hampaté Bâ published a Bambara myth on the origin of the world in which a character named Nonsi serves as the messenger of Massa Dambali (Uncreated King; God) (Bâ, "Animisme," 142–52). The myth characterizes Chameleon as the emblem of prudence and agreeable cohabitation, the symbol of adaptation. It also explains how, using the rainbow, the celestial bridge, to travel while on duty, he appropriated its colors. While this story is clearly presented by Bâ as a myth, Dakubu's analysis is based on folktales. Yet in both texts, the animal figures function as messengers (and confidants) of God. Dakubu notes that in "the central episode of the tale in all three versions, . . . Spider establishes himself as the one who can discover and relay the divine will. He disguises himself as a bird to do so, . . . because birds are recognized as inhabiting the space that separates heaven and earth" ("Spider," 41).

It is worth noting that Chameleon also can climb up trees (toward the sky) as well as walk on the ground. As a messenger of God in the Bambara text, he travels between the sky and the earth. However, Spider appears as the ideal messenger-friend of God. His self-imposed task of discovering God's will and then carrying it out, making sure his will is done without being asked to do so, makes him the perfect messenger-friend. His ability to read God's mind creates an intimacy in knowledge between the two. Spider's characteristic deviousness may be the characteristic reflection of human bewilderment and inability to apprehend his behavior since he is not bound by social rules.

Another important contribution made by Roberts concerns the term of address commonly used for Spider and Rabbit in *Brer Anansy* and in *Brer Rabbit.* Roberts demonstrates the fallacy contained in the assertion that *brer* is a diminutive form of *brother,* a title of respect used by African-American storytellers when speaking of Spider or Rabbit. He maintains that "the word is an address of familiarity" and "that the pronunciation suggested by the spelling of *brer* is . . . inconsistent with the phonology of Black English or West Indian non-standard English" ("Misinterpretations," 101). The sources of the misinterpretation may be found in the transcription efforts (such as Joel Chandler Harris's Uncle Remus stories) and in the urge of commentators to associate English titles with African-American speech patterns. This urge may have clouded the etymological tracking of the word to Cambridge, Norfolk, and Essex, where the word *bor,* also spelled *bo',* was used as "a term of familiar address, applied to persons of either sex and all ages," according to the *English Dialect* (1898; in "Misinterpretations," 100). Roberts adds:

> The spellings *brer* and *bro'* and others such as *bro'er* can be regarded as attempts to relate the folktale word to a known English word, a

> practice which was a general one in the presentation of non-standard dialects. Such spellings contrast with early Afro-American phonology which showed a distinct preference for consonant-vowel-consonant-vowel word structure, thus reducing many initial consonant clusters. In addition, *brer Rabbit,* with post-consonant r, a final r and initial r in sequence, is clearly contrary to Afro-American phonology. (br) most likely came about in the following way: b ranansi—branansi, and was generalized before other names. ("Misinterpretations," 100)

Considering the general, consecrated use of *brer* and *bro'* as meaning brother in the U.S. today, it is amazing that a total fabrication has gained the unquestioned respect of thousands, perhaps millions of users. The use is an extraordinary case of cultural invention.

The indisputable importance of Anancy stories in the New World is proved, once again, by the wonderful stories collected by Darryl Dance in Jamaica. Dance compares Anancy to the "American brer Rabbit" and states that "Anancy is generally a figure of admiration whose cunning and scheming nature reflects the indirection and subtleties necessary for survival and occasionally victory for the Black man in a racist country" (Dance, *Jamaicans,* 12). She also notes that some Jamaicans distrust Spider stories for their wicked contents and believe that "Anancy's rascality and deceit are bad for the national character" (*Jamaicans,* 12).[3]

Is it possible that Spider stories only reflect contemporary social concerns? In other words, is it possible that an emphasis on cunning alone was necessitated by the conditions for survival prevalent at a specific moment in Jamaican history? Like music and sports, folktales may have served and may continue to serve perceived contemporary needs. These needs, depending on the urgency of the response to social and political crises, may emphasize one aspect of the character traits of Spider—ranging from the sacred to the profane—at the expense of others. This may explain the current distrust of some Jamaicans for Spider because in their view "the admiration for unscrupulous cunning is encouraged by Anancy stories" and these stories "express an unhealthy trait of character" (*Jamaicans,* 12). In other words, what may have been sanctioned by the community during slavery and colonialism may be perceived generally as unacceptable by a segment of society today. The question becomes: Whose perceived needs are now being expressed?

To put the evolution of Anancy stories to a test would require comparing versions of the "same" story over a long period of time. These versions may reveal patterns of composition and treatment that reflect precise contemporary interests. One etiological story collected by Dance demonstrates the Promethean trait of Spider in Jamaican society. It is a story about the origin of sorrel in the Jamaican diet, and Brer Anancy is credited with the discovery of the red flower as well as of the recipe for making the drink at Christmas (*Jamaicans,* 9–10). Since the preparation and serving of this drink at Christmas is a Jamaican tradition, it appears that Brer Anancy is, at the same time, credited with the invention of a tradition. This tale can be grouped among those that focus on "the magic man"[4] in Spider or God's messenger-friend of the Dagaare story. Yet there is an important difference between the two manifestations of Spider. In the Jamaican tale, Spider is uncertain of the outcome of his action. His discovery is a purely accidental event, and the process of the discovery itself is full of danger for Spider and for the community. It is clear in the story that he is unfamiliar with the flowers he is selling and that sorrel petals fall accidentally in a boiling pot, thereby turning the water red. He does not know the attributes of the plant he has carried to the market for sale. It may be poisonous and cause harm to the people he has encouraged to drink it, and in that case, he will have to face unpleasant consequences. Therefore, he frets, the story tells us, while the mysterious drink is being tested. The difference between this tale and the Dagaare tale is the uncertainty of the trickster and the nervousness he displays during this trial. While the Dagaare Spider remains cool, the Jamaican Spider is agitated, possessed by fear.

Nevertheless, the story remains an important etiological tale, a myth in which Spider acts as an agent—an unconscious agent, it is true—of discovery. Furthermore, his discovery benefits the whole community as is customary in such instances. Although God is present in the Dagaare drama, he is not mentioned in the Jamaican story. However, it is not an exaggeration to say that God is embedded in the evocation of the Christmas celebration that opens the narrative. The event explains Spider's desperate move to make money in order to purchase Christmas gifts by selling an apparently worthless bush to the people in the marketplace.

Contrary to Spider, Bouki the hyena is not a trickster. He is included in this study as the alter ego of the trickster. In West Africa, in Louisiana, and in Haiti, Bouki functions as the victim of the endless ruses of Hare-Rabbit, and in that sense, he is the ultimate symbol of the dupe in all three areas, although with notable differentiating characteristics in each. Bouki is the emblematic figure of the dupe, because every trickster needs a Bouki. Diop describes him as "Bouki-the-Hyena, that thief and coward, whose hind-quarters always seem to be sagging beneath a shower of blows" (Diop, *Tales,* xi). Consistently described as an ugly creature (both morally and physically), and defined primarily by his belly, Hyena has absolutely no redeeming qualities in West African folktales. The audience actually expects him to blunder and be ridiculed. The laughter his blunders provoke among children is essential to any story in the cycle of Hare. *Stupid, gluttonous, ugly, shameless, selfish, stinking*—these are some of the terms applied to Hyena in folktales. The fact that this wild animal of the savannah is a hunter and a scavenger who is too easily inclined to dig up cadavers in the cemeteries for his meals does not endear him to humans. It is believed that no creature would eat hyena flesh because it is poisonous. To most people of the savannah, the hyena is not, in reality, laughable at all; it is a dreadful beast. When someone is called a hyena, it implies excessive ugliness, brutality, stupidity, stubborn perseverence, and greed—all of which inspire fear.

As Marcia Gaudet has noted (Gaudet, "Hyena," 66–72), the hyena inspired fear among the ancient Egyptians and among the Greeks and Romans who were baffled by its hermaphroditic appearance and its alleged bisexuality. This fear of the hyena may have earned him a permanent place as the dupe in African folktales. But what could explain his endurance in Louisiana and in Haiti?

According to Gaudet, Hyena's presence in Louisiana as Compair Bouki was first documented in 1895 by Alcee Fortier in *Louisiana Folk-tales.* A linguist, Fortier identified the etymology of *bouqui* as deriving from the Wolof for *hyena.* It seems appropriate and natural that Hare should become Lapin or Rabbit in America as a first step in the adaptation and eventual transformation of a popular African character in the New World. But can Bouki endure as a hyena in America? What is the true identity of Bouki in America? According to Gaudet, "the African term bouki was obviously maintained in Louisiana tales because there were, of course, no hyenas in Louisiana, and thus Louisianians had no way of attaching the English or French (*l'hyène*) to the animal they knew as bouki. The term is still maintained today, whether the tales are told in English or in French. The word is still applied frequently in Louisiana French (metaphorically) to an ugly person or ugly baby" ("Hyena," 68).

It is clear from this description that Bouki is not a hyena in Louisiana folktales, despite his remarkable resemblance in character traits to his Senegambian namesake. If the physical appearance of Bouki remains undefined in Louisiana, it is as clear in Haiti as it is in Senegal. While Bouki in Wolof folktales is a hyena, in Haiti, Bouqui is a person, according to Suzanne Comhaire-Sylvain, who states that the term *bouqui* is found in the Dominican Republic, in Louisiana, and in the Bahamas. Furthermore, she notes that tales of Native Americans and French colonists were incorporated into the cycle of Bouqui that she has collected into a book entitled *Le roman de Bouqui* (The Romance of Bouqui). She maintains that these tales are much more than the sum of their original sources, assuming that none was created in Haiti; they constitute, nonetheless, a national monument and the romance of Bouqui is profoundly Haitian in character.

Comhaire-Sylvain, who worked for a long time in folklore (she successfully defended her dissertation on Haitian folktales in 1937), underlines major differences between, as she puts it so perceptively, "Bouqui and the African hyena." In Haitian folktales, Bouqui is a person who is described in the following terms: "a sort of a big, fat, ugly, voracious brute with a long tail, a carnivorous creature who is unafraid of eating carcasses, and whose characteristic bad odor has made Louisiana folkorists assimilate it to the he-goat" (Comhaire-Sylvain, *Bouqui,* 13).

This composite physical appearance is fascinating on two levels. First, the fusion of person and animal makes Bouqui into a very strange character, indeed a hybrid. The animal part of Bouqui is made of a combination of some traits of the hyena—an ugly beast, a brute, and a scavenger—and the he-goat whose strong smell is legendary. Also, the association with the he-goat does more than release bad odors, it problematizes somewhat the etymology of Bouqui and the Wolof origin of the word. After all, it is perfectly conceivable that French-speaking Louisiana had either transformed the goat into a new character or, more likely, had managed to merge some of the traits of the hyena and the goat into its own composite character. It is important to note, however, that the French word *bouc* (he-goat) could have generated *bouqui.* Secondly, it is worth noting that neither of these animals has a long tail. Yet the creature with a long tail is a familiar Christian representation of the devil. Hyena may have absorbed this physical trait of strangeness associated with the devil into its new Haitian emblematic image. Along with this composite, syncretic physical appearance of Bouqui, the character traits of the Haitian companion of Lapin also set him apart from the hyena in many ways. His cruelty is due only to excessive stupidity, not to an innate or compulsive penchant for meanness or violence. Whereas it would not occur to a Senegalese to identify with Hyena in a folktale—so strong is his negative image—Haitian folktales tend to depict Bouqui as a person worthy of compassion. He inspires pity, because in Haiti, Bouqui the dupe and Malice the trickster are inscribed inside a different paradigm where the peasant is opposed to the city dweller, the illiterate person to the educated person, the Creole slave to the newly arrived slave (*Bouqui,* 14).

Bouqui's eternal victimizer in Haiti is known as Compère Lapin or Malice. In Senegal, it is his cousin Hare who shines as the trickster-hero in the cycle that bears his name. He is immediately identified by his short tail, his long ears, and his small size. He is clever, often generous, and obsessed with punishing and torturing Hyena. He is admired for this, since most people think Hyena deserves to be punished for thoughtlessly breaking the most sacred social rules. In his cycle, Leuk, the Senegambian hare, emerges as a hero whose small size is fully compensated by his unparalleled intelligence. Whereas Spider is a combination of the profane and the sacred, Hare is a secular figure in the folktales. If he was once a mythological character, as Comhaire-Sylvain contends, this aspect of his identity has been lost for such a long time that there remains no memory of it in West African tales.

Contrary to Ananse, there are no traces of Hare's Wolof name in the New World. Hare is a trickster known as Lapin or Rabbit or Malice in the Americas. In Haitian folktales, whether he is named Lapin or Malice, he is thought of as a person, the trickster-hero who constantly tries to ridicule Bouqui. Like Anancy in Jamaica, he is not always admired for his tricks. There is a degree of resentment among the peasants, in spite of their "idolatry of intelligence," against some of the excesses of Malice (*Bouqui,* 15).

According to Joëlle Laurent and Ina Césaire, Compère Lapin is the most popular and complex animal character in the folktales of Martinique. As in Haiti, he is a person but is described in Martinique as a mulatto. And like the Jamaican Anancy, his speech is marked by a certain nasal quality (which in Senegambia is ascribed to Hyena). He is clever and unscrupulous. He endorses the local symbols of power: He speaks French like an educated fellow, and knows some Latin. In a sense, he is a metaphor for the good-talker type of man of words so well described by Abrahams: "The decorated and decorous verbiage of the good talker arises at serious community events: weddings, arrivals and departures, political gatherings, *thanksgivings* (parties given after a sickness or some such trial), and many other sentimental occasions. The good talker usually expresses himself in toasts, speeches, or recitations" (*Man-of-Words,* xv).

Furthermore, Compère Lapin as described by Laurent and Césaire is very similar in character to Malice (*Contes,* 13–14). He is the Creole slave who looks down on the field slaves. He identifies with the boss and his symbols of power, which, in addition to the dominant, prestigious language, include such positions of authority as overseer and guardian of the king's dominion. In light of this additional definition of the character, it is easy to understand why the peasants feel compassion toward Bouqui, who emerges as a real victim of this African-American trickster's cruelty.

An extremely resilient character, Leuk (the hare) has successfully undergone another regional and cultural metamorphosis to become Brer Rabbit. In his new identity, he was and remains one of the most familiar animal figures in American culture. Although the trickster's ambiguous character has long been a subject of great interest, his American specificity is now increasingly documented and meticulously defined by scholars of African-American culture. In his essay on "Structural Analysis of the Afro-American Trickster," Jay Edwards defines the African-American trickster as "a power-broker" who deceives for "his own benefit or that of others" (Edwards, "Analysis," 81–103). He goes on to say that while trickster tales served the entertainment needs of African slaves on the plantation, they also provided a means of coming to terms with the dilemmas posed by bondage. According to Edwards, these tales taught that "trickster strategies involve the maximization of short-term (economic) gain at the expense of long-term social cohesion" ("Analysis," 92). Moreover, in their daily lives blacks were "fully prevented from developing cooperative social contracts for their own long-range self-improvement" ("Analysis," 92). The precarious quality of a life of constant danger militates strongly in favor of a trickster's views. However, the trickster is always at risk of being unmasked by the dupe for the false friend that he really is and of being punished for his greed. Edwards observes that "unlike the majority of European folktales, Afro-American tales terminate in disharmony between the two principal actors caused by the violation of an agreement and unreciprocated exchange of value" ("Analysis," 92). This note of disharmony is no doubt the consequence of the dialectical tension in a hostile social environment between the imperatives of survival and death and the individual and communal interests.

In a full-length study devoted to the folk hero in African-American expressive culture ranging from the folktale to the spiritual, John W. Roberts puts a special emphasis on the transformation of the original African trickster animal figure into a distinct African-American trickster-tale tradition. Much of the informative context is located in the period of African slavery in America, and the trickster tales are seen as a response to existing conditions. And from the perspective of the enslaved, the transparency of the role distribution in this tradition was a clear sign of the injustice of their condition. In general, the trickster was a small animal such as the rabbit; the dupe, a much larger one such as the wolf or the bear. In the wild, the former would be the prey of the latter, whereas in the folktale, the prey becomes the trickster, while its hunter becomes the dupe. Naturally, developing skills in and relying on trickery and wit is primarily a matter of survival for Rabbit. In this sense, the trickster stories offered the enslaved Africans a modus operandi, a manner of proceeding in difficult times, and a way of beating the odds in the plantation culture.

However, as attractive as they may be, the character traits of the animal trickster were not meant to become a lifestyle, much less a world view. The indiscriminate adoption of the trickster's ways as a communally sanctioned code of behavior was the consequence of a misinterpretation of the set of survival codes the trickster came to embody in the U.S. As a result, the trickster's way became a way of fending for oneself regardless of who might become the dupe. Further, Roberts suggests that it is this development that accounts for Brer Rabbit's readiness and willingness to dupe even animals such as Partridge, who are not only harmless toward Rabbit but may also be allies in the wild. As an aftereffect of the increasing crystallization of trickery and ruses around Rabbit, the tales were decontextualized from their initial ethical principles.

As a corrective measure, it became necessary to move the spiritual power of the African trickster into a more controlled and more reliable host. John, the new host, is the human epitome of witticism, who is able to repeatedly dupe Old Master in their dangerous encounters. John (Ti-Jean in the Francophone New World) is transformed into a popular hero whose memorable lessons are carefully etched in intelligent and witty formulas.

The transformation that Roberts has outlined in his important study is not meant to dismiss Rabbit. He was and remains a worthy and admirable character, perhaps even a model for generating trickster-type characters in American popular culture. What the transformation shows is a concern with the continuity, adaptation, and firm grounding of the African trickster in American soil in an original manner. While the moral ambiguity of the trickster is left intact, a new character is created to extend into the future the moral code that could no longer be preserved in Brer Rabbit. In this sense, the transformations that African animal figures have undergone in the expressive cultural traditions of the New World are a testimony to the creative genius of the African-American peoples and a historical record of their accomplishments.

H. Nigel Thomas also sees the African-American trickster as an exemplary figure for survival whose cunning was "marshalled against white society" and "was firmly established long before the abolition of slavery" and who continued to serve in this role through the Jim Crow era (Thomas, *Folklore,* 82). But he also notes a certain degree of syncretism in the merging of character traits from other American trickster traditions into the African-American trickster. For example, the African-American trickster has absorbed aspects of both the Euro-American trickster (confidence man) and the Amerindian trickster. According to Thomas, the Euro-American trickster is defined mainly by the fact that his "rationale is deception for its inherent power and control." He is also a linguistic manipulator, a feature that is reminiscent of the West African trickster's "linguistic dexterity." In the end, the character that has progressively developed out of this cross-fertilization is uniquely African-American, and "the peddling of assurance, faith in self, and the sanctity of capitalism—all germane to the American ethos—bring interesting ramifications to the Afro-American trickster tradition" (*Folklore,* 83).

While there may be a palimpsest of character traits in every trickster standing today at the busy crossroad of American cultures and identities, the relation of the African tricksters who have survived the middle passage and constitute the focus of this paper to their American counterparts may best be described in terms of a triptych as a metaphor for literature and art. The triptych is commonly defined as literature written on a tablet of three leaves tied together or as a carving, a design, and/or a painting made of three panels that are hinged together in such a way that the two side panels may be folded over the central one. In this way, the triptych becomes a set of portable tableaux during travels, and as an altarpiece, it can be easily opened during rituals and closed afterward. The triptych as a metaphor is significant in several ways in the present context.

At the purely geographical level, it is significant that the three animal characters that this essay is concerned with are emphatically distributed to the three regions, with the Caribbean islands nestled between Africa and the Americas. The role of geography itself in the unfathomable historical tragedy that has befallen African peoples through the Atlantic slave trade is still a subject of profound meditation for the poet. In the first stanza of Senghor's poem "Prayer for Peace," Christ crucified embodies Africa as his right hand, America his left side, and Haiti his heart (Senghor, *Poetry,* 69). From the island of Gorée's corridor of no return off the coast of Senegal through the infamous middle passage to the plantation experience in the Americas, the African peoples have carried, transformed, and created a new and complex literary tradition from the fragments of this triptych of animal figures in folktales.

If Ananse and Leuk or Rabbit are the representations of the two side panels of a triptych, *Bou(k)qui,* by virtue of his catalytic function, stands as the middle panel of a vast text. It is this inscribed middle panel that offers the surface on which the tricksters rest. Bou(k)qui, as a symbol of the dupe, provides them with a base from which they can spring back to life. He also provides them with the hinges that anchor them solidly to an inscribed landscape without which the tricksters are only fragments of a larger text. Historically, the relation that binds the African animal figures to the ones that subsequently flourished in the Americas can be likened to the relationship between the Byzantine triptych and the European tradition that developed over the centuries in the hands of German, Spanish, and Flemish artists of the fourteenth, fifteenth, and sixteenth centuries. In the Americas, Hyena, Hare, and Ananse have undergone profound transformations that underscore the emergence of new and original characters. Together, *Bou(k)qui,* Brer Rabbit, and Ananse form a very large triptych of African-American oral culture that invites a more detailed reading.

As an altarpiece and a pictorial representation of scenes from the Bible, the triptych has an obvious religious function. The fact that both the inside and outside of the panels are decorated suggests an invitation to read both sides of the triptych for a thorough apprehension of its message. While the outside of the panels is usually offered to everybody's gaze, it is only during church rituals that the inside pictures spring to life when they are opened for the initiates. Likewise, many scholars have hinted at the mythological and spiritual functions of both Ananse and Hare in West African stories. And although John W. Roberts has recently emphasized the absence of this function in Brer Rabbit in the U.S., the magical character of Anancy was recognized by Louise Bennett in Jamaica. Only an initiate can extend the present liminal reading of this triptych of animal figures into the core of African-American wisdom and provide a deeper understanding of their spiritual significance.

NOTES

1. All translations from the French are my own unless otherwise indicated.
2. Abrahams quotes a tape-recorded exchange between Frazier and Herskovits.
3. A Rastafarian condemnation of Anancy in Jamaica is cited by Poynting in the essay that precedes this one.
4. Dance citing Louise Bennett in *Jamaicans,* 12.

REFERENCES

Abrahams, R. D. *The Man-of-Words in the West Indies.* Baltimore: The John Hopkins University Press, 1983.

Bâ, Amadou Hampaté. "Sur l'animisme (A travers les mythes de l'Afrique Noire)." *Présence Africaine* 24–25 (1959): 142–52.

Bremond, C., et al. *Recherches en Littérature Orale Africaine. Cahiers d'Etudes Africaines* 12, no. 45 (1st cahier 1972); 15, no. 60 (4th cahier 1976).

Bremond, C. "Principes d'un index des ruses." *Cahier d'Etudes Africaines* 15, no. 60 (1976): 601–18.

Comhaire-Sylvain, S. *Le Roman de Bouqui.* Ottawa: LEMEAC, 1973.

Dadié, Bernard B. *Le Pagne Noir.* Paris: Présence Africaine, 1955.

———. "Le conte, élément de solidarité et d'universalité." *Présence Africaine* 27–28 (1959): 71–80.

Dakubu, M. E. Kropp. "Why Spider is King of Stories: The Message in the Medium of a West African Tale." *African Languages and Cultures* 3, no. 1 (1990): 33–56.

Damas, L.G. *Veillées noires.* Paris: Stock, 1943.

Dance, Darryl Cumber. *Folklore From Contemporary Jamaicans.* Knoxville: University of Tennessee Press, 1985.

Diop, Birago. *Les Contes d'Amadou Koumba.* Paris: Fasquelle, 1947.

———. *Tales of Amadou Koumba,* trans. and ed. Dorothy S. Blair. London: Oxford University Press, 1966.

Edwards, Jay. "Structural Analysis of the Afro-American Trickster Tale." In *Black Literature & Literary Theory,* ed. Henry Louis Gates, Jr., 81–103. New York: Methuen, 1984.

Fortier, Alcee. "Bits of Louisiana Folklore." *Transactions of the Modern Language Association* 3 (1887): 100–68; reprinted in *Louisiana Folk-Tales.* American Folk-Lore Society Memoirs. Vol. 2. Boston: Houghton Mifflin, 1895.

Gaudet, Marcia. "Bouki, the Hyena, in Louisiana and African Tales." *Journal of American Folklore* 105, no. 415 (1992): 66–72.

Irele, Abiola "African Letters: The Making of a Tradition." *Yale Journal of Criticism* 5, no. 1 (1991): 69–100.

Laurent, Joëlle, and Ina Césaire. *Contes de mort et de vie aux Antilles.* Paris: Nubia, 1976.

McKay, Claude. *Banjo.* New York: Harcourt Brace Jovanovich, 1957 [1929].

Paulme, Denise. "Typologie des contes du Décepteur." *Cahier d'Etudes Africaines* 15, no. 60 (1976): 569–600.

Roberts, John W. *From Trickster to Badman: The Black Folk Hero in Slavery and Freedom.* Philadelphia: University of Pennsylvania Press, 1989.

Roberts, Peter A. "The Misinterpretations of *Brer Anancy.*" *Folklore* 99, no. 1 (1988): 98–101.

Senghor, Léopold Sedar. *La Belle Histoire de Leuk-le-lièvre.* Paris: Hachette, 1953.

———. *The Collected Poetry,* trans. by Melvin Dixon. CARAF BOOKS. Charlottesville: University Press of Virginia, 1991.

Seydou, Christiane. "L'Analyse des rapports entre la culture et la littérature à travers un corpus de contes homogène." *Cahiers d'Etudes Africaines* 12, no. 45 (1972).

———. "Introduction." *Cahier d'Etudes Africaines* 12, no. 45 (1972).

Socé, Ousmane. *Contes et Légendes d'Afrique Noire.* Paris: Nouvelles Editions Latines, 1962.

Thomas, H. Nigel. *From Folklore to Fiction.* Westport, Connecticut: Greenwood Press, 1988.

Turner, L. D. *Africanisms in Gullah Dialect.* Ann Arbor: University of Michigan Press, 1949.

A. James Arnold

Animal Tales, Historic Dispossession, and Creole Identity in the French West Indies

The traditional tale, told in Creole in a communal setting in the evening, often during the wake held for a deceased member of the community, shares a cast of animal characters with numerous African societies and with African-American culture, as Kandioura Dramé has shown. His presentation has raised the question of whether it makes sense to read the characters of Rabbit, Spider, and Hyena as being somehow the same in these three geocultural regions. My own remarks will extend this general examination of the question into one specific area, the dependent Creolophone West Indies, that is to say, the Overseas French Departments (départements d'outre-mer) of Guiana, Martinique, and Guadeloupe. The Creole spoken in Martinique is essentially identical with that of Saint Lucia, Derek Walcott's home.

It is self-evident that the French West Indies are located geographically *in* the Americas, but the extent to which their popular culture has continued to be an integral part *of* the Americas has been a subject of debate. V. S. Naipaul wrote in his Caribbean travel book *The Middle Passage* that on disembarking in Fort-de-France, Martinique, he found himself no longer in the Caribbean at all but in a provincial corner of France (Naipaul, *Passage,* 197). After making allowances for the arch style of Naipaul's writing on the Caribbean, we are still left with a troublesome suggestion. Naipaul is not the only Caribbean person to see French West Indians in this way. A few years ago, at the fall reception for new fellows of the Carter G. Woodson Institute for Afro-American and African Studies of the University of Virginia, I was making small talk with a Ph.D. candidate from Jamaica who asked me what my interest in the Caribbean was. When I explained that I had been working for some years on the Martinican poet and playwright Aimé Césaire, she responded, "Those people are French." She was perfectly serious. The point of her objection was the degree of assimilation of Martinicans, Guadeloupeans, and Guianese to the metropolitan French culture as seen from a Jamaican perspective.

It should be clear from Dramé's paper that the interpretation we place on the meaning of an Afro-Caribbean or African-American animal tale or set of tales will depend finally on our assumptions concerning the relations obtaining among the tale, the teller, and the audience taken in its most general sociocultural sense. However scientific the investigation, our very perspective or angle of approach will necessarily draw us to structure the meanings we find in the tales according to our underlying assumptions. When literary scholars examine such a body of tales, we all too often take our prejudices for a natural state of affairs, and we are prone to draw universal conclusions that are ultimately indefensible. Since the original occasion for these essays brought together such a distinguished assemblage of literary scholars and anthropologists, as well as practitioners of the storytelling art, it seemed to me appropriate to seek a common ground.

I shall pursue the hypothesis that the animal characters discussed by Dramé have been transformed under the pressures of a peculiar colonial and neocolonial history. Unlike the great majority of their sister islands in the Lesser Antilles, Martinique and Guadeloupe—and French Guiana on the South American mainland—have not known a period of independence since the tumult of the French Revolution and the Napoleonic wars. Colonized in the early seventeenth century, these three Caribbean territories passed directly from colonial to neocolonial status in 1946, when they were officially proclaimed overseas departments of France (the status held by Algeria until the success of its revolution fifteen years later).

A minimal awareness of the conditions of economic production in the islands will provide a useful background against which to understand the importance of the creole folktale and its history. In a colony (and, today, in a neocolony), the only culture that matters to the metropole is agriculture. At first, sugarcane provided the wealth of the islands as well as the necessity for its salient characteristic, the traffic in African slaves on which the plantation economy was built. The plantation society specific to the cultivation of sugarcane in the Caribbean provided the structures within which the transplanted African animal characters acquired their new creole (and, thus, American) reality. As long as the plantation economy survived more or less intact, the creole folktale remained its living expression among the people. But large-scale sugarcane production disappeared from the French West Indies in the course of the nineteenth century and was replaced by pineapple and banana production, which are now largely mechanized. In a word, the landscape and the human relations that gave their meaning to the French West Indian animal characters have been transformed by historical and economic processes.

The vestiges of the folktale as the cultural expression of the plantation system were studied in 1978 by Maryse Condé in her essay *La civilisation du bossale* (The Culture of Colonial Blacks). She analyzed a corpus of ten traditional tales in which the paired characters of Rabbit (Compè Lapin) and Zamba—one of the French West Indian modifications of Hyena of West Africa—occur together. Of the ten tales, three are set in a period of famine where survival is the central issue, three more involve the theft of food, and yet another involves trickery by Rabbit to insure that he can eat without stopping work. Fully seventy percent of the tales turn on the value of trickery for survival under conditions of extreme penury.

Condé had already lived and worked in West Africa for some time when she prepared this essay. Her experience with both cultural regions—West African and West Indian—permitted her to show that the paired characters of Rabbit and Zamba had undergone a profound transformation under conditions of slave labor and extreme economic hardship. In the West African corpus available to her, she found a consistent opposition between Hyena and the other animal characters. Hyena was regularly punished for his cruelty and greed, whereas in the French West Indies, both Rabbit and Hyena are gluttonous characters. She observes that "the voracity that draws [Hyena/Zamba] into so many misadventures is shared by his companion [Rabbit]; both think only about stuffing themselves with meat; but the superiority of Rabbit is in his knowing how to avoid getting caught" (Condé, *Bossale*, 38). She concludes this contrastive examination of Rabbit and Zamba by arguing that in the new West Indian context the animal characters do not illustrate a shared moral code typical of a stable community but rather a pedagogy for survival in extremis. The two characters are, however, differentiated by other traits in the traditional tales of Guadeloupe and Martinique. Whereas Rabbit is a ladies' man (so to speak), Zamba loves his wife and children. Rabbit is a good public speaker, singer, and musician (a man of words, to pick up the consecrated expression used by Dramé). Zamba lacks all these qualities, and he is gullible. Rabbit, of course, is clever; but he is also vengeful, cowardly, and proud. Finally, in Condé's view, both characters have the same desires and goals. All that separates them fundamentally is success. Zamba's virtues cannot assure his success, whereas Rabbit's faults do not prevent him from succeeding.

Condé notes that the animal characters of the Rabbit/Zamba cycle of tales in fact have relatively few positive traits. She tends to interpret this naturalistically. Slaves had little need for positive moral traits (as other societies judge these), but skills and talents such as those possessed by Rabbit could assure escape from the grinding misery of field labor to a more favored existence in and around the big house.

In an interesting aside concerning Haitian interpretations of these same characters, Condé also notes that Jacques Stéphen Alexis, in his *Romancéro aux étoiles* (Star-studded Songbook), took Malice (the Haitian equivalent of Rabbit) to be a mulatto, whereas Zamba was a black. This may be the result of the quite different history of Haiti, after its independence in 1804, and the French West Indies. Alexis's interpretation, which has its roots in the work of the pioneer scholar of popular culture in Haiti, Jean Price-Mars, sees only two groups in Haitian society: the great mass of black laborers and the tiny mulatto minority who rapidly set themselves up as the elite of the nation early in the nineteenth century. Whites had essentially been removed from the scene in the course of the Haitian revolution. The situation in the French West Indies was quite different. An equally tiny white Creole elite, called *békés* in Martinique, held nearly all the arable land and all the levers of economic power in island life. Mulattos constituted, from the mid-nineteenth century, an educated middle class that came to dominate the professions. Blacks had to struggle to rise out of the mass of field hands in the sugarcane economy. In this context, Condé vacillates between seeing Zamba as the freshly arrived slave who is no match for his acculturated Creole companion in servitude, Rabbit, and, alternatively, asking whether Zamba may not represent Massa, who appears to be all-powerful, but who is gullible and easily fooled by the wily slave.

More important to Condé's argument is the inescapable fact that, in all these possible interpretations, the characteristics of Rabbit are those the slaveholding class attributed to the slaves. In other words, conceived in the slaves' interiorization of the image their masters had of them, the animal characters of the traditional tales constituted the very face and expression of the culture of slavery. Through their own folktales, the slaves had incorporated and expressed others' stereotypes of them. In Condé's analysis, that which seems to be indisputably the slaves' own popular cultural production—the traditional folktale—has its origins in someone else's vision.

In his groundbreaking study *Caribbean Discourse,* published three years after Condé's essay, Edouard Glissant made the case that the creole folktale in the French West Indies is no longer the well of inspiration of the popular culture, that it is incapable of providing a dynamic that can be transformed conceptually by the arts of painting, sculpting, and writing. The folktale in Guadeloupe, Martinique, and French Guiana has become, in his view, the expression within popular culture of the neocolonial system that governs the entire society of the overseas departments of France in the Caribbean, importing everything of value from the metropole. Glissant's theoretical approach is cross-cultural; it assumes that retention studies—as Dramé's analysis has already demonstrated—have little to tell us about the French West Indian tale today.

Glissant agrees with Condé concerning what was lost in the Middle Passage by the Africans who had to put together out of the available materials—*bricoler,* Claude Lévi-Strauss would have said—the vocabulary, grammar, and syntax of the creole folktale. The heroic dimension of the communal history that each future slave left behind, in the form of the epics related by African *griots,* are nowhere reconstituted in the French West Indies. Nor did the putative local heroes, the maroon leaders, find their way into epic works in Guadeloupe, Martinique, or French Guiana. All that remains is a deep "longing for the ideal of history" (Glissant, *Discourse,* 79). Glissant puts the lack of a constructive relation between the creole folktale and history this way:

> The fragmented nature of the Caribbean folktale is such that no chronology can emerge, that time cannot be conceived as a basic dimen-

> sion of human experience. Its most used measure of time is the change from day to night. During the night, Brer Rabbit will set the traps in which Brer Tiger [another avatar of Hyena] will be dramatically caught when day comes. Thus night is the forerunner of the day. Obscurity leads transparency. The rhythm of night and day is the only measure of time for the slave, the peasant, the agricultural worker. In a great number of folktales heard during childhood, the storyteller tells about receiving at the end of the story a kick in his bottom that hurled him into his audience. This final ritual in the tale does not only attest to its lucidity (the storyteller is not important, the story told is not sacred), but also to a discontinuous conception of time. As opposed to myth, the tale does not hallow cultural accretion and does not activate it. (*Discourse,* 84)

Glissant points to other features of the creole tale that constitute a nonuniform whole: asides to the audience by the narrator (Laurent and Césaire, *Contes,* 28–35); repeated breaks in the narrative; abrupt changes in tone (*Discourse,* 85). He also agrees with Condé concerning the lack of morality of the creole tale in the French West Indies. He puts it this way: "The economy of its 'morality': its shrewdest maneuver consists of repeating each time the same situation and to be careful not to propose exemplary 'solutions'" (*Discourse,* 85). This detail fits nicely with the absence of any high seriousness in the representation of the "sacrificial victim"—Zamba or Brer Tiger in the examples mentioned above. On the contrary, the victim is "nothing but a joke." Glissant's observation on the sacrificial victim relates to his interrogation of the sense of the tragic in French West Indian culture, which is inaugurated by the negritude movement in the 1940s but is absent from the folktale.

Ultimately, what the traditional folktale points to for Glissant is, ironically enough for this genre, the absence of a self-conscious collectivity: "We have here the embattled, nonexistent group that consequently makes the emergence of the individual impossible. The question we need to ask in Martinique will not be, for instance: 'Who am I'—a question that from the outset is meaningless—but rather 'Who are we?'" (*Discourse,* 86). Since Dramé has pointed out the link between the negritude movement in Africa and the literary flowering of the traditional tale, it is appropriate here to linger a moment on the reason for the lack of such a flowering in the French West Indies, even after the negritude movement sought to stimulate a new collective consciousness. Once again, it is Glissant who goes to the heart of the matter in *Caribbean Discourse:* "The most obvious difference between the African and Caribbean versions of negritude is that the African one proceeds from the multiple reality of ancestral yet threatened cultures, while the Caribbean version precedes the free intervention of new cultures whose expression is subverted by the disorder of colonialism" (*Discourse,* 24).

I alluded earlier, in discussing Condé's essay on the creole folktale, to the different identity attributed to Rabbit and the local equivalent of Hyena (Zamba or Bouqui) in the French West Indies and in Haiti, respectively. Glissant's examination of the language and the landscape of folktale, and their relation to the economy, goes some way toward explaining how similar characters may function differently in societies where the tale is regularly told in Creole. We can usefully juxtapose Glissant's description of the creole folktale's relationship to the plantation system with Condé's detailed examination of the transformation of Rabbit and Hyena in the French West Indies. Glissant writes:

> Creole was in the islands the language of the plantation system, which was responsible for the cultivation of sugar cane. The system has disappeared, but in Martinique it has not been replaced by another system of production; it degenerated into a circuit of exchange. Martinique is a land in which products manufactured elsewhere are consumed. It is therefore destined to become increasingly a land you pass through. In such a land, whose present organization ensures that nothing can be produced there again, the structure of the mother tongue, deprived of a dynamic hinterland, cannot be reinforced. Creole cannot become the language of shopping malls, nor of luxury hotels. Cane, bananas, pineapples are the last vestiges of the Creole world. With them this language will disappear, if it does not become functional in some other way. (*Discourse,* 127)

Glissant's treatment of landscape, which no one else seems to have dealt with, deserves our attention here.

> What is striking is the emphatic emptiness of the landscape in the Creole folktale; in it landscape is reduced to symbolic space and becomes a pattern of succeeding spaces through which one journeys; the forest and its darkness, the savannah and its daylight, the hill and its fatigue. Really, places you pass through. The importance of walking is amazing. "I walked so much," the tale more or less says,

> "that I was exhausted and I ended up heel first." The route is reversible. There is, naturally, vegetation along these routes; animals mark the way. But it is important to realize that if the place is indicated, *it is never described.* The description of the landscape is not a feature of the folktale. Neither the joy nor the pleasure of describing are evident in it. This is because the landscape of the folktale is not meant to be inhabited. A place you pass through, it is not yet a country. (*Discourse,* 130).

With respect to the principal trickster figure of the French West Indies, Rabbit, Glissant has come to the same conclusions as Condé. His socioeconomic analysis is much more broadly based, whereas Condé did more of a literary content analysis. We have seen that Condé concluded that the transformation of Rabbit and Zamba/Hyena in the new creole society resulted from a moral and psychological interiorization of the masters' view of the slave. Glissant's analysis reaches the conclusion that "the Creole folktale has *verified* the nature of the [plantation] system and its structure" (*Discourse,* 131). Or again:

> In such a context, man ([or] the animal who symbolizes him) has with things and trees, creatures and people, nothing like a sustained relationship. The extreme "breathlessness" of the Creole folktale leaves no room for quiet rest. No time to gaze at things. The relationship with one's surroundings is always dramatic and suspicious. . . . You must run without stopping, from a past order that is rejected into an absurd present. The land that has been suffered is not yet the land that is offered, made accessible. National consciousness is budding in the tale, but it does not burst into bloom. (*Discourse,* 131)

Concerning Rabbit, then, Glissant concludes: "The proposed ideal is from the outset shaped by a negation of popular 'values.' One can only escape by ceasing to be oneself, while trying to remain so. The character of Brer Rabbit is therefore *also* the projection of this individual ingenuity that is sanctioned by a collective absence" (*Discourse,* 130).

There is an abundance of evidence to support Glissant's theory beyond what he provides in *Caribbean Discourse.* My favorite example of the importation into the Creole language of Martinique of a French cultural product is the translation of a selection of La Fontaine's fables by Marie-Thérèse Julien-Lung-Fou in 1958. These so-called *Fables créoles* are the perfect illustration of the neocolonial process. The prestigious cultural product, La Fontaine's fables, comes from France and brings with it meaning and significance. Transposed into Creole with illustrations by the translator, La Fontaine's original animal characters then provide an authoritative model for Martinicans young and old, but nothing of these so-called creole tales has in fact been creolized (that is, made to conform to local reality). On my first visit to the one bookstore in Fort-de-France in 1970, this is the only volume of animal tales I could find. If a hypothetical collection of Martinican tales in Creole existed, it was not offered for sale. In fact, the efforts of a new generation of folklorists would begin to bear fruit a decade later, with "Tales of Death and Life in the Antilles" (*Contes de mort et de vie aux Antilles)*, edited by Ina Césaire, the daughter of the founder of the West Indian negritude movement.

In 1981, at the same time that the Paris edition of *Caribbean Discourse* appeared, I published a book on the poetry and poetics of Aimé Césaire, in which I demonstrated that the poems Césaire wrote on subjects taken from creole folklore became more dense, hermetic, and learned in direct relation to the popular nature of his subject matter (that is, the more widespread or humble the "creole" subject, the more learned, hermetic, and "French" the poem). The text I chose for extended discussion of this principle, "Beautiful Spurted Blood"—"Beau sang giclé" in the original—treats a well-known creole folktale (Arnold, *Modernism,* 253–54). One of Césaire's earliest exegetes, who probably got her information directly from the author, relates the plot of the creole tale as follows: "to feed his children . . . Yé climbs a palm tree to kill the enchanted bird" (Kesteloot, *Césaire,* 51–52), which, "after it has been eaten, resuscitates [giving the family severe indigestion] and forces the man, his wife, and their children to give back every feather" (*Césaire,* 53).

Here is the text of the poem in the translation by Clayton Eshleman and Annette Smith:

> trophy head lacerated limbs
> deadly sting beautiful spurted blood
> lost warblings ravished shores
> childhoods childhoods a tale too stirred up
> dawn on its chain ferocious snapping to be born
> oh belated assassin
> the bird with the feathers once more beautiful than the past
> demands an accounting for its scattered plumes[.]
>
> (A. Césaire, *Poetry,* 307)

Only in the last three lines, beginning with "oh belated assassin," is there any narrative thrust to the poem. "Beautiful Spurted Blood" is otherwise so thoroughly marked by the poetics of semantic ellipsis and the paratactic juxtaposition of apparently unrelated elements (a technique characteristic of surrealist poetry) that only the most alert reader will even guess at the ghostly presence of its creole subject. Indeed, as I argued in 1981, it is finally unnecessary that the reader recognize the creole subject matter in order to appreciate "Beautiful Spurted Blood" as a successful modernist poem. Even very well prepared readers of modern poetry are much more likely to comprehend the poem in terms of a tradition that begins in France with Stéphane Mallarmé and runs through André Breton and the surrealists. Yet the poem does speak of and to French West Indian culture and identity, but so tortuously, so painfully that all we can grasp is the agony related to an absence. The creole story of Yé and the enchanted bird can be grasped and understood in Césaire's version only as the result of a sophisticated hermeneutic process, which is to say that its significance is inaccessible to the primary audience of traditional creole folktales. If we choose to read Césaire's poem as a cultural document, it becomes the sign of a severe dysfunction, of an inability to relate elements of a shared creole tradition in such a way that the art form remains accessible to a general readership. The lack of a continuous narrative thread ties in nicely with Glissant's notion of "longing for the ideal of history," which cannot overcome its "epistemological deficiency" (*Discourse,* 61) in order to create an effective link between present and past.

Like French and other modernist writers before him, Césaire turned his back on historical writing (which was, for him, impossible) and interpreted the simple narratives of the creole tales as modernist myth, attempting to infuse into them precisely that ritual, sacrificial function that, as Glissant has shown, they lack. Rather than the reappropriation of an (as yet) impossible history, the creole tale thus becomes, for the father of the French West Indian negritude movement, the raw material of an agonistic tragedy in which the enchanted bird must die and be reborn in order to transform the consciousness of the ordinary folk, of whom the peasant Yé is the representative. Consequently, Césaire's poetic rendering of this tale constitutes a closed text of the modernist sort. It cannot open onto a community's shared values because these are seen as nonexistent in any positive sense.

If we are given to psychoanalytic theorizing, what we see in "Beautiful Spurted Blood" is a violent return of the repressed creole culture, which can express itself at all only through its extreme opposite, the most rarified modernist poetics in French (which was, of course, the linguistic instrument of the original cultural repression). Whence the tortuous syntax of the poem, where only the interstices of the text, the ellipses, permit the passage of a creole cultural subject in the form of a mysterious, enigmatic eruption. And that only for the most patient of readers. With respect to the problematics of animal figures in New World cultures, I propose that "Beautiful Spurted Blood" and a number of similar texts of Césaire's are the sign of an impossibility.

In my view, no French West Indian writer could use the creole folktale creatively, as the West African writer Birago Diop did, among the generation born, as Césaire was, on the eve of the First World War. The reason for this can be found in the cultural disruption brought about by the official policy of assimilation practiced by the French on their subjects in the "old" colonies of the West Indies (those dating from the seventeenth century, whereas the French colonization of West and Central Africa dates from the late nineteenth century). When we factor the policy of cultural assimilation of French West Indian people of color in with the economic transformation of the landscape that we considered earlier, the result is a historical pressure that paralyzed the imagination of the first generation of French West Indian intellectuals who came to an awareness of themselves as the heirs to the African diaspora. My argument is, of course, a way of talking about what the negritude movement meant in the French West Indies, where its significance was essentially different from the meaning it could have for Africans who had never been entirely cut off from their traditional culture.

The notion of generations is useful to us here. It is in fact only with the generation of Guadeloupeans and Martinicans born after the end of the Second World War that one finds serious researchers in folktale (Ina Césaire), novelists who incorporate elements of folktale into fictional plots (Daniel Maximin), and writers of fiction who regularly use a form of marvelous realism akin to that found throughout Latin American fiction (Patrick Chamoiseau). It is significant that these writers have no memory of the colony. They know only the *département d'outre-mer,* which gives them a sensation of belonging to France in a special, and unequal, way while preventing them from constructing a national identity. In *Caribbean Discourse,* Glissant has called the literary imagination that is possible under such circumstances "forced poetics": "I define forced or constrained poetics as any collective desire for expression that, when it manifests itself, is negated at the same time because of a *deficiency* that stifles it, not at the level of desire, which never ceases, but at the level of expression, which is never realized" (*Discourse,* 120).

Daniel Maximin's first novel, *Lone Sun,* published in 1981, demonstrates the ruses and detours that French West Indian writers of the younger generation—Maximin was born in 1947—have come to adopt. *Lone Sun* attempts to reappropriate, indeed to rewrite, the history of the island of Guadeloupe from the period preceding the French Revolution to the Black Power movement of the 1960s. His cast of characters includes *bossales* (newly arrived African slaves); white, mulatto, and black Creoles; and the French invaders of the Napoleonic armies who reimposed slavery in 1802. The novel illustrates a number of Glissant's theses. Maximin uses Creole extensively in his French text, mixing in presumed African chants and incantations that provoke mysterious reactions. Most important, for our purposes here, he weaves a number of creole folktales into his plot. One in particular, devoted to an animal character called Armored Fish (*Poisson armé*), precipitates the cure of a profoundly troubled child who had seen her father's small boat pulled under the sea by the wake of a German submarine during the war.[1] The analogic argument is clear: By making anew the connection with the sources of our popular culture, we can cure ourselves of our collective instability.

Maximin is also a great admirer of Césaire, whose poem "Beautiful Spurted Blood" he uses in his text to provide the secret code that permits a band of Guadeloupean and Martinican patriots to trigger an uprising against the local Vichy French government of the colony. Maximin's reading of the poem, however, displaces the enchanted bird in favor of the young revolutionaries whose beautiful blood is spilled in an ill-conceived and poorly executed uprising. Like Césaire, whose inspiration he so closely follows, Maximin posits a human sacrifice as necessary to galvanize the spirit of the community. The form of Maximin's novel tells us much about the perils of a forced poetics in neocolonial Guadeloupe, Martinique, and French Guiana. The closest Maximin can come to rewriting the lost history of the descendents of slaves in his native island is a mosaic of fragments attributed to very different narrators separated in space and time. Moreover, the dense network of intertextual references relies far more heavily on French literary texts than it does on creole folktales; and in this respect, the intertextuality is clearly an adaptation to the novel of Césaire's own poetics.

Such a poetics makes considerable demands upon the reader, whose literary culture is expected to be extensive and sophisticated.

Maximin, who was largely educated in France, is exceptional in finding a potential healing function in animal tales from his region. Most writers conform much more closely to the description given recently by Jack Corzani: "[French] West Indian culture, dominated by fear and injustice, reveled in an essentially teratological imaginary. The inventory of their monsters is particularly large and their heritage significantly weighted down by these beings since the West Indians generally associated the terrors of African witchcraft and the horrors of their American slavery with the demons of Christianity" (Corzani, *Mythology,* 134).

We have reached the point where the teratological imagination of the Europeans, laid out by Michael Palencia-Roth in his essay, can be shown to have so thoroughly penetrated the collective imaginary of the descendants of African slaves in the dependent French West Indies (Guadeloupe, Martinique, and French Guiana) that in all probability the individual strands of tradition can no longer be differentiated. The issue now is whether French West Indians will be able to forge an idea of the nation that will permit a collective exorcism of their folkloric monsters, as in the Trinidadian Earl Lovelace's *The Dragon Can't Dance,* or whether they will remain tied to a static conception of the inheritance of plantation society that excludes non-"creole" elements, as in the vision of not-Acadia one finds in Antonine Maillet's *Pélagie-la-charrette.*

NOTES

1. Behind the German submarine of the Second World War plot stands the slave ship dating back to the Middle Passage, which Lilyan Kesteloot saw in this French West Indian folktale (see Kesteloot, *Césaire,* 51).

REFERENCES

Arnold, A. James. *Modernism and Negritude: The Poetry and Poetics of Aimé Césaire.* Cambridge: Harvard University Press, 1981.

Césaire, Aimé. *The Collected Poetry.* Trans. Clayton Eshleman and Annette Smith. Berkeley; Los Angeles: University of California Press, 1983.

Chamoiseau, Patrick. *Texaco.* Paris: Gallimard, 1992.

Condé, Maryse. *La civilisation du bossale.* Paris: L'Harmattan, 1978.

Corzani, Jack. "West Indian Mythology and Its Literary Illustrations." *Research in African Literatures* 25, no. 2 (1994): 131–39.

Glissant, Edouard. *Le discours antillais.* Paris: Seuil, 1981.

———. *Caribbean Discourse.* Trans. J. Michael Dash. CARAF BOOKS. Charlottesville; London: University Press of Virginia, 1989.

Julien-Lung-Fou, Marie-Thérèse. *Fables créoles transposées et illustrées.* Fort-de-France, Martinique: Editions Dialogue, 1958.

Kesteloot, Lilyan, and Barthelémy Kotchy, *Aimé Césaire, l'homme et l'oeuvre.* Classiques Africaines. Paris: Présence Africaine, 1993 [1973].

Laurent, Joëlle, and Ina Césaire. *Contes de mort et de vie aux Antilles.* Paris: Nubia, 1976.

Maximin, Daniel. *L'isolé soleil.* Paris: Seuil, 1981.

———. *Lone Sun.* CARAF BOOKS. Charlottesville; London: University Press of Virginia, 1989.

Naipaul, V. S. *The Middle Passage.* London: Deutsch, 1962.

Derek Walcott

AFTERWORD

Animals, Elemental Tales, and the Theater

When I was very young, I had an aunt whom we called Sidone who would tell us stories. She was an old woman—I can't remember her face too clearly, but she was a powerful woman and a terrific storyteller. My brother is also a playwright, we are twins, and the remarkable thing is that the big thrill was for Sidone to scare you with stories about the African night that was there in the country in Saint Lucia, in the fireflies and the funny-looking banana trees and the superstitions, or what people call superstitions and which are myths. And that in itself was magical. I've written about it in a book called *Midsummer*.[1] There is in it a poem about her, and we would go and expect her to sit on the back step and start to tell these stories. And two boys sitting there, not knowing that they wanted to write . . . or maybe beginning to be writers, listening to these amazing stories that were a combination of French and Creole, that obviously had African roots. And the role that she played was really a traditional tribal, sibylline role of the storyteller. And she was tremendous, because she could scare you. There were songs in the narration that she would sing, and they were very plaintive and very frightening, very beautiful songs. That would be normal or expected in the West Indian setting in the country. It may still go on.

What is really remarkable, remembering it, is that my brother and I would go there in daylight after school sometimes and head up the hill that she now lived on, to go and hear her tell those stories. It wasn't that there weren't movies, there were, but to go and hear Sidone tell stories was part of our memory as writers. I mention this because it's predictable somebody would say that's where a lot of Third World and West Indian literature comes from: that narration and dramatization. Actually, it wasn't just storytelling; it was dramatization. She would change roles. So she became very frightening, but beautifully frightening. If ever there was a visible and audible Muse, then I think she must have been it, this woman, who probably could not write . . . she may have been able to read, but certainly she was a very powerful storyteller, and she had this reputation within the family for that. For us to do that in the afternoon, after school, as growing children meant that there was something absolutely compelling in going into her presence and waiting for dusk, when it would be the best time to begin to tell these stories.

So that's part of something, a memory that—I am sure, when I think of it—generated in the theater particularly, not necessarily in the poetry, but certainly in the theater, the impulse to tell stories based on the folk imagination and the folk memory, and in a setting that was turbulently beautiful in terms of what the landscape looked like, particularly at night in the moonlight. You've heard all these things and you say: "Yeah, we've heard that. Children tell the stories, dancing in the moonlight, that sort of stuff, right?" That's great that that happened because that's the source of all literature.

And just to jump around a little bit, I've just done a play, an adaptation of the *Odyssey,* for the Royal Shakespeare Company.[2] And in the course of an interview somewhere, the figure of Odysseus came up and Odysseus's qualities are precisely the qualities one ascribes to certain animals in folklore. There is a feeling that even if he is a man, and he's maybe the first humanist if you wish—*The Odyssey* certainly is the first modern novel. At the core of the *Odyssey,* there is something that has folkloric qualities. But I tend to think of Odysseus as the equivalent of someone in Jamaican or Caribbean folklore, as someone elusive and small, as someone who can get out of things. And the confrontation between Odysseus and the Cyclops is the same confrontation that might happen between a small animal and a very big one: the cunning that is there as opposed to size. So without making a case for somebody to try to say: "Oh, I see what you're saying, terrific anthropology or whatever," I just think that figures that have come out of large emblematic figures certainly have their basis in a lot of animalistic sources or emblems. And I'll just take one example.

The elusiveness of Odysseus probably is a quality one would ascribe to a figure or the animal confronting a larger one, if you think of the Cyclops, for instance, in that way. All right. Well, that's Greek, and it's very easy to jump from Caribbean to Greek to make the parallels because they are there; but to take specific examples of what happened, in my case, later . . . I'm thinking of this not as a sort of public, international thing; I'm really having a chat here with people who I think would like to ask questions that I'd love to answer about the subject of this conference.

I could divide my work, maybe to its detriment, into two styles, in a sense. I've done plays that are based very obviously on what we would generally call folklore, which is a very patronizing phrase. The present definition of *folk* has been seized by a lot of defensive academics, a lot of aggressive politicians, or you could switch adjectives: aggressive academics, defensive politicians; defensive academics, aggressive politicians. But the point is that the property of reaching the people and preserving what belongs to the people, all that stuff, is sometimes very dangerous because it has elements of a curious kind of patronage in it. In Saint Lucia recently, two young writers gave me a tape of somebody singing folk songs—there we go—folk songs from Saint Lucia, and it was astonishing to hear this woman and how she was singing. And I tried to explain to another artist the other night in Trinidad that I'm not talking about *folk*. When you talk about *folk* as a writer, then the danger there is you tend to say: "Well, we've got to preserve what we have, you've got to be rootsy, X or Y, you've got to talk that way." You know, that kind of thing; it's all very dangerous and ephemeral, that kind of aggressiveness. It turns into anthropology; and you can't patronize genuine people by making them anthropological specimens, like saying: "Oh, you are a great representative of the folk. Now you keep doing that." Right? While you've been watching *Days of Our Lives*. Right? Each person has the right to go to the movies and to turn on to any channel or to watch a soap opera or sing country songs, instead of being a damned representative of the *folk* for the rest of his or her life. So anyway, there's that, that we have to look out for.

And the same thing can happen in reverse to writers who are very aggressive and say: "Why you doing write in English?" All that sort of thing, you know? The thing to notice about these people who are very defensive about dialect is that when they write profound essays on preserving the dialect, they're all written in Jamesian English. You say: "Well, why you all write things like that?"—"Well, you see, the t'ing of this man writing here is that he should'a really said . . ." You don't get that. You get very measured polysyllabic sentences saying why you must defend the dialect. So it's all a contradiction, you know?

Anyway, so what I'm talking about is there are two sort of strains that go on still in Caribbean writing, and in the theater particularly. One is that there is the strain of the *folk*, let's use that damned word, of folk origin, mythical origin. One of them is *Dream on Monkey Mountain*. The other one, for instance, is *Ti-Jean and His Brothers*. (I'm talking about my plays here because presumably the people who will be asking me questions may have read them—I'm not just advertising them—I'm just saying that maybe as you know them you might want to ask me things about them.) And the other kind of play, which is a naturalistic play, generally has a historical or a contemporary setting, but not necessarily with such obvious dimensions of folk sources in terms of either song or fear or stories that you draw on.

Now, since the subject is about animal figures that appear in literature, in *Dream on Monkey Mountain* the man, Makak, is a monkey and the other figures in the play are Tigre, a tiger, Souris, a mouse; and there are other figures there, but I'm just giving you the animal ones. Now, Makak in the play is based on a man I knew who terrified us when we were very young in Saint Lucia, a man called—and that's the tough thing about this—he was called Makak Roger. Roger was not his name. I think he may have worked for somebody called Roger, so it really was this that people were calling him: "This is Roger's monkey," which is terrible; but that's what he was. He would get very drunk. He was an ugly, short, ferocious man who would be bellowing up the street, and you would hear him coming and everybody was terrified of Makak Roger. Well, when I remembered this particular man, I thought what a degrading thing for him to be called that. There was something in that man, however drunk and however degraded, that was extremely powerful. In other words, it's as if his power had been aborted in some way and that that strength may have been the strength of somebody who basically could have been an Attila the Hun. If you need an Attila the Hun, why not? Everybody needs an Attila the Hun; every country after a while says, "Hey, where is our Attila the Hun?" There is a deep yearning in countries for . . . , well, I won't get into that. Anyway. You have your own problems right now. Looking at a couple of Attila the Huns instead of some of the things we see now. But anyway, what I'm saying is: The man had such elemental power that I thought I would like to do something about him. But the central thing, of course, is the figure of the ape. The African is the ape. The African is the baboon. Tarzan and the apes. It is not only Tarzan and the apes; it's Tarzan and all of the apes, meaning not only Cheeta, but Cheeta's buddies. Meaning those wild guys coming through the jungle screaming. So it's Tarzan and the apes; that's the attitude that's in "Tarzan . . ." That's the African. That's the African we were shown in the Caribbean. Not Benin, nothing like that.[3] However, if you take the image of the monkey, as the comic, laughable, pathetic mimic man that Makak was, then that's what's there in the play [*Dream on Monkey Mountain*].

In the other play, *Ti-Jean,* there's a more direct parallel between the ordinary kind of West Indian . . . or any fable that goes in acts of one, two, three: big brother, medium-size brother, little brother. And the little brother is the one who is the smartest. All fables have this: three sisters, act one, act two, act three; that's the rhythm of the folktale just as it is the rhythm of anything. Somehow in the human heartbeat, in the human oral imagination it's got to be one, two, three: beginning, middle, end. Birth, fornication, and death . . . copulation and death, sorry, same thing. Copulation sounds more dignified. It has a deeper intent. But that rhythm that's there in the folktale is the same structure that exists in the novel. . . . There is so much to be said in the Caribbean that the West Indian novel is now simply interested in wanting to go from beginning, middle, and end, and it's great that the West Indian novelist is still in the nineteenth century. It's wonderful because the twentieth century has such terrible literature it's better to stay there. As Joseph Brodsky once said, "What are we doing with the twentieth century when we already have the nineteenth?" A great remark. And of course the nineteenth-century novelists include Balzac, Dickens, the Victorian novel, Hardy. These are massive writers. And Joyce can be looked at not as the first twentieth-century novelist but the last nineteenth-century novelist. That's what he is, honestly. So that the scale of the Joycean novel, of *Ulysses,* is really the summation of the nineteenth century, not the beginning of the twentieth. That's a one, two, three even there.

I'm not drifting away from the subject of the animals because in *Ti-Jean* the chorus is an audible chorus of a frog, a cricket, and a bird. When I was doing this story, I thought: Okay, we need musicians so we'll have a frog doing the bass, a cricket playing the maracas, and a bird doing the flute. And when we did the play, that's what they were. So the three musicians were the three animals and that's said in the play. Those songs are there in the Caribbean night. If you heard the orchestration of the Caribbean night, you'd be amazed how rich it is in terms of the sound that goes on.

As another example apropos of nothing too profound, here is the way I heard this story, *Ti-Jean and His Brothers,* which is a figure that goes through French Creole literature. "Little John and His Brothers" is what it means. And he's a figure, I think, even in French-Canadian literature. I heard this story when I was at college. There was a terrific storyteller and here again is an example of the oral storyteller. Now I'm not getting into one of those things where there is going to be . . . if you divide the room in half, there'll be somebody saying "oral," somebody saying "written," and then there'll be a small civil war. I'm not talking about the difference between oral and whatever. There's no difference in the Caribbean between oral and written. No matter what the anthologists and the anthropologists may say, they are the same thing. Nor are there two languages; there's only one, one melody. This is how I heard the story. There was a boy at school called Mock because he was a very fast talker, very agitated, and that was a shortened name of Democracy, because he was an orator so he was called Mock. Anyway, he told the story and this is the point about trying to make things translatable, which sometimes they aren't. There are three brothers: Gros Jean, meaning "Big John," Mi-Jean, meaning "Middle John," and Ti-Jean, meaning "Little John." And the whole point of that is that the Devil challenges them: If they get annoyed with the Devil, if they lose their temper, the Devil will eat them. Very simple. Now that's a story Sidone may have told; but this is one Mock knew, and he told it to us. He would tell it beautifully. But the whole story is based on the exaggeration of a positive, comparative, superlative; in other words, three degrees in expression of anger, which are purely a question of vocabulary. And I'll tell you how I mean that. The first brother is challenged by the Devil. He blows up; he loses his temper. The Devil says to him: *"Ous fâché?"*—"You're vexed." And the guy says, *"Oui, moi fâché!"*—"Yes, I'm vexed."[4] So the Devil eats him. He lost. The second brother—the Devil gets him into a trap—the Devil says to him: *"Ous enragé?"* Meaning, "You are enraged?" Notice the distinction. It's growing. *Fâché,* "angry," *enragé,* "enraged," that's the second brother (Walcott, *Ti-Jean and His Brothers,* 130). So you say, "What's going to be the third one?" The third one is a joke and it's purely verbal. Ti-Jean now does something to the Devil—the bet is mutual—so the Devil loses his temper. And Ti-Jean says to the Devil: *"Ous fâché?"* And the Devil says: *"Moi fâché tout seul, moi désolé,"* meaning, "I'm not only enraged, I am desolated!" (*Ti-Jean and His Brothers,* 159–60). Now, this may not be funny to you because you don't have French Creole; but when you hear him tell the story in the one, two, three . . . Everyone is saying: "Oh, you have to be there." Yeah, you have to be there. But I was there, and it was great the way he said it. And the whole story was based on that anger and I used that story told to me by a schoolboy; I built the play around this thing. It doesn't work in an English translation and it's a full-length play, so you can't base a play on a noun or an adjective. However, I'm just showing you that this is one sort of origin. Plays of the other kind—which are based on observation, reality, and sociology, or whatever kind of -ology you want to talk about—are plays that are realistic. They're comedies or tragedies but they don't have that clear identity of being out of the *folk.*

I'm going to read the beginning of *Dream on Monkey Mountain.* This man Makak is arrested by a corporal who does not have an animal's name. And that's part of the point of this enlarged fable. The corporal's name is Lestrade. Lestrade is a real name meaning "somebody who is astraddle of both worlds," sort of balanced between both worlds.[5] And the names of the other fellows in the play are Tigre, "tiger cat," and Souris, "mouse." Each has the qualities ascribed to those animals: Tigre has a bad temper; Souris is small and cunning. And Makak of course is this phenomenal, legendary idea of the black man and the wild ape. And that's how he sees himself—or is made to see himself—as ugly and apish. So when he's arrested by Lestrade—who, by the way is a mulatto, a man from both worlds, black and white, that is, in the middle—when he's arrested then, the other fellows are in the prison. And Lestrade brings him on. I use in this play a chorus of people: a *conteur,* or "singer-narrator," who sings when they bring him into the prison. And on one side is an empty cell; on the other side is a cell containing these two prisoners: (Tigre and Souris). The play begins with the chant of the chorus and the people singing.

[Reading from *Dream on Monkey Mountain*]

The cast list in *Ti-Jean* has a cricket, a frog, a firefly, a bird, Gros Jean, Mi-Jean, Ti-Jean, a Mother, a figure called a bolom.[6] The bolom is a figure—one of these words that you grow up saying but you don't know what they mean—only recently I realized that perhaps bolom is really *beau-l'homme* (fine little man). Maybe, I'm not sure. So I just made it *bolom,* without the French. It could have been that, bolom, you never know. An old man, a *papa bois,* an old man of the woods, like Pan. And there is a terrible, an embarrassing pun at the beginning of the play: *Greek-croak, Greek-croak*; it's lousy but it's nice. It's like making a reference to the fact that Aristophanes has a play called *The Frogs;* and this frog knows Greek and he knew that he was in Aristophanes so he said "Greek-croak." Oh, my god! So it is in the evening in the heights of a forest; a cricket, a frog, a firefly, a bird.

The other thing about the folktale is that it simplifies the theater considerably. You don't need props. Time changes any way you want. It's a figure, the body, duration. . . . The psychological reality of most modern theater is that (it's really very silly the theater, if you think of it, and I think to someone coming from another tradition, people who are alleged to be "uncivilized" or who have never seen a theater) it is very, very stupid for people to go into a room like this and spend a lot of money in pretending that if I built a street here, under this roof, and it cost me a lot of money to get a designer to simulate a street and a house, that Western theater spends a lot of money on the simulation of a reality that nobody really believes. You don't really—you say, okay, this is a street in Hong Kong—but I'm not going to look at the roof. . . . Now what kind of fantasy is that. All Western theater is based on this detail of reality, which is totally stupid. A lot of theater, Oriental theater, doesn't depend on this nonsense of pretending that we're going to simulate reality down to the last nail and have an expert painter. But I do it. I write that kind of play as well. But when you think of it, basically, it is remarkably idiotic to pretend that you really have New York under this real roof and four walls.

But that is part of the psychology that has made theater realistic, so that if you have that kind of set, you can't talk like Shakespeare because nobody talks like that. Or you can't talk even in the highest kind of literature because it's a contradiction of the furniture, of the design. Whereas the power of folk theater, as in Greek theater, where there's no scenery and people don't sit down—you don't sit down in Shakespeare either, or, if they do sit down, they get up right away: The king gets vexed very fast, right?—so it's a theater that is not based on leisure and sitting down and exchanging conversation. . . . What I'm saying is that the tradition that is very strong in the theater gets its vitality not from the finish and reality of Realism, it gets it out of another source:

a primal source. And a lot of Western directors return to that source, people like Peter Brook or Jerzy Grotowski, they go back to that power of narration that is there in the presence of the storyteller or the story being told by the dance and the bodies and the music that's happening. The theater that is poor has a greater chance of being imaginative than the theater that is rich.

[Reading from *Ti-Jean and His Brothers*]

[The presentation concluded with a question and answer period, the best of which has been included in the editor's introduction. Ed.]

NOTES

1. "Her leaves were the libraries of the Caribbean. / The luck that was ours, those fragrant origins! / Her head was magnificent, Sidone. In the gully of her voice / shadows stood up and walked, her voice travels my shelves. / She was the lamplight in the stare of two mesmerized boys / still joined in one shadow, indivisible twins." *Midsummer,* XIV (New York: Farrar, Straus & Giroux, 1981), unpaginated.

2. Derek Walcott, *The Odyssey,* first performed by the Royal Shakespeare Theatre, Stratford-upon-Avon, at The Other Place on 24 June 1992, and at The Pit, London, on 16 June 1993.

3. The allusion is to the Benin bronzes that so mystified the Europeans who first saw them. Europeans of the imperial era could not conceive of an African society so advanced as to have had the technology and the artistic impetus to create the Benin bronzes in the distant past.

4. The Creole text related here is parallel to the English text elaborated in *Ti-Jean and His Brothers* in *Dream on Monkey Mountain and Other Plays* (New York: Farrar, Straus & Giroux, 1970), 114. The Creole text is closer to the version told by Mock. (Parenthetical references in the text indicate where to find the corresponding passage in *Ti-Jean . . .*)

5. Lestrade is, of course, also the name of the bumbling Scotland Yard detective in Sir Arthur Conan Doyle's Sherlock Holmes stories. A straight French derivation would suggest *Stage* (*l'estrade*), the *boards* of theatrical parlance, rather than a man astraddle of both worlds, which is typically Caribbean and American.

6. The bolom is a small figure that wears a hat, with feet reversed, just like a fetus, an unchristened child.

Contributors

Index

Contributors

A. JAMES ARNOLD is Professor of French at the University of Virginia. He is the series editor of New World Studies and was the founding general editor of CARAF BOOKS, both at the University Press of Virginia. Under the aegis of the International Comparative Literature Association, he edits the three-volume *History of Literature in the Caribbean.* The author of *Modernism and Negritude* and the editor of Aimé Césaire's *Lyric and Dramatic Poetry, 1946–1982,* he is on the international advisory board of the *New West Indian Guide.* He has held major grants from the American Council of Learned Societies, the National Endowment for the Humanities, the Fulbright Commission, and the National Humanities Center.

KANDIOURA DRAMÉ is Associate Professor of French at the University of Virginia. He was a founding editor of the CARAF BOOKS series. He is the author of *The Novel as Transformation Myth: A Study of the Novels of Mongo Beti and Ngugi wa Thiong'o* and is a freqent contributor to the journal *Research in African Literatures.*

GARY H. GOSSEN is Professor of Anthropology and Latin American Studies at the University of Albany (State University of New York). A renowned specialist of Mesoamerican cultures, his work based in Chiapas,

Mexico, received international attention with the outbreak of the civil war there in early 1994. His books include *Chamulas in the World of the Sun* and *Symbol and Meaning Beyond the Closed Community*; his most recent major project is an edited encyclopedia volume entitled *South and Mesoamerican Native Spirituality: From the Cult of the Feathered Serpent to the Theology of Liberation.* His recent articles have appeared in *Cultural Anthropology* and *American Anthropologist.*

VI HILBERT is the founder and director of Lushootseed Research in Seattle, an institute devoted to the preservation and dissemination of the Lushootseed language and culture. She is the author of *Haboo: Native American Stories from Puget Sound, Ways of the Lushootseed,* and *Aunt Susie*; she is the coauthor of the two-volume *Lushootseed Grammar.* She is an Upper Skagit Elder and a Living Treasure of Washington State.

DELL H. HYMES is Commonwealth Professor of Anthropology and English at the University of Virginia. Since 1964, he has authored or edited fourteen books, including *Reinventing Anthropology, Pidginization and Creolization of Languages,* and *"In Vain I Tried to Tell You": Essays in Native American Ethnopoetics.* He has held fellowships from the Center for Advanced Study in the Behavioral Sciences at Stanford University, the American Council of Learned Studies, and the National Endowment for the Humanities.

JAY MILLER is currently on the board of Lushootseed Research and on the faculty of Native American Educational Services in Chicago. He has authored five books, over thirty articles, and many contributions to edited collections. He is working on a study of Coast Salishan culture to be entitled *Saleehalee / Soulside.*

JOANNA OVERING is Senior Lecturer in Anthropology at the London School of Economics. She is a foremost specialist of the Piaroa culture of the upper Amazon. Her books include *Reason and Morality.* She is a frequent contributor to the journal *Man.*

MICHAEL PALENCIA-ROTH is Professor of Comparative Literature and Latin American Studies at the University of Illinois. He is the author of *Perspectives on Faust, Gabriel García-Márquez,* and *Myth and the Modern Novel.* He recently served as president of the International Society for the Comparative Study of Civilization.

JEREMY POYNTING is the publisher of Peepal Tree Press in Leeds, England. He has been an Associate Fellow at the University of Warwick, Centre for Caribbean Studies. He is the author of *The Second Shipwreck: A Study of Indo-Caribbean Literature* and of articles on several Caribbean writers, including Wilson Harris. He has contributed to the *Journal of Commonwealth Literature.*

BRINSLEY SAMAROO is Professor of History at the University of the West Indies in St. Augustine, Trinidad. He is the coeditor of *India in the Caribbean.* His contributions to the history of Indians in Trinidad have appeared in *East Indians in the Caribbean.* From 1987 to 1991, he served as the minister of agriculture and marine exploitation in the government of Trinidad and Tobago.

CANDACE SLATER is Professor of Spanish and Portuguese at the University of California, Berkeley. She is the author of *Stories on a String, Trail of Miracles, City Steeple, City Streets,* and *Dance of the Dolphin.* Her articles have appeared in *Comparative Studies in Society and History, Romance Philology,* the *Latin American Research Review,* and the *Journal of American Folklore.*

DEREK WALCOTT received the Nobel Prize for Literature on 8 October 1992. The talk included here as an afterword was his first as Nobel laureate. Born in Saint Lucia and long identified with the Trinidad Theatre Workshop, which he founded, Walcott is among the most honored poets and playwrights in English. He has been the recipient of the Guinness Award, the Royal Society of Literature Award, the Cholmondely Prize for Poetry, and several fellowships, including a MacArthur Foundation grant and a Rockefeller Foundation fellowship. He is the author of seven volumes of poetry, including *Omeros* and *Another Life,* and several prize-winning plays, including *Dream on Monkey Mountain, Ti-Jean and His Brothers,* and *The Odyssey.*

Index

New World Studies

New World Studies publishes interdisciplinary research that seeks to redefine the culture map of the Americas and to propose particularly stimulating points of departure for an emerging field. Encompassing the Caribbean as well as continental North, Central, and South America, the series books examine cultural processes within the hemisphere, taking into account the economic, demographic, and historical phenomena that shape them. Given the increasing diversity and richness of the linguistic and cultural traditions in the Americas, the need for research that privileges neither the English-speaking United States nor Spanish-speaking Latin America has never been greater. The series is designed to bring the best of this new research into an identifiable forum and to channel its results to the rapidly evolving audience for cultural studies.

New World Studies

A. JAMES ARNOLD, SERIES EDITOR

Vera M. Kutzinski
Sugar's Secrets: Race and the Erotics of Cuban Nationalism

Richard D. E. Burton and Fred Reno, Editors
French and West Indian: Martinique, Guadeloupe, and French Guiana Today

A. James Arnold, Editor
Monsters, Tricksters, and Sacred Cows: Animal Tales and American Identities